ℛ

GIT-R-DONE

GIT-R-DONE

LARRY THE CABLE GUY

 THREE RIVERS PRESS • NEW YORK

All rights reserved.
Published in the United States by Three Rivers Press,
an imprint of the Crown Publishing Group,
a division of Random House, Inc., New York.
www.crownpublishing.com

Three Rivers Press and the Tugboat design are registered
trademarks of Random House, Inc.

Originally published in hardcover in the United States by Crown Publishers,
an imprint of the Crown Publishing Group,
a division of Random House, Inc., New York, in 2005.

Library of Congress Cataloging-in-Publication Data
Larry, the Cable Guy.
Git-r-done / Larry the Cable Guy.—1st ed.
1. American wit and humor. I. Title.
PN6165.L375   2005
818'.602—dc22   2005024243

ISBN-13: 978-0-307-23767-5
ISBN-10: 0-307-23767-2

Printed in the United States of America

Design by Leonard W. Henderson

10 9 8 7 6 5 4 3 2 1

First Paperback Edition

DEAR READER,

Thank you for buying this highly anticipated book that absolutely no one is talkin' about. I hope you can put aside the brief 23 minutes it will take for you to sit on the toilet and read it. Remember, though, this is not a kid's book. As much as I love kids, and as much as I'd love to write stories about rabbits and rainbows, this is mainly for adults. You see, it's not that I don't want to do a book that kids can enjoy. I do. I'm actually in production now on a book for kids called *Farts Are Funny*. But in this book, every now and then I'm going to have to deal with evil commie libs and politically correct uptight cry babies, and when I talk about them, I sometimes get irritated, and when that happens, as in most families, you tend to say things you shouldn't. Even though this book isn't real bad in that department, I still wouldn't want it to fall into the hands of kids.

Now with the warning label out of the way, lets open 'er up and git-r-done!

CONTENTS

Foreword by My Mother ix

Introduction by Lewis Black xi

Chapter 1: GIT-R-DONE!!! 1

Chapter 2: THE ORIGIN OF GIT-R-DONE! 19

Chapter 3: LORD, I APOLOGIZE! 38

Chapter 4: LAWRENCE THE TELEGRAPH GUY . . .55

Chapter 5: MEDIA MADNESS 81

Chapter 6: RODEO RIDERS NOT NAMED CODY . . .97

Chapter 7: NASCAR 98

Chapter 8: NOW WHAT DO I
WRITE ABOUT? 116

Chapter 9: DOREEN'S DIARY 118

Chapter 10: MY DIARY 129

Chapter 11: I'LL DIET TOMORROW 150

Chapter 12: EVERYDAY OBSERVATIONS 165

Chapter 13: POLITICAL RAMBLINGS 200

Chapter 14: THAT'S FUNNY,
AND I DON'T CARE WHO YA ARE . .230

Chapter 15: RELATIONSHIPS, LOVE,
AND FOUR-WHEELERS 240

Chapter 16: HODGEPODGE 251

End Credits 265

Rum Balls Recipe .267

FOREWORD BY MY MOTHER

Well. . . . There's really not much I can say here except for I apologize to everyone ahead of time for the crap you are about to read, and actually kinda wish he'd have left me out of it! Enjoy . . .

INTRODUCTION BY LEWIS BLACK

Why does Larry the Cable Guy's book need an introduction? I haven't a clue. And if you don't know who he is by now, then this isn't going to help. Suffice it to say, if his photo scares you, then you should read this book, because it will really scare you. And if comedy scares you, then you need some form of counseling. And who knows, maybe if this book freaks you out, then the stuff that shouldn't freak you out, but freaks you out, won't freak you out anymore.

Why did Larry ask me to write this introduction? God only knows. I certainly can't add to his fan base. For crying out loud, more people are going to read this introduction than read my book. (Yes, I wrote a book, too. Why don't you drop this book where you found it and go look for mine? Larry won't notice.) Actually, I think Larry wanted me to write this because he thinks I am a communist. Jesus, there are hardly any communists left, unless you want to count the ones in China, and they are all so into cash now that it's just a matter of time till they start up their own version of NASCAR. (Larry is the only person, by the way, who could write a chapter on NASCAR that I would read.) To set the record straight, I am a socialist, which means I have no political affiliation at all since there are only three of us in the country and no one except us knows what socialism is. When Larry finds out what "socialism" means, he will probably try to kick my ass. If he can find a minute when he's not touching himself. On second thought, maybe it's because I am the only Jew he knows.

I'll tell you this, writing an introduction to a book is harder than writing a book. For God's sake, you actually have to read the book. I wish they had told me that.

I learned a lot about my friend from reading this book. Apparently Dan is the creator of Larry the Cable Guy. Wow, that was a shock. I always thought he was gay. So gay, in fact, that he was actually Dr. Phil. And I didn't know you could buy a bull to be ridden in rodeos. I have no idea what I can do with that information. Maybe it could work as a pickup line in, let's say, Montana. Apparently he stole my catch phrase, "git-r-done," and made it his. Mine was a little different, though. It was, "Could we try to accomplish something here . . . people . . . is anyone listening?" Also, it's not "Lord, I apologize," it's "Yahweh, I am really, really, really sorry."

But seriously, I have known him for years. I met him when he opened for me at the Comedy Corner in West Palm Beach. He was a funny kid and a terrific guy. I have watched over the years as he evolved into the comic force known as Larry the Cable Guy. He worked his teats off to get to where he is today. (And lucky for him that he was able to make enough money to purchase prosthetic titties.) He has always made me laugh because of his profound sense of silliness, which, no matter how biting and nasty his commentaries may get, keeps everything in perspective. Like every good comic, Larry knows that the laugh is what counts. I am also impressed by the humility he brings to his work. He is always the first one to laugh at himself. And he always makes me laugh.

I enjoyed the hell out of this book. We may stand on completely opposite sides of all sorts of issues, but in the end we have enjoyed each other's company for years. Larry would say that's what America is all about. It certainly is.

WARNING: Reading this book may cause you to think like Larry the Cable Guy. The reader may experience short periods of confusion or madness. Do not read before going to work, out on a date, or speaking before a group.

GIT-R-DONE

Chapter 1

GIT-R-DONE!!!

WELL, HERE WE GO. This is the first book I've written since 1975, when I was in the 7th grade and wrote *Boogers Are Good Eatin'*. Regardless of the title, that 27-page pamphlet earned me a C+ as well as several ass beatings from the class bully.

When they approached me to do this, I thought there's no way I could possibly find the time. I have all these other projects. I have a CD to put out. I have my tour schedule. I have to get a lawyer in Florida to help me fight the Supreme Court so I can keep the air hose in my blowup doll. So little time.

But after several days of . . . meditation . . . medication . . . masturbation! That's it! I not only decided to do it, I promised myself that this book would make *Boogers Are Good Eatin'* look like a seventh grader's pamphlet.

Set the bar high, that's what I always say.

I figure the thing most people want to know about me—other than how I keep my ass so muscular and hard—would be how I came by the name Larry the Cable Guy, and how I started doing social commentaries for radio stations across the country. Good questions, so let me get into this incredible story full of intrigue and dick jokes. (I'm glad no one is askin' about that time I was sodomized by Dick Van Patten.)

Since I don't want to waste your time with that boring "good old days" crap, I'll give ya a brief summary of how I came about in this world. My dad was a preacher; my mom ran the Tilt-a-Whirl at the fair. Somehow they met, had some teeth fixed, and got married.

I was born in 1963, as a C-section baby. I was born in section C of a Waylon Jennings concert! My dad thought they had good seats until my mom's water broke. They were great parents and the only blemish was when my dad beat me after reading my 7th-grade pamphlet *Boogers Are Good Eatin'*.

I started doin' stand-up comedy in 1985 right after I blew out my knee doing porno movies. Speakin' of the porno industry, there's a drive-in porno theater next to my log trailer here in Florida. It's pretty big. They call it the Herpes Simplex 2. Last week I went there to see a double feature, *Red Patch Adams* and *Citizen Cankor*. Before the second feature, I got arrested for car jacking!!!

(Already this is either the funniest book you've ever read or the dumbest, and I know it ain't the dumbest if you've read *Boogers Are Good Eatin'* or Al Franken's last book.)

OK, time to fess up: I actually didn't work in the porn industry. I blew out my knee tripping over an *Alice Does Anal* tape while runnin' for the phone.

Which reminds me . . . I used to date a girl named Alice. I met her at Hooters. She was really unique. She didn't have big boobs, but she could turn her head in a circle just like an owl.

But enough about Alice (isn't that an old Glen Campbell song?), let's get back to my story.

In 1991 there was a radio station in Tampa called 95 YNF. It was an awesome station that at the time no one could touch in the ratings. The station had hired a good buddy of mine, a comedian, to be a sidekick. He called me one day and said he needed some friends to call in and do some comedy.

I wanted to do this so bad that I had the phone checked on the top of the pole. Every day I would climb up and down it just to be heard by households across the bay.

I started callin' in as Iris, an old Jewish woman from Boca Raton. She was a fun character to impersonate until my throat started hurting from doin' her raspy voice all the time. I then became alarmed when I suddenly found myself stealing food and Sweet'N Low packets from buffets; I also developed this obsession with playing bingo and started askin' strange questions like who was running for the condo board.

And I didn't even own a condo.

I had to do something. I tried changin' my character's name from Iris to Rose. Unfortunately, I was still using that same raspy voice, so I ran into the same problems except for one thing: Rose didn't like Sweet'N Low.

For the next few months I would do all these different characters for the station. Some I rated as pretty good: the Fartin' Retard (pure genius), Cowman, Pigman, and various queer voices. Some came out pretty bad: Penis Pete, the Human Turd (that could have been funny if just given a chance), and various queer voices.

I could never find one I really could put my heart into until I realized I could call in as myself if I just changed my name. WOW! What a brilliant concept! Be myself and change my name! Y'all are probably already asking how I could possibly get away with that, right? Let's read on!

To understand how I came up with my name, y'all first need a little background on how I grew up. Ya know, when I did the Blue Collar Tour, I was the only guy there that wasn't born in the South. I was the only guy that wasn't born with the accent. And I was the only guy that had auditioned for *Hustler on Ice*.

I was, however, the only guy on the tour that actually grew up on a farm and lived the life.

My parents raised me on a pig farm outside a little town called Pawnee City, Nebraska. Ya might say it was a small town. The city hall came up to my chin. Pawnee City had around 1,200 people at the time. However, if ya counted critters, we would have been only a little smaller than China. But since we're not countin' critters . . . But come to think of it, Mildred Green could have counted as a critter considering she had more body hair than most collie dogs, so let's put the population at around 1,199.

Anyway, to make a long story even longer, I grew up in this town doin' most things country boys my age do: ridin' horses, feedin' cattle, lettin' the dog lick peanut butter off your privates . . .

I know. That sounds disgustin' but, hey, gimme a break! There were only 12 girls in my whole class. Besides, I was young and needed the money. I do regret the peanut butter thing, though. I can just see that turnin' up on TV one day and ruinin' my career:

"LARRY THE CABLE GUY'S PEANUT BUTTER TAPES ON THE NEXT *ACCESS HOLLYWOOD*! FOLLOWED BY AN ALL NEW *EVERY-BODY LOVES RAYMOND*."

The other boys in Pawnee City hunted a lot. I was never that big a hunter. Don't get me wrong, I love to hunt; I just never have time. When I was a kid, I did get a BB gun after I got confirmed, and my dad said to only shoot what I wanted to eat. So I went out and shot my neighbors' redheaded daughter in the ass. Hey, I was hungry for some pumpkin pie, by God! Nothin' wrong with a little dessert for the holidays.

I do like to hog hunt a little down at the country bar after 2 a.m., but ya don't need guns for them girls. Just put a couple of oatmeal creams in your pockets and they follow ya around like you're the fat girl Willard.

I don't know what my point is here. I just love the sound of the phrase "fat girl Willard"!

Like I said earlier, I never actually grew up in the South, but I've always loved everything about that part of the country. I love the people, the food, the weather, the way the girls talk to ya when they're moving their fingers seductively through your back hair at the strip club on Fridays (totally nude by the way after 10).

I actually acquired my accent back in '79 when I moved from Nebraska to Sanford, Florida. Since I grew up around livestock and Mildred Green, I automatically gravitated to the farm kids. They all sounded like they had just come from a *Dukes of Hazzard* casting call. I've always been a dialect chameleon, so I started speaking with a thick accent. From that point on it was my way of speech and I love it. Don't get me wrong: I can come in and out of it anytime I want; I just feel more comfortable in a southern dialect.

The cool thing is my family actually has a strong connection to the South. A great-great grandpa (there might be another great in there, I'm not sure) offered a gun and a horse to anyone that would join the Confederacy back in '64. Who cares if it was 1964. Give the guy a break. He had Alzheimer's and thought he was Jefferson Davis.

I know, ya think that's sad. Well, how do ya think I felt havin' to empty Jefferson Davis's bedpan every night?

When I went to college at Baptist University of America in Decatur, Georgia, my roommates were from Beaumont, Texas, and Dalton, Georgia. They pretty much frosted the dialect cake for me. By the end of my college years I sounded like a roadie for the Marshall Tucker Band.

I had a blast in college. I had a double major. Everyone had to major in Bible Studies and one other thing. My one other thing was looking at Andrea Koler's titties. (Lord, I apologize.) By the end of the school year I could quote the entire book of Luke AND get a bra off with 2 fingers in under 11 seconds.

Those were the days.

So now ya know a little bit about where I grew up and how I acquired my accent. That brings us to how I created my next character for 95 YNF, the guy who was really myself only with a different name (man, this is getting complicated).

This is how it happened: I was sitting on the couch at home

watching *Three's Company* and wishing I was Jack Tripper when my phone rang. It was my buddy from the radio station. He said they had been waiting on some cable guy to call them for a few days but they hadn't heard from him. So he asked me to call in and pretend to be the cable guy.

At the time I did a five-minute bit in my act about a cable installer coming to your house. I never thought of doin' it on the radio, mostly because I was tryin' to get my voice back from impersonating that old Jewish woman character. I also still had two months probation left after goin' down to the dinner theater, stripping naked, and sticking my wiener in between my legs to taunt Rosie O'Donnell.

But after much thought and half a bottle of Jim Beam, I agreed to call in the next day. That night I wrote out a bit where I would do social commentary as the cable guy. Then I went to bed and dreamt I was Jack Tripper nailing both roommates while Mr. Furley was at the Regal Beagle spreading rumors about me being a homosexual.

I'll never forget my first time on the air. Just before the phone call my stomach got upset from the seven bowls of Cap'n Crunch I had consumed the night before. I was miserable the whole morning. I could have pooped through a screen door and not touched a wire. However, throughout all the complications from the Captain and his crunch berries, I persevered through three minutes of radio hilarity.

I really can't remember right now what exactly I talked about; evidently it was funny enough, 'cause they asked me to do it again. In the beginning, I just introduced myself as the cable guy and never really attached a first name with it. When someone finally asked me to give one, I didn't want to use my real first name; I just popped out with Larry. That was kinda easy. Lawrence was my middle name, taken from my grandma.

I know. It's weird havin' a grandma named Larry, but just think how her mom, Earl, felt.

Names from the old days were weird. I've actually met old dudes named Connie and Sue. Back in the day, Bertha and Mildred were really popular names. I've never met anyone under 75 who was named either one of those, but I bet there used to be a Bertha that was a piece of ass. Somewhere back in 1932, I'm sure there was some pathetic sumbitch rubbin' one out while thinkin' about Mabel and Mildred and Bertha. The antique Charlie's Angels.

Today, ya wouldn't think of a Bertha bein' hot. You never see a sexy Mildred or Bertha. I'm sure I'll never be watching the country music awards over at my brother's log trailer and hear the announcer say, "And now here are the nominees for female country singer of the year: Faith Hill, Shania Twain, and Bertha Cramps." It just wouldn't sound right.

Back in 1932, I'm sure Bertha Cramps was turnin' heads left and right. Nowadays, though, she's that fat old lady wearin' the hairnet and servin' up mac and cheese in the lunchroom.

But gettin' back to my grandma, ya know, the one I got my middle name from? She actually was a stripper in a brothel back in '41. Grandma Lawrence is kind of losing it as she gets older and every now and then she gets back into the stripper frame of mind.

Last week, for example, she accidentally sent two naked pictures of herself to *Good Housekeeping* magazine. Then she sent a picture of her peach pie along with the recipe in to *Hustler*. The good news is that she won pie of the month in both publications (we're so damn proud of her).

But enough of my prostitute grandma, let's return to me. . . .

After those first few call-ins to the radio station, the name Larry the Cable Guy began to stick as a recurring character. I never realized how popular my calls were becoming because I phoned in while I was touring the country with *Riverdance* and doing a little stand-up. I never had time to hear the broadcasts.

Meanwhile, I ended up quitting Riverdance; I enjoyed per-formin' but the costume pinched my nuts so bad during the leg kicks, I ended up herniating myself. I swear my left nut swelled up to the size of one of those medicine balls. It was very painful, but for 11 days I got a great workout.

With my dancin' career behind me, I concentrated on doin' stand-up and pursuin' my first love: making scenic murals out of nipples cut from various porn publications. I actually made a beautiful forest scene out of vaginas I cut out of *Gallery Magazine*. I gave it to my parents for their anniversary. It's hanging up in their living room right next to the John Wayne I made out of penis tips. Every year I give 'em a new one and they just go to squallerin'!

Sorry. I've been drinking and it's late.

Anyway, I ended up doing call-ins at this radio station for about a year. It got to the point where I was doing social commentary three days a week without getting paid a red cent. Ya see I never really cared about the money too much, but it was actually becoming a pain in my muscular Dolph Lundgren–lookin' ass to do these things so often. I know makin' phone calls doesn't sound like much work, but trust me, it wasn't easy. Besides, all my time was being taken up by my latest project: the city wanted me to create a canyon scene for the courthouse. Made entirely out of buttholes.

Ya know how many magazines ya have to buy to find enough buttholes for a mural? Let me tell ya, it ain't no walk in the park.

I asked the station to cough up a little cash to at least cover the expense of all those phone calls I was makin'. They refused. I still continued doin' them but with my tail between my legs.

Then, after a bit of thought, a lightbulb went off in my head. I decided to run for president of the United States and get the station to publicize my campaign. They'd get a great promo out of it, and I'd make a little cash selling campaign T-shirts. What you might call a win-win situation.

We began selling *Larry the Cable Guy for President* T-shirts at convenience stores all over central Florida. I made campaign stops and gave speeches on the radio that I wrote myself. I even made a *Larry for President* mural out of tits from a Heather Locklear photo shoot.

I tell ya, things were kickin' until it came time to get paid for the shirts. When we first agreed to do the promotion, the station said they'd give me a buck for every shirt they sold. I figure they must have moved around 40,000 shirts.

In radio math, that meant they owed me seven thousand dollars.

Boy, was that an instant education. The thing I never realized about the radio business is that most of the people in charge are brain-dead morons. Don't get me wrong, I love radio. The jocks and the people that are just regular employees bustin' their asses and making the station tick are great. But the people in control of the cash, those guys drivin' around in sports cars and Hummers while the rest of the air staff is getting towed, are the ones I got a problem with.

Some radio stations like to treat their talent like orange-pickin' immigrants. They seem to forget that if it wasn't for the on-air personalities bringin' in the listeners and pushin' up the ratings, they'd be on the same level as the retard workin' the fry machine down at Wendy's. Not all of 'em, mind you. There's still a few good ones out there that care about their employees, but the majority of 'em can kiss my eye-watering ass.

After the shirt fiasco, I told the station to kiss my buns of steel, which, by the way, have been known to set off metal detectors at airports. I stopped callin' in altogether and retired to the comedy clubs. I also worked on a contract with the school board to make butthole murals for a new high school.

Just when I thought I was done with radio, a competing station invited me to call them with my commentaries. I hesitated until they said that I would not only get to compete against my old station, I'd also get paid AND they'd let me run the police siren at the St. Patrick's Day parade.

Well obviously this would be something I'd like to do! So I told my girlfriend and her husband that I was goin' to move out and once again work for a radio station, doin' what I loved.

I worked at WDIZ in Orlando for almost four years and it was a much better experience than my YNF days. The people at WDIZ greeted me with warmth and kindness; I even got to dry-hump the receptionist on casual Fridays.

At WDIZ, I could cluelessly lay the groundwork for my new character, which was really me just bein' me with a fake name. Everywhere I went, people were talkin' about my commentaries from the night before. I figured if these listeners got off on me, either they were big fans or else they were really starved for entertainment. I mean, after all, we're talkin' about a day and age when *Alf* and *Silver Spoons* were the talk of the town. The cool thing was that people were listening to me and actually liking what I did.

Whenever I thought about how my work was finally earnin' some notoriety, I rubbed myself so hard a genie popped out. Before that, the only time anyone ever recognized me for anything was in a police lineup after I got my wiener stuck in the birdhouse at the zoo. I would have gotten away with it, only some women from a local bird watchers club were there and they had told the zoo attendant they'd seen a beer-bellied woodpecker.

I felt bad because I normally don't act like that. However, my brother had just been baptized the night before and we had thrown a big blowout for him.

Ya know, it coulda been worse. We were gonna take him to Hooters, but I'm kinda cautious about goin' there. Call me nuts, but I do believe that if the shorts get any shorter on them waitresses the FDA is gonna start makin' em wear hairnets between their legs. I mean it's a little ridiculous. Two weeks ago I went there with a buddy and my chicken wings needed a comb over!

I ain't BS'n. I was literally two bites from coughin' up the kinda hairballs Rosie O'Donnell might barf after an Indigo Girl meet-and-greet.

I tell ya what, though, Hooters has been great for my career. Even though I've got a better shot at gettin' laid at a N.O.W. convention while wearin' a shirt that says "Show Me Your Penis," Hooters kept me busy while I did stuff for the radio station. I could always count on bringin' in an extra 400 bucks a week hosting their bikini contests. Any time a comedian can get onstage and make 400 bucks, you grab it. Usually only strippers and deformed cripples can make that kinda stage cash.

Actually you can make pretty good cash on stage without being a comedian or a stripper. My brother once won a talent contest by fartin' the song "Dixie" through an oil funnel. He not only took home 500 bucks, he got to meet Regis after the show.

Who says dreams don't come true?

But God bless Hooters for the 400 bucks I received every third Thursday of the month. It helped pay for the medicine to treat the herpes I also received from Hooters every third Friday of the month.

By the way, did y'all know Hooters has its own airline? Hooters Air! I flown 'em five times and already have seven thousand frequent boner miles. It's the only airline I've ever been on where I requested an aisle seat and prayed for turbulence!

It's also the only airline where the flight attendants can use their tits as flotation devices! (I could do this all day!)

Those flight attendants piss me off, though. They have to be dumber than a box of dumb stuff. I asked one girl if I could see the cockpit. She pulled her little green shorts down. The guy next to me peeked down her shorts and asked, "Is that the black box they always talk about on these airplanes?" That was the last straw. First, the dumb flight attendants, then a drunken preacher! That was the last time I flew that airline!

But enough about big tits and black boxes; let's get back to how my name came about. We still gotta cover how I started tourin' with that name and how I got Kate Bosworth to fondle my testicles at a truck stop.

Excuse me, did I say Kate Bosworth? I meant to say how I saw Tom *Bosley's* testicles at a rest stop. I ain't kiddin'. Okay, I made the nuts thing up, but I really once seen Tom Bosley from *Happy Days* at a rest stop. Although to be honest, I actually thought it was David Doyle from *Charlie's Angels*.

I bet that sucks for those guys. They both had totally separate successful careers, yet everybody thinks Tom Bosley and David Doyle are the same guy. Ruben Studdard and Star Jones often suffer from the same kind of mix-up. And I don't even want to tell you about all the people who mistake my ass for George Clooney's.

Many in the entertainment field call this the Oak Ridge Boys–Statler Brothers disease. They are both country singing groups and everybody confuses one for the other. I once made a big mistake by yellin' "Sing 'Elvira' " during a Statler Brothers performance. They got all pissed. Granted, I forgot the Oak Ridge Boys actually sang that song AND the Statlers were singing at a friend's funeral, so my request might not have been appropriate. However, I do love that song and I didn't quite understand their reaction.

I mean, for God's sake, we sang "East Bound and Down" by Jerry Reed at my grandpa's funeral, so what's the big deal?

By the way, before leavin' this fascinatin' subject, I want to state for the record that I've seen Melissa Etheridge at a gym doin' squats.

And, yes, I did see her nuts.

Now where were we?

Oh yeah. Four years after I started doing commentary on WDIZ, the Clear Channel Corporation bought the station. You may have heard of Clear Channel. They don't own every radio station in America, just those whose call letters start with K or W. Clear Channel and Ticketmaster are the musical mafia. If you're in entertainment, you can't wipe your ass without one of these two corporations spreading your cheeks.

Both of 'em have been good to me, but they do some crap that I'll never understand. For example, Clear Channel fired some morning DJ's after the company claimed it couldn't afford to pay their 28-thousand-dollar-a-year salaries. The very next day, the station started givin' away a thousand dollars an hour as part of a month-long promotion.

Hello, McFly! That's like armin' Rosie O'Donnell with a rape whistle. It doesn't make any sense. They just fired a guy 'cause they couldn't afford his 28 grand and they end up givin' away thirty times that over the next month? Why didn't they just keep the guy and give away 500 bucks an hour? And that ain't just Clear Channel, that's a lot of stations.

Clear Channel's policy reminds me of the joke I tell where a company puts out a suggestion box and offers to give a hundred dollars to any employee that comes up with a way to save the company money.

So somebody writes "Make the reward 50 bucks." DUH!!!!

I swear, somebody could make a fortune selling drool cups to corporate execs. How do companies survive with these retards runnin' the front office?

And don't even get me started on Ticketmaster. Look, I know I need 'em. Ya gotta have a way to sell tickets, but they got all these extra fees and ya wonder what in the hell they're all for. I took this

oriental piece of ass and her interpreter out to see ZZ Top one
year. The tickets were 42 bucks apiece! By the time they added in
all the extra charges, I was up to 210 bucks. And to top that off, the
Chinese chick didn't even put out. Her interpreter, however, is
completely shaved.

Oh, and for the record, I used to work at Ticketmaster. I quit
after two weeks and they charged me a 50 dollar quittin' fee!

Sumbitches.

After Clear Channel bought WDIZ, the new management decided
to keep me around. Well, how could they not want me? At the time
I was the highest rated feature on the show. It mighta also helped
that I pretended to be crippled and they were scared of gettin'
sued if they dumped me.

This was awesome! The station not only raised my salary, they
threw in a bad-ass handicapped spot in the front for the days I
showed up. My contract allowed me to call in the radio bits from
wherever I was touring. When I was off the road, though, I had to
come in and do the morning show live.

Since they never knew whether I could really walk, this was the
best of both worlds. I traveled and made fans all over the country
doing stand-up. When I came home, I'd visit the station and get
waited on. How cool is that? It's amazing how much ass you can
get with a wheelchair. I was Ron Jeremy on wheels!

It almost came to an end, though, one Friday when the general
manager caught me running for some Krispy Kremes. I told him I
had just seen Benny Hinn, the faith healer, and he had cured my
paralysis.

Luckily he fell for it. The good news was that I felt better about
not livin' a lie anymore. The bad news: I lost my handicapped
parking spot and they kicked me off the wheelchair basketball
team. That doubly sucked because I was high scorer and was all set
to nail the cheerleader with the clubfoot.

I spent the next several years perfecting my commentaries while my popularity continued to grow. That was cool. I enjoyed writing them, and performing the bits improved my stand-up routines.

This is a good time to describe what my commentaries sounded like. As I said earlier, the cable guy is a character I created, but at the same time, he is me. I changed only my name and, by now, people know that name and relate with it. If I'da known it was gonna take off like this, I might have done it different—maybe used my real name—but ya play the cards you're dealt. Besides, my middle name fits better on a cable guy. I've met way more cable guys named Larry than Danny, which happens to be my first name. Hell, my friends call me L.D. for Larry-Dan, so what's the big deal?

One thing was certain. I couldn't use the name my dad called me: Dickweed. And that was on a good day. I've never met a cable guy named Dickweed; THAT I am sure of.

I could have called myself Lance the Cable Guy, but 90 percent of all Lances are either starring in gay porn or gettin' their asses kicked at recess.

When I give interviews, the same questions about The Cable Guy keep croppin' up. "Is it true Shania Twain uses you as a sex toy?" That's usually the first question. The second question is always "How much is you and how much is the character?"

Here's my replies. To the first question: No, Shania Twain does not use me as a sex toy. However, a girl that looked like Mark Twain once let me see her titties behind a Long John Silver's (by the way . . . NASTY!).

As for question number two, in some ways I'm just like my character and in others I'm not. The real "me" is first and foremost an American and proud of it. I grew up in a small town on a pig farm in Nebraska. I like country music, Iron Maiden, Lynyrd Skynyrd, four-wheelin', and bird huntin', I believe Alf's TV talk show is hilarious AND I do believe in Jesus.

I love John Wayne and the *Andy Griffith Show*. I also love this show that's on Playboy TV right now as I write this book. I love Ted Nugent, all the branches of the military and the NRA and I think at least two cast members from *The View* have penises. My hero is Ronald Reagan. I think if ya live in America you should learn the language AND I got no problem with the rebel flag on the General Lee.

Now that you know all that, you decide how close I am to my character. I just don't know.

Okay, now it's my turn to ask a question. What's that chick's name that was in *Joe Dirt*? Damn, whenever she crawled off that horse in them Daisy Dukes I'd run right out and hump my toolshed! She damn near made me forget about that crippled cheerleader with the clubfoot!

That, of course, brings me to my commentaries. But hold on first, I'll be right back. I have to poop. All this writin' makes me so constipated that when it hits, ya gotta run to the toilet, so hold on.

OK, I'm back.

Before we start, let me ask you another question. This just came to me while sittin' in there. Ya ever fart so hard your back cracks? Well guess what? TADA! Next time your back hurts, forget aspirins or other pain relievers. Eat a corn dog! I'm tellin' ya, it works.

Now where were we? Oh, yeah, the commentaries. Here's how they started. I've always been pretty opinionated and I loved watchin' political shows. I love *The O'Reilly Factor*. I love *Hannity & Colmes*. I watch Chris Matthews and the *Naked News* on Showtime. I know naked chicks doin' the news may not really be top-notch news reporting but it's thc only ncws source that actually gave me a boner while coverin' the pope's funeral.

Now ya know how ya get pissed while watchin' news shows like these. It doesn't even have to be the news, it could be reruns of Whoopie Goldberg's piece of crap show, whatever. That's me every night, gettin' pissed off over something in the news. So I figured I'd write down my feelings about a particular story and read 'em to the audience.

Hence the birth of my radio commentaries.

From the start, I knew I couldn't just call and bitch seriously about a topic. Preachy is boring. Since I was calling mainly rock and alternative stations, I also knew the audience would accept material that was a bit rough. This of course was way before Janet Jackson popped out her nasty decorated Christmas nipple and ruined everything.

So here's the formula I developed for writing my commentaries:

1. I'd grab a pen and paper;
2. I'd check my scrotum for ticks from playin' with my dogs; and
3. I'd write down anything that pissed me off about a certain news item.

I always wrote how I honestly felt about a topic. Then I'd review the material and "Larry" it up a bit. The idea was always to make a point, but, first and foremost, I wanted the piece to be funny and outrageous. I wanted people shakin' their heads and saying "I can't believe this guy just said that on the radio."

For example: one day I read an item in the paper ('cause my neighbor got up late) about Kim Jong Il of North Korea mouthing off about having nuclear weapons and threatenin' to use them. I hated that little flippin' commie and what he said just pissed me off, so I used him as my topic for the day.

Here's how the first draft looked:

Ya know I can't figure out this North Korean leader. This sorry communist could care less about human life as long as he can threaten everybody and keep 'em under his mercy. I'm not scared of the little asshole. So maybe he has nuclear weapons. He ain't gonna use 'em. He ain't even got anybody tall enough that could press the button anyway unless he gets somethin' to stand on. The hell with him.

Pretty basic, huh? It's not really funny, it's definitely not outrageous, and there's really no point to it.

Now watch the changes as we "Larry" it up:

What's up with that sweet-and-sour commie gook Kim Jong Ill Cream Cheese, whatever the hell his name is? I oughta go over to them rice paddies and wax on and wax off an ass whoopin' on that rice fartin' commie fag. He says he's gonna use nuclear weapons—big deal! I say good luck findin' anybody tall enough to reach the button over there!! Gee, I hope they don't get phone books or we are screwed.

Now, that's good commentary.

Is it politically correct? Of course not.

Is it outrageous? Yes.

Is it funny? It is to me.

Is it time to get the binoculars and watch my neighbor wax her privates by her bathroom window with the shades open?

DAMN RIGHT!

Okay, we made it. All the way to the end of the first chapter. I am real sorry that I left out the part about the time I had Heidi Klum bent over a workout bench; maybe I can work that in some later chapter. Now it's time to tell you how the phrase *git-r-done* came about and changed my life. I'll do my best to explain its influence on American culture while also touching on a more important topic: how the cancellation of *Hee-Haw* dramatically affected my friends and family.

Chapter 2

THE ORIGIN OF GIT-R-DONE!

IN THIS CHAPTER I'm gonna not only give out the secret recipe for Kentucky Fried Chicken—which tastes better than a cheerleader on game day— I'm gonna reveal how the phrase "git-r-done" (which, by the way, is sweeping the nation faster than illegal immigration) came about. I'll also share some experiences, so you'll discover how it has affected my life.

So grab a Jack Daniels fruit punch cooler and a hanky, 'cause it's gonna be tear jerking. This is one of the most important chapters in the book because the main question that people always ask me after my shows, other than "Is your sister really covered in moles?" and "Are you the model from the Sloflex commercial ads?", is "What is the origin of 'git-r-done'?"

The first time I called in as the cable guy to 95 YNF in Tampa I ended my call with "git-r-done." I just made it up on the spot and never really thought anything about it. The jocks thought it was funny and when they asked, "What's that mean?" I said "Well whatever ya do, just git-r-done!" I didn't know it then, but that was the day a life-changin' phrase was born.

It was also the day my nephew was born, but this book ain't about him so the hell with him! Actually, I have three nephews,

John, Ricki, and Heather. John and Ricki are pretty normal but Heather is a little weird.

OK, back to the book.

"Git-r-done" is a phrase that basically sums up a good American work ethic. Meaning whatever ya have to do, don't complain, just git-r-done. Do what ya gotta do, do it good, and git-r-done! It's a great phrase. I feel it carries way better staying power than other cultural phrases, such as "Where's the beef?" or "Bounty . . . the quicker picker-upper," because it's one of those phrases that you can use anywhere.

Think about it. Ya can't be at a ball game with two outs in the ninth inning and yell to the pitcher "Bounty is the quicker picker-upper!!" It makes no sense and you'd look retarded. But you could yell "Git-r-done!" and everyone would know what ya meant.

That's why "git-r-done" is perfect for any occasion. With "Bounty is the quicker picker-upper" and "Where's the beef?" ya have to pick your spots. "Git-r-done" is universal. Well, almost universal. Seems that in Japanese, the phrase roughly translates into "you're hung like an eggroll." Which explains why I was fired two years ago from a Mitsubishi corporate function. The conversation that got my ass canned went like this:

"Larry, this is Mr. Tagogee, president of Mitsubishi."

"Nice to meet ya. Git-r-done!"

Oh well, at least I didn't miss the Braves' game that night.

The thing I love about the phrase is its versatility. For example, you can use it to relay happiness . . . git-r-done! Sadness . . . git-r-done! Horror . . . git-r-done! Surprise . . . git-r-done!

Of course, you can't hear all those subtle differences on paper. You'll have to add your own inflections to each matching emotion, but if you take the time its tons of fun for the entire family! I'm even thinking of putting out Git-R-Done!: The Boardgame.

Just think of the bonding that will inspire. Dad lands on the Git-R-Done space while Mom and the kids yell "Git-r-done!" and slap high fives. Then Dad draws a Git-R-Done card that says, "Advance two spaces to the titty bar box and pay each female employee 100 bucks."

Fun for the whole family!

I never started sayin' "git-r-done" thinking, *Wow I'm gonna create this phrase and the whole country is gonna love it.* I mean I tried that before and it didn't work. Way before I did stand-up, I worked at a place for the hearing impaired. Every afternoon for five years, after we all ate lunch, I'd stand up and yell, "That was titty-lickin' good," thinkin' that it would catch on and all these hearing-impaired folks would soon be motioning "titty-lickin' good" in sign language. Unfortunately, my attempts fell on deaf ears. (I could do this all day.)

I actually had tried other phrases, but they never took off. For twenty years I yelled "Yipper dipper ripper stripper." It garnered a few laughs, but what it mostly got was lots of stares. Even I didn't know what it meant, but it flowed off the tongue real good and had *stripper* at the end of it. I thought anything that ends in *stripper* was bound to sell. This didn't. Maybe it was the *yipper* that threw people off. I know it couldn't have been *dipper* or *ripper*. I'll never figure out why it didn't work. However, every now and again I still use it at parties, hopin' to work out the kinks.

Here's another phrase I used that sure sounded funny to me: "If I was a sculptor, but then again, no." That wasn't mine, though. I ripped it off from an old Elton John song. You know the one where the lyrics go "if I was a sculptor, but then again, no?" I can't remember the name of that song, but I used the phrase randomly in my act. I didn't that much, though. Only after a joke bombed.

Which meant I used it about 85 percent of the time.

I guess it was funny only to me because, after I said it, the crowd would just stare back at me like a buncha skinheads watchin' *The Jeffersons*. That was demoralizin'; I began to think maybe I shouldn't even be a comedian. Maybe I should go into a different line of work.

Maybe if I was a sculptor . . . ah, but then again, no.

The "git-r-done" phrase literally fell in my lap. I used it for almost three years without even knowing it was becoming so popular. I didn't even think much of it until the day I walked through the mall with a buddy, checkin' out high school ass. We heard somebody yell "Git-r-done" to his friend as he left the store.

My buddy asked, "Did you hear that?" Well, of course I didn't. My mind was preoccupied with a fantasy it was concocting that had me and the girl I had just seen at the Orange Julius 69'n in a hammock. He said, "Dude, that guy just yelled 'Git-r-done.' Ain't that your phrase?" I said "Yes." Then I put the bag I was carrying over my crotch to hide my Orange Julius boner and went over to talk to the guy who yelled. I was like, "Dude, where did ya hear that phrase?"

First off I shouldn't have said "Dude" because it wasn't a dude; it was actually a chick that looked like T.J. Hooker. Anyway he, she, whatever replied, "I got it from Larry the Cable Guy. He says it all the time on the radio."

I thought that was the coolest thing. Not that people were starting to use my phrase, but that I actually had met a girl that looked like T.J. Hooker.

I started noticing people saying it all over the place, no matter where I went. That's when I thought, *Man, I gotta copyright this thing*. I hadn't tried to copyright anything since 1978 when I came up with Farrah Fawcett–flavored lick sticks (somethin' else that coulda worked, given half a chance).

I finally copyrighted my new phrase after spending a lot of time and taking a lot of verbal abuse. By verbal abuse I mean I couldn't go anywhere without runnin' into some copyright office employee who would yell, "How'd the Farrah lick sticks turn out?" Regardless of the lick sticks, I knew this was worthy of copyrighting, so after investin' several thousand dollars—which, by the way, I won during a Clear Channel radio station cash giveaway—I got the copyright for "git-r-done."

By then no one within earshot of me could say the phrase without my noticin'. During the 2000 election, I thought I heard George W. use it, but I might have been mistaken. I do remember the first time somebody major used my phrase nationally. It was the Arizona Diamondbacks baseball team. Luis Gonzalez, the left fielder of the Diamondbacks known as "Gonzo," is a good buddy of mine. I met him in Tampa Bay way back in the '80s when I was a small black man performing under the name of "Smokes."

Luis said that I was so funny offstage, I should just be myself when I performed. So I sold my rims, broke up with the fat white chick I was livin' with at the time, and went back to appearing as me. Luis would come to my shows all the time and I'd go help him with his swing. He won't admit this, but if not for my awesome hitting instructions, he'd never be in the majors today.

OK, that's all BS, but I did show him how to make a potato gun, so kiss my redneck ass. At least I did something for him.

I'll never forget the 2001 season, when Luis and the Diamondbacks won the World Series. That was also the year my ugly friend Tina got a tattoo on her privates that said "Downgrade . . . watch for other truckers."

But we won't get into that here.

I was working at the Improv in Phoenix during the first week of June that year. Nice booking! Phoenix in June! Why didn't my manager just give me 1,200 bucks and kick me in the nuts. The week I played there, it was 123 degrees out and people were melting at the park.

I had just walked into my hotel room when the phone rang. My second cousin and his ex-wife were the only people I knew in Phoenix. Those two hated each other so much, they used to visit Vegas every first week of June just to renew their divorce vows, so I knew they weren't around to call me.

It was Luis. We hadn't seen each other since the Tampa Bay years. He invited me to Bank One Ballpark to hang out with some of the players in the clubhouse and help Mark Grace hone his swing. It was a blast. I fielded, hit some balls, and, after the game started, I stayed in the locker room and made 430 bucks goin' through various wallets and satchels.

Turned out most of the Diamondbacks were huge fans of mine. They called the following week and asked if they could play a recording of me saying "Git-r-done" every time Luis came to bat during a game and every time their lefty reliever Greg Swindell came into pitch.

They also wanted to play it every time they showed some girl with big tits on the jumbo screen.

I said yes to everything except Swindell (he once cost me 300 bucks in a Strat-o-Matic game draft). That was the first big boost for "git-r-done." The D-backs even adopted the phrase for their 2001 World Series run. They had signs everywhere that said GIT-R-DONE DIAMONDBACKS! After the Series ended, Luis sent me a picture of him getting the Series-winning hit against the New York Yankees. In the background on the jumbo screen it said "Got-r-done!"

Luis also sent me a picture of a huge turd from Randy Johnson, Arizona's ace pitcher. You coulda sat 15 marines comfortably on that damn thing. I mean I've had some bowel movements that coulda took some major awards, but that thing! Ripley would have been scratchin' his head in disbelief. How cool is that, though? I'm not talkin' about the turd. Something I created was startin' to go mainstream.

I was so damn proud. I hadn't been that excited since *Mama's Family* came out on DVD!

The year 2001 was a very good one for me. People everywhere were saying "Git-r-done," especially after I hooked up with the Blue Collar Comedy tour. I was performing before bigger crowds. I was perfecting my act. I was playing with myself every night in some of the nicest hotels in America. My tests came back negative.

Things were looking up.

Then it hit. One night I was laying in bed practicing some penis puppetry for an upcomin' *Tonight Show* appearance. I was all set to twist my wiener into a poodle dog while watchin' a Shania Twain video for inspiration.

That's when I found the lump.

I was like, *This is just great. Just as I'm startin' to get famous, I'm gonna die of tumors.* But after a few brief terrifyin' minutes, I realized I had accidentally sat on a Werther's Original hard candy and it had wedged up my crack pretty good. It was so far beyond my reach, I just let it melt out over the course of the following day. I actually didn't mind it. It was painless, and when I farted, it sent out a nice butterscotch aroma.

Funny how life works, ain't it? Here I went from thinking I was gonna die to actually improving my life. I even thought of maybe getting a second copyright on a thing called the Butterscotch Fart Buster. I never did copyright it, but whenever I eat BBQ or watch reruns of Urkel, I always stick a Werther's Original up my ass. Sometimes I'll use cinnamon for the ladies!

It took over 14 years of radio calls and performances plus the Blue Collar Tour to popularize my phrase. The Diamondback thing helped tremendously and I thank them for that. In 2002, the Los Angeles Dodgers asked permission to use "git-r-done" during spring training. Then I noticed other pro teams adoptin' it. I noticed school and college players began sayin' it.

And I noticed that I had put on so much weight, I now had big-ger tits than Gwyneth Paltrow.

I needed to lose some of that weight. I had gained over 50 pounds that year. Some mighta blamed that on eatin' too much. I blamed it on Janet Jackson, that skank. Ever since she popped her titties out at the Super Bowl halftime show I couldn't stop drinkin' chocolate milk.

Even if I hadn't put on all those pounds, I would have been pissed off at her anyway. Here we are watchin' the Super Bowl on the big screen down at Best Buy and outta nowhere this moron pops out her big, nasty, pierced party tits in front of God and everybody around the country. I didn't even hardly think they were that sexy, except for maybe I did a little.

OK, maybe I did a lot, but I'm just sayin' . . .

I'll tell ya a big thrill I got after "git-r-done" achieved some fame. I'm a huge NASCAR fan, and one day I was in Charlotte, North Car-olina, waiting for a ride to one of my shows. My tour manager called and said, "Somebody downstairs wants to give you a lift."

"Well, who is it?"

"It's a surprise. Just get downstairs right away."

Boy, I was excited! All kinds of thoughts went through my head. Could it be Faith Hill? Could it be that the Playboy Channel was there because they needed a fat redneck in some sorta shower video with Jenna Jameson? Maybe it was the patent office wanting to know about the Butterscotch Fart Buster.

Turns out it was Michael Waltrip, the racing car driver! That was cool, though I kinda wished it had been the patent office. Michael told me that he said "Git-r-done" all the time and that he wanted to take me to the show and hang out. WOW!! Now we got the folks at NASCAR repeatin' my phrase and Michael Waltrip, one of my favorite drivers, turns out to be a fan! Awesome! I figured I could die and go to heaven and see if the Lord really looks the way pictures portray him in the churches. Ya know, like the drummer from Foghat, or if he's wearin' a more businesslike look, kinda like Ben Stein.

I had a blast hangin' out with Michael Waltrip; he's one of the coolest dudes around. It was unbelievable for me to be spendin' time with so many famous people. You could see that I was truly blessed. I mean I'm the guy that cried when he met the actor James Best (Roscoe P. Coltrane from *The Dukes of Hazzard*) at a diner called Mel's in Sanford, Florida!

The most neato part (can't believe I wrote that—what am I, Beaver Cleaver?) was having NASCAR people saying "Git-r-done!" Now if I could just persuade the Pope to say it in 70 different languages (provided he doesn't use it in Japanese).

Not everyone had fun with the phrase. There was some dick-weed principal of a high school outside of Albany, New York, who banned kids from saying it. He thought "git-r-done" was an offensive phrase that meant to "git *her* done." While "git-r-done *could* mean that under the right circumstances, it doesn't. Just like Nikes "just do it" isn't telling ya' to have sex, neither does "git-r-done." Both phrases can have double meanings dependin' on how someone uses 'em. In that regard, they're a lot like Wendy's "Where's the beef?", which actually started out as a joke about Dave Thomas's penis.

Lib public school administrators like this principal crack me up. They work in a field that encourages free thought and then they ban things without usin' common sense. I mean if a kid is walkin' around school with a shirt that says "Ass inspector," common sense would say maybe he hadn't oughta wear that shirt to school.

I mean, let's face it. A shirt like that should be worn only maybe at a fair or water theme park.

But you'd think this guy would have researched the phrase before he did the communist thing by banning it. So I called this principal and in a good Christian way said, "Hey asswipe, don't ya think ya oughta check into somethin' before ya ban it?"

This guy workin' at Radio Shack had no clue what I was talkin' about, which is when I realized I had dialed the wrong number.

I did reach the school on my next try and this is what I got: "For English press 1. For Spanish press 2."

Man, I was madder than a pervert with palsy tryin' to draw a pair of tits on an Etch-a-Sketch. Here was this voice mailbox for a public school offerin' instructions in Spanish. I mean, God bless Spanish-speakin' folks. If it wasn't for them, the Atlanta Braves would have sucked for the last ten years. But give me a break. This was an *American* public school, not a *Spanish* public school. Even if they do got a lot of Spanish kids, shouldn't these students be learnin' the English language? I bet ya tickets to Judy Juggs that answer-phones in Mexican schools ain't playin' no English recordings!

I tell ya, I haven't been that irritated since I tried watchin' *Busty Cops* on a VHS player with bad tracking! Don't get me wrong, I'm all for anybody that wants to come to this country. But it ain't my fault English is the spoken language. *For English press 1. For Spanish press 2!* Here's an idea. How 'bout puttin' button #3 on there to push in case ya want the feller that pushed 2 to learn English! It's downright ridiculous!

I finally got the principal on the phone and cordially explained what "git-r-done" meant. His response was totally deadpan. He kinda mumbled somethin' about bringin' it up at the next meeting. Then he hung up. You just know this is the kinda guy that acts all goody-goody in school. Then he goes home and nails himself with the handle of a hairbrush while he's bent over a footstool. I knew he had already made up his mind; I gave it a shot anyway. I even tried tellin' him my Butterscotch Fart Buster idea, but he sounded disinterested.

Luckily, the kids (God bless 'em) stuck up for the phrase and the ban actually did more good than harm because ya couldn't go anywhere outside the school limits without seein' "git-r-done" written on something.

As for those kids that use it in a bad way, whatever, it's a free country. I can't control what people mean when they say it. Use it anyway ya like. But the phrase is actually talkin' about a blue collar work ethic and nothing more. It just chaps my ass that educators in a school system as bad as ours have nothing more to worry about than a phrase some comedian made up.

Mind you I'm not knockin' all public school officials. There are some good ones that want to do right. But it seems like the majority of school administrators are so wrapped up in political correctness that their common sense has disappeared like a fat girl playin' dodge ball.

I'll give ya an example of what I mean by no common sense. There was recently a story about a kid in Florida that snapped another student with a rubber band. The school expelled him because they said he had used the rubber band as a weapon and that broke the school's rule against havin' weapons in school.

You gotta be shittin' me! A rubber band a weapon? I have never seen a rubber band hurt anyone in my whole life.

However, I did see a wedding band do some damage to my brother last year!

Here's another example of what I'm talkin' about. Not long ago, some school suspended a girl after a security guard saw a butter knife sittin' on the passenger seat of her car. I ain't making that up. A butter knife! What did they think she was gonna do? Go berserk and peanut butter and jelly somebody to death?

That's what I'm talkin' about. No common sense.

I will say that even though that principal from Albany was too brain dead to get the meaning of my phrase, the United States Military understands it. I love these guys. My dad was in the military.

He saw action in Korea, Vietnam, and a Wal-Mart in Jackson, Mississippi.

The Wal-Mart thing was rough. Dad was buying stool softener when he flashed back to the time he got shot in his wipin' hand while taking a poop in the jungle. Soon as Dad saw the Korean cashier, he snapped. Dad tried to stab her with a Jimmy Dean pure pork sausage. Customers had to wrestle him to the floor. I hadn't seen such a flusterclut since my fat sister caused a 12-tray pileup in front of the caramel nut rolls at the country buffet.

I never served in the military. However, I did catch syphilis from a Vietnamese girl named Cathy Ming in college. I was stupid, I guess, but I was so horny. She was workin' at Jiffy Lube and kept tauntin' me with her leg hiked up while she worked that foot jack. I mean give me a break.

I would have served in the military but we weren't fightin' any wars at the time. None of my friends were joinin' and there was this new invention for your TV called the remote control, so not even Pam Anderson layin' naked in a bed of Frosted Flakes could get me outta the house back then.

But it's not as if I don't have any military experience. I used to shoot toy soldiers with my BB gun. I'd set the Americans on one side and the German-lookin' ones on the other. Every now and then, I'd put up a picture of Jane Fonda just to make it interesting. Then my brother would grab my gun and shoot me in the ass until I ran cryin' to the house and my fun for the day was over.

What made it really sad was that I was 31 at the time.

I love the military and support everything they do. Far as I'm concerned, we should pay those soldiers in Iraq a lot more money. You know that 40 billion dollars we're givin' the Iraqis to rebuild their country? Let's cut that by about two-thirds. The Iraqis won't be hurtin'. With all that oil bubblin' under their country, they've got plenty of their own money already.

I ain't yankin' on the people of Iraq. God bless 'em, they got rid of a dictator and now they have a chance for democracy. I'm all for 'em! I hope they all get new wicker baskets full of snakes for Christmas, but they oughta pay for some of that stuff themselves. It's called the price for freedom. With all the brave lives we've sacrificed, you'd think they could cough up some cash! We oughta take some of that money we're sending to Iraq and give every soldier that fought a million bucks. It'd for sure total up to be less than the 40 billion we're throwin' to a country that don't need it.

By the way, my nuts itch!

The military has been great to me. When my last CD, *The Right to Bare Arms,* came out, the army put in the first big order. Our soldiers have sent me all sorts of pictures showin' "Git-r-done!" plastered on tanks, jeeps, Humvees, helicopters, and the titties of Iraqi whores. That's awesome! Just another example of how the phrase has caught on.

I hope that that principle and anyone else who thinks it's a sexual phrase are payin' attention. Obviously the soldiers aren't putting that phrase on their tanks to say "We're Americans and we're coming to hump your women!" They're saying "We're Americans and we're comin' to kick your dictator's ass so you can have some sense of freedom. GIT-R-DONE!"

And, believe me, those soldiers will git-r-done, guaranteed. It's really a humbling experience knowing that what I do (whatever the hell that is) lifts up their morale a little bit. I can't commend the men and women in the armed forces enough for the way they perform.

I'll tell ya who else I commend: the guy that wrote the film *Stroker Ace*. If there ever was a make-out movie made in this world, that's one of the best. Just bring a girl to your apartment after takin' her to Long John Silver's and pop *Stroker Ace* into the DVD player. Whoo Lord, if you ain't got her top off in the first 20 min-utes then you got a dud 'cause that damn movie kicks ass!

One day I was sitting in my house trying to think of a surefire product that I could sell to novelty stores. I came up with this Roman soldier named Farticus. He'd be just like any other plastic toy solder, except when you pulled a string, he'd fart. Very clever indeed.

Before I could write down my idea, a football game came on the tube and immediately sidetracked me. I love football. However, even though I was big enough to play the sport as a kid, I joined the marchin' band instead. Caught a lot of crap for that. All the jocks called me a sissy and a pussy and every other name in the book. I stuck it out even though I hated the band costume. It kept wedging up my asscrack and after every parade my nuts would be chafed. Boy, there's nothing in this world worse than chafed nuts (I actually think that's a line from a George Michael song).

Still, I have to admit I loved twirlin' that baton.

Now if I may for a minute stray from this particular topic, I just have to get this out, "Yipper dipper ripper stripper!"

Sorry but I'm still tryin' to work the kinks out on that.

As I was saying, I love football. I love all sports, but football is number one, followed by baseball, NASCAR, rodeo, bull riding, and gymnastics. Gotta stick a qualifier on that last one. I love gym-nastics, but only when they get up close on the splits and flying camels, which me and my friends refer to as "flying camel toes."

I know, we're so childish, but I swear the bar routine oughta be on Pay-Per-View. Why, I seen this one gal from Germany stick 'er legs so far behind her shoulders, she looked like she was givin' birth to her own damned head. I taped her entire routine for our next poker game.

I've heard that the Olympic committee wants to ban those skimpy outfits the gymnasts wear. Somethin' about preservin' the dignity of the events. This comin' from the same group of folks that requested whores in their rooms when they went to interview cities bidding for the Olympics. I hope they don't pass the ban because the Olympics' ratings'll suffer if we don't get a few days of Debbie Cho in a red thong spread-eagled on a floor mat.

Okay, back to my original point.

What was it, anyway?

Oh, yeah. So I'm watchin' the football game and working on my Farticus idea when I hear Terry Bradshaw on Fox Sports NFL Sunday say "Git-r-done!" I about swallowed my Skoal berry blend! I'm thinkin', *He didn't just say what I thought he did, did he?*

James Brown must have read my mind, 'cause then he said, "Git-r-done," too. When Bradshaw asked him "Do you listen to Larry the Cable Guy?" Brown replied, "I love that guy . . . git-r-done!"

Holy Dick Trickle! They're *both* sayin' my phrase on Fox NFL Sunday!

I immediately called my buddy and said, "Did you hear what they just said on Fox NFL Sunday? They said 'Git-r-done!'" Then I realized I had the wrong number again. Either my phone is really screwed up or I'm just an idiot. Probably the latter, so I checked the number, called my buddy, and asked if he'd seen it.

For some reason, he was breathing real heavy. He said that he wasn't watchin' football that day because his wife was gone and another network was broadcasting a gymnastics tournament. Then he hung up. I'm left standing with the phone in my hand listening to a dial tone, thinkin', *Ya know its really cool that they said my phrase and all on* NFL Today, *but I forgot about the gymnastics! Hell, if I hurry up, I can still catch the floor exercise. Yipper dipper ripper stripper!*

Hey, that sounds better there.

Anyway, I actually didn't put on gymnastics. No way I was switchin' from Terry Bradshaw and James Brown. I mean, who woulda thunk it! I had made it to the National Football League! Now if that didn't solidify git-r-done as a national phrase, then I'll kiss your ass. It was just really awesome to see all my hard work pay off. When I used the saying on that radio station in Tampa Bay back in 1991, I never dreamed it would make its way into American Culture. And the best part is that it's a great phrase and it's still going strong.

I guess this is the time to tell y'all (all three of you people that bought this book) where the phrase really has a home: the Professional Bull Riders. That really means a lot to me. I've been a fan of rodeo and bull riding my whole life. I swear, if I weren't such a fat ass, I'd climb up on a bull tomorrow. But I don't ride bulls, I eat 'em.

Way back in 1994 A.D. my buddy, Tator Porter, was trying to earn a living as a professional bull rider. We met at a bikini contest in a country bar in Kissimmee, Florida. I was the emcee; he was a contestant. Tator came onstage that night in a slinky rebel flag T-back. It sounds wild, but he took fourth place, which should let ya know how ugly the rest of the competition was. Tator was drunk, so he might not remember the contest, but I'll never forget how he looked. It was two whole days before I stopped throwin' up.

Tator was a talented bull rider but he needed a sponsor. So while I was unhooking his rebel flag bra, I offered to back him. He agreed and history was made. It was the first time that anyone had ever helped a bull rider out of a rebel flag thong bikini and it was the first day I became actively involved with a sport I dearly loved.

I really lucked out with Tator. The first year I sponsored him, he went on a roll and rode better than ever. He coulda gotten on Rosie O'Donnell and dangled a bag of Fiddle Faddle from a fishin' pole in front of her without gettin' thrown off. His ass was stickier than Ricky Martin's after a meet and greet.

Tator rode with a big red "Git-r-done" on the back of his vest. I hadn't been that proud since I saw my sister on Jerry Springer takin' that DNA test to determine that the Puerto Rican guy she was seein' wasn't the real father of my niece. I was tearin' up. Not at Tator, at Springer. Every time Tator would come out of the shoots, the crowd yelled "Git-r-done!" and the announcers would talk about me. I was not only getting great press, but I was getting involved in a small way with bull riding! Yipper dipper ripper stripper!

Wow, it worked twice.

I called the PBR and offered to do a joint T-shirt promotion with them. I figured somethin' like "The PBR Gits-R-Done" might work. That or "Show Me Your Tits." Even though I liked "Show Me Your Tits," I didn't have a copyright on that phrase; I'd already seen that shirt worn to about every biker rally and church ice cream social in the country.

I called the fine folks at the PBR and said, "Hey, would you like to do a joint T-shirt with me?" Once again I had the wrong number, but the lady at the convenience store was nice. She even told me about her pregnant 14-year-old daughter.

By now, I figured I needed a new phone 'cause I never got the right number on that stupid Oakland Raiders helmet phone. I got a sleek Panasonic and finally reached those great folks with the PBR. We ended up doing a joint T-shirt featurin' the PBR logo across the front and *larrythecableguy.com* underneath it. On the back, we stuck a big red "Git-r-done!" flanked on both ends by the PBR bull logo.

Things really got exciting. Those shirts sold like spinnin' rims in a Detroit neighborhood and Tator went on to win the Professional Bull Riders' finals in Las Vegas. I was proud as a trailer trash dad listenin' to his son say the F-word for the first time. To think only six years earlier, a good night for Tator was winnin' 25 bucks and a bar tab for wearin' a rebel flag bikini.

OK, for the record and so Tator doesn't kick my ass when he reads this, I was the one that actually wore the bikini, but who gives a damn? He did win the PBR finals, OK?

My next step was to buy a bull and name it. A bull named Theresa struck me as an obvious choice since she was the girl that no one could stay on in high school. Just kidding. I wanted a bull named after my phrase. Tell me a bull named "Git-r-done" wouldn't kick ass. So I got a hold of a fella named H.D. Page. He owned buckin' bulls and he set me up with my first bull sponsorship.

That's where my story gets so cool. All this was possible because of some phrase I just made up. Well, it also helped that people thought I was funny. I mean, if I didn't show up and deliver the goods, "git-r-done" would be buried in the catchphrase graveyard right next to "Plop plop fizz fizz!" and "Gee, your hair smells terrific." Instead, "git-r-done" is right up there with "Can ya hear me now?" among the most recognizable phrases around.

This may be biased, but I consider my phrase way more honest than "Can ya hear me now?" They're fricken lyin' to ya with that "Can ya hear me now?" on the cell phone malarkey. Here this moron is leadin' us to believe he's standin' by the Eiffel Tower talkin' to his buddy in America while gettin' perfect reception. In reality I can't call a friend two blocks away without calling him back 47 times because my commie cell phone has such poor reception! Let me tell ya right now, "Can ya hear me now?" doesn't git-r-done!

So that's Chapter 2. I wanna thank all those fine sports teams, military folks, and everyday Americans for usin' my phrase. That principal outside of Albany can kiss my Playgirl-lookin' hind end, but to everybody else I am truly grateful and happy. It's just a fun catchy little thing that sticks in your head. Kinda like the first time ya saw titties in *National Geographic*. No matter what you're feeling on any particular day, it works for all occasions. So remember, whatever ya do, don't complain and don't quit.

Just give 100 percent and GIT-R-DONE!!

Hey, I just remembered somethin'. I forgot to give out that secret recipe for Kentucky Fried Chicken. Okay, maybe I'll put that in Chapter 3.

Chapter 3

LORD, I APOLOGIZE!

IF YOU MADE IT THROUGH the first two chapters of this book, that means you're really enjoying it or else you're just reading because you want to tell friends you just read the dumbest thing since the biography of Hulk Hogan.

This chapter will explain the origin of the phrase "Lord, I apologize" and my special prayer, "Be with the starvin' pygmies down in New Guinea." You will meet the famous Boobla Boobla, the pygmy that I adopted several years ago. Time permitting, we will also cover why fat lesbians dress like mountain men.

Everyone—and I'm no exception—has done something that they have had to apologize to the Lord for. Everyone except atheists. They don't believe in God so they never use his name unless they say "God damn" or when they get in a bad car wreck.

I always thought that was kinda hypocritical. Here ya got these atheists that don't believe in God, but when their lives are on the line, like say they're laying in a ditch after a crash with a truck layin' on the top of their torsos, they yell, "God, please help me!"

The way I figure it, these sumbitches spend their whole lives spouting, "There is no God." Then in the critical hour they yell for something they don't believe in! They may as well be under that truck yellin' "Daffy Duck, please help me" or "Bugs Bunny, please help me."

Let me tell y'all commie non-believers somethin'. I believe in God and I really think he's got a way better miracle track record than Daffy Duck or Bugs Bunny. Don't get me wrong. I love Daffy and Bugs, but when I need a miracle I feel way more at peace talking to God than I do the Cartoon Network.

The "Lord, I apologize" thing came about because of my upbringin'. My dad was a preacher and, boy, could he get into some long conversations and sermons. He's the only guy that could make a Jehovah's Witness look at his watch and say he had to really be leaving.

One Saturday evening, we went to the Waffle House right after leavin' a titty bar. I was, oh, I don't know, maybe 12. Ya better believe goin' to the Waffle House for an egg and hash skillet after seein' some titties was a big thrill for me and my friends.

Before we started eatin', Dad stood up to pray and it was not only long, but loud. It was just a few decibels softer than when my mom used to listen to Paul Harvey on the stereo with the windows open while goin' down the interstate at 50 miles an hour in the grain truck. About 10 minutes into the prayer, my brother stood up from his wheelchair (he often pretended to be crippled, so we could get into the Waffle House whenever it was crowded) and whispered in my ear, "Man, he's prayin' for everybody but the starvin' pygmies."

Fast forward about 25 years later. I'm onstage in a club doin' a joke that I knew my dad wouldn't approve of, so I said, "Lord, I apologize." Since my brother was in the front row sitting in his wheelchair (the club was sold out that night), I added, "and be with the starvin' pygmies in New Guinea."

Hence another phrase was born.

At first only he laughed at it, but after the third time I said it, the crowd laughed and didn't even know why. That happens a lot in my act. People howl over that phrase, but they can't figure out why. Don't get me wrong. It's funny. There's just no explainin' why it's so funny! That's a mystery that will last longer than the secret of the pyramids.

Every time I'd go onstage, I'd pop out the phrase "Lord, I apologize" and then add the pygmy part. It's really crazy how stuff like that catches on. It got to the point that if I did a joke and the crowd thought it was over the line, somebody would yell, "Ya better apologize." It was awesome. I was used to people yelling out things like "You suck" or "Bring back the first guy," but I was finally on to something.

It was funny. I took something my dad said and used it as an inside joke between me and my brother and it caught on with everyone. The phrase became so popular, I ended up calling my first album *Lord, I Apologize*. And you know what? Even though we released that album back in 2001, people still come to my shows and yell out "Ya better apologize." Of course, they also yell, "Bring back the first guy," but that's not the point of this story.

Now in everyday life when I do somethin' stupid or get pissed off at somebody, I always say "Lord, I apologize" and hope that the Lord in some goofy way is thinking, *Well, at least he realizes he shouldn't have acted that way*.

I remember one time at band camp . . .

Oh, sorry, this paragraph is meant for *Hustler*!

When I was a kid livin' back on the farm, I had my own truck. That thing kicked ass. It was a regular farm-kid truck with big tires and a sticker that said "No Fat Chicks" and a rebel flag. My only problem was it had no engine. That didn't stop it from bein' a great date trailer. On Friday nights, my dad would pull me and some chick around town with his Massey Furguson. We got around fine and it didn't cost me a nickel in gas.

One night I was with this fat chick from the 11th grade, breaking the "No Fat Chicks" rule from the sticker. Dad was haulin' ass down

a gravel road when the back tire from his tractor threw up a rock.
It smacked Loretta right in the head and knocked her out cold. I
ended up pullin' her home, but not until I copped a feel off one of
her mush melon–sized boobs.

Lord, I apologize.

Stickers that said "No Fat Chicks" always cracked me up. Thing
is, you'd see the sign, then you'd see the guy driving and you'd
wonder why he's being so damn picky. Most guys with that sticker
on their trucks or cars usually don't have much choice in the matter. It works both ways, though. I saw this bumper sticker on a
girl's car as it was leavin' the Kmart. It said "Single and Loving It!" I
pulled up next to her and she looked a little like one of the
Judds. . . . Cledus T.

I thought, *Damn, single and loving it. Well it looks like she's
gonna be loving it for a long long time!*

Lord, I apologize.

It ain't like I'm claimin' to be all sexy like one of the Duke boys,
but damn, at least I don't put a stupid sticker on the back of my
car. I did have the "No Fat Chicks" sticker back in high school, but
I was 26 for God's sake. You tend to grow out of that goofy sticker
phase. All I have on my car now—I mean truck, I ain't no pussy—
are stickers with George Strait, a Jesus fish, and George Bush
pissin' on an Iraqi flag.

By the way, for the record, putting a Jesus fish on your car still
does not stop cops from pullin' ya over after leavin' the bar, just so
ya know.

Lord, I apologize.

"God Is My Co-Pilot!" Boy, there's a sticker that pisses me off.

I love the Lord, OK, and I think it's cool that people want everyone to know they love the Lord as well. But I'd rather tell people
with my actions than with some car stickers. I'm sure God really
enjoys watchin' his name broadcast on a car bumper right after the

driver flipped the bird to some old lady for cuttin' him off. If God truly was his co-pilot, he'd pop him in the mouth and tell him to shut up and respect his elders.

Come to think of it, I saw a car with one of those co-pilot stickers in a ditch one time.

Evidently God took a few minutes off that afternoon.

Pardon me, but I think the Lord has more important things to do than hop in the shotgun seat of Herb's Plymouth and go to the Wal-Mart on a Saturday to get trash can lids and various creams for his hemorrhoids. I saw one dude with that sticker on his car. When I looked in the co-pilot's seat, he had a black guy sittin' there. I thought, *If God's your co-pilot he sure does look different than the church photo.* I ain't never heard of or seen one picture of the Lord lookin' like a defensive tackle for the Lions.

I mean everybody knows God looks like the drummer for Foghat. You know it, I know it, and the American people know it!

Lord, I apologize!

While I'm on the stupid bumper sticker thing, let me share this story. Remember that good-lookin' teacher in Tampa that had sex with the 6th grader? First time I saw her on the news, I thought, *She's hot!* But my second thought was how sick is that? And it's happening in this country all the time! Teachers are even startin' to get ballsy about it. The other day I saw this teacher pulling out of the parking lot at the local grade school. Plastered right across the front bumper of her car was a sticker that said "I Slept With Your Honor Student!"

Lord, I apologize!

Having your teacher sleep with you could be a great stay-in-school incentive. I mean these teachers ain't like the hairnet old bags we had when I was a kid. If I got seduced in 6th grade, I woulda been scared! I would have had to throw ole lady Jackson outta her wheelchair, rip out her breathin' tube, and tie her tits in a knot under the desk just to get the hell out!

But some teachers nowadays look like supermodels and they're real aggressive. They oughta change that slogan "No Child Left Behind" to "No Child's Behind Left Alone"!

It's really a shame what's happening in our public school system these days and I'm 'specially sad that I'm not a part of it.

Now here's the deal, I love old folks and they love to laugh. I actually did a show one time and made this old lady laugh so hard she peed her pants; I felt really good knowing that the older folks dug my material. Then she pooped her pants and I began to realize I actually had nothing to do with either one of those reactions. So I called up my manager and told him to stop bookin' me at any more old folks' homes!

Never seen it comin', right? Lord, I apologize.

A while back, I saw a sticker on the rear bumper of some old couple's car that asked, "What Would Jesus Do?" I got to thinking about that. They were doing about 25 miles an hour down the freeway at the time and I thought, *What would Jesus do?, I bet he'd do the fricken speed limit! I mean come on speed it up to at least 40.*

I used to have to say, "Lord, I apologize" a lot while I was drivin'.

To be honest, though, I never really get too pissed at anything. However, back in the early '80s, when *Hee Haw* got thrown under the bus and canceled by a bunch of corporate L.A. fag executives, I went out and looted my brother's barn. Then I burnt down his shed. That was about the only serious blowup I've ever had in my life.

I'm basically a mild-mannered, ill-tempered guy with a muscular hind section. However, I do admit that driving down the road and coming in contact with other drivers tends to make me a bit

cranky. I remember one time I was driving down the road, diggin'
on the radio and in my nose. I was doin' about 60 miles an hour,
minding my own business, when I had to brake real fast 'cause this
guy in front of me is doin' around 10! My finger about went into
my brain.

I normally don't pick my nose a lot when I drive, but this was
one of those dry-air days and those make for some awesome
boogers. I felt like a miner that had just hit the mother lode. There
I was listenin' to Toby Keith, havin' a great nose-pickin' day, and
then some slow-drivin' jackass ends up ruinin' everything.

When I honked to get his attention, the guy flipped me off. So I
just kinda nudged him a little from behind with my truck. He
totally overreacted and went flyin' over his handlebars! Hey, I
don't care if it was a cop, ya gotta speed it up some times!

Lord, I apologize!

Let me go back to the dry-nose thing. I always envied the people
in the western part of the United States, especially west Texas, Arizona, and Nevada. They have all that dry air and booger season
lasts almost year-round. In Phoenix, boogers are so common,
you'll even see well-mannered, uppity folks diggin' one out at the
opera or at a wine tasting. It's just part of their western culture.

Here in the South it's pretty humid, so if you enjoy a good pick
you really only have a limited season. Sure, we have better bass
fishin', but it doesn't even come close to a nice nose pick in the
middle of watchin' a Braves game. If there's only one complaint
I've ever had about living in the South it would be that booger season is too short and there are too many fat Canadians wearing
Speedos on the beaches. I believe that Speedos are a privilege, not
a right! I wore a Speedo once at the beach and went to eat. The
manager of the local convenience store accused me of stealin' a
roll of dimes!

Lord, I apologize!

The cell phone industry also pisses me off enough to say something I'm not proud of in public. I hate these damn things worse than the old *Moesha* show. I read in the paper one time ('cause my neighbor got up late again, Sunday edition) that cell phones put microwaves into your head. People say that's all BS but I gotta tell ya I talked to my cousin last year for an hour straight and the next day I pooped a Hot Pocket. That's no joke. I don't want to act un-Christian when I say this, but all cell phone salesmen should burn in hell and the whole time they're burning they should be gettin' their asses rammed with the wood end of a pitchfork while the devil screams, "Can ya hear me now!"

Lord, I apologize!

I hate that little weasel in those cell phone commercials. I just wish for once a bus would slam into that little bastard while he's in the middle of braggin' about his cell phone reception. Here I got the same phone he does and I couldn't hear the sumbitch I was talkin' to if I stood next to him. I think all those cell phone assholes sit around their boardrooms just laughing their asses off about all the people who keep buyin' their products even though the damn things never work.

A recent survey of cell phone customers yielded some not-so-surprising results. The researchers found that people were most likely to say one of three phrases the first time they used their cell phones. The phrases were not "Hello," or "Hey I finally got a cell phone!" or "Guess where I'm calling you from?" No, the first thing most people say is, "This piece of shit!" Second place went to "Hello? Can you hear me? Hello? Son of a bitch! Hello? Dammit!" Window breaking followed by silence ranked a very close third.

And that's just from people at my church!

Lord, I apologize!

I saw this TV commercial the other day while I was working on a

Dick Trickle NASCAR butthole mural for my brother-in-law's Christmas party. It was a T-Mobile commercial that offered customers 1000 "Whenever Minutes."

Wow, a thousand "Whenever Minutes."

Yeah, WHENEVER you can get fricken reception!

Lord, I apologize.

I hate people that use cell phones while they drive. A representative from the Make a Wish Foundation called my house one day and asked if I could spend a few hours with some sick kids who were really big fans of mine. It was totally cool. We had an awesome time with a remote control fart machine that we planted at an old folks home and then I took 'em all to the bass pro shop to eat some stink bait.

At the end of the night, we wound up at a local titty bar. Now maybe you think that was inappropriate, but I was the guardian and when I asked this one kid what he wished for, he asked for a lap dance. I thought, *Hey anything to help out. I'm all about the kids.* Turned out he wasn't even sick but just some jackass hormone-enraged 6th grader pretending he was dying so he could see some titties.

Anyway, we leave the titty bar, get on the Interstate, and pass through a construction site. Here comes some moron on his cell phone, changin' two, three lanes at a time. He had no turn blinkers and he took out more cones than Oprah at the Dairy Queen. That's the kinda guy the cops oughta go after! The guy was a menace! I bet I spilled four beers followin' that sumbitch!

Lord, I apologize.

Boy we've come all this way but I still haven't talked about my friend Boobla Boobla. Ol' Boobla is quite a kid. I first saw him about four years ago in a photo taken with Sally Struthers right after she had finished shootin' another one of them starvin' children commericals. Sally had been eating a turkey leg and runnin' to her helicopter when Boobla got tangled in her legs. Instead of gently pulling him off her, she kicked him outta the way and he rolled down a hill into a mound of fire ants.

Somebody from the *National Geographic* snapped a picture and got it all down on film. Here was Sally, climbin' in her helicopter and waving to the crowd with a turkey leg the size of Bamm-Bamm's club. Meanwhile, in the background, you see this pygmy kid jumpin' in the air and slappin' himself about the body and face, trying to get rid of all these fire ants that are just kickin' his ass! He kinda looked like a retarded Webster floppin' around like that. It was priceless.

I decided to contact Boobla as soon as I seen that picture. I called Pygmies R Us, a company that specialized in importing orphaned pygmies to the US for circuses and adoptive parents. They also sold sandals, wicker hats, and giant ceramic lion heads. Except for the pygmy adoptions, it reminded me of a Pier One store I seen in Detroit.

A friend of mine thought I should do business with someone a little more reputable than this firm. He had once ordered a pygmy through Pygmies R Us and the boy they sent gave him nothing but trouble from day one. My friend threw a party for the boy right after he arrived in America. He even gave him a pony as a welcoming gift. The boy gutted it with a steak knife. Then he stabbed the clown. This kid was only four years old, but, man, what a pistol!

Though Boobla turned out to be more manageable, he also could be a handful at times. As soon as the adoption was approved, I sent him some cash to cover his rabies shots; he spent it all on a Boutros Boutros-Ghali bobble-head doll. Then he nearly died after a coyote bit him.

When he finally visited me, his head was so swollen from the rabies, he looked like a *South Park* character. It was kinda embarrassing. I made him stay in his room for most of the trip so he wouldn't scare the other children in the neighborhood. But after some medication and bed rest, we finally reduced his head to almost the size of a normal retarded kid.

We ended up having an enjoyable time together doing things most fathers and sons do. Playing baseball and football and blow darting bums and hookers down by the Christian center. Boobla Boobla is now back in New Guinea and I hear from him every now and then. The last time he came to visit was Christmas 2002. The cool thing about him at Christmas was he was so low maintenance. While the other kids were bitchin' about not getting the games they wanted for their PlayStations, all he had to do was unwrap a couple of flour bags and he was like a pig in slop. He actually poured one whole bag on his head and ran around without showering for two days.

It was so cute. I looked like I was babysitting Edgar Winter's kid. I've received a lot of letters from Boobla over the years but nothing was as touching as this one that I just received in 2004 after sending him a box of Christmas stuff.

DEAR LARRY,

Thank you so much for the fly swatters. They sure do come in handy during those muggy nights. My brother, Boobla Bingda DudaDdoda Allah Hakim Hasem-Bbola Bada Jackson, got hit in the head last night by a flower bag during a food drop. He will be OK. However, he has a big knot on his head and will no longer be able to carry fruit on his head to the market.

My mother is all excited because *National Geographic* is gonna show her tits on the cover of their February edition. She was so excited she went and told the elders and got her mole pierced and her armpits braided. Last week the members of the hunting tribunal took me out hippo giggin'. It's almost like when you took me frog giggin', only we gig hippos. I threw my back out, however, half way thru the giggin' because they made me carry the decoys.

Well I need to go now because they just started tootin' on the warning horns that there's a tiger somewhere in the camp and we have to run for shelter. If you're not where you need to be when they spot a tiger and sound them horns then you're really in a lot of trou . . .

Well, that was the letter. I still ain't heard from him, but I'm sure he's fine.

Lord, I apologize for that whole pygmy story as well as for the "Be with the starvin' pygmies in New Guinea" prayer.

Now I gotta question: Why is Sally Struthers beggin' for food for starvin' people? It's a wonder those natives didn't string up that human Ho-Ho on a BBQ pole in the first hour thinkin' they was killin' a stray hippo! I think if you're gonna raise money for food, the person doing the raisin' shouldn't weigh more than a third of the population combined.

Here these kids is eatin' bugs and grass and in comes "Double Cheeseburger" Struthers walking around like she's the pygmy Jesus about to lead 'em all to the land of biscuits and gravy. If you're gonna plug folks for money, at least have somebody that looks like they need to eat too.

Let Mick Jagger raise money for starving folks. Hell, that dude is so skinny, when he dies they're gonna have to bury him in a poster tube. I'm worried about him. I wouldn't be surprised to turn on Fox News one day and learn he just died by falling through his own butthole and strangling himself. But I'd give money to a feller like that. Sally Struthers don't make me wanna write a check for starvin' kids. She makes me wanna turn on *All in the Family* to remind myself what she used to look like before she became the only human to have OnStar installed!

Lord, I apologize.

Here's another thing you should apologize to the Lord about: a tattoo. I really hate tattoos. I mean they look good on some people, but I can't think of one I'd like. When my sister was a teenager, she got a Herbie the Love Bug tattooed on her ass. Now here she is, 32 years later, and that Love Bug has turned into a van. What the hell was she thinkin'?

My sister also got a tattoo on the back of her head that said "Warning: Not for People with Heart Problems. May Cause Dizziness." Can you believe that? Fourteen years old and a tattoo like that?

It's a wonder the state didn't take her kids away from her.

Don't the people gettin' these tattoos realize that they will be old one day or are they just oblivious? Ain't nothin' more exciting than takin' the kids over to their grandparents' house and Grandpa greets ya at the door with a big "F-y'all" tattooed across his forehead. Then Grandma shows you somethin' she just got at the flea market; a tattoo of butterfly wings around her vagina!

Lord, I apologize.

And just like where there's smoke, there's fire; or where there's thunder, there's lightnin'; or where there's Barbra Streisand there's assholes; where there's tattoos, there's piercings. This is something I'll never understand. One time I saw a guy with a pierced penis! I've been known to faint whenever I zip myself up in my pants, so I could never drive a bolt thru that thing. I mean what possesses a man to have his penis pierced? I already have a hard enough time tryin' not to pee on the toilet lid; I can't imagine trying to do it with a hitch pin stickin' through my privates. Is it supposed to be sexy?

I was with a girl that had 32 piercings all over her body. I felt like I was makin' love to her and working on my truck at the same time. I didn't need a rubber, I needed a grease gun to stick up her crack!

One of my nieces had nine bolts put in her vagina. Ya believe that? That's as disgusting as Star Jones's wedding pictures. One time my niece was standing on the front porch of the house in a sundress and the wind kicked up out of nowhere. Sounded like we had wind chimes out on the front porch! At least put some pants on if you're gonna turn your vagina into a construction site.

I will admit, though, that I sorta got pierced in the 9th grade. I stapled a piece of construction paper to my nuts just to get my buddy Doug to show me pictures of our math teacher's daughter all naked and spread-eagled in a hay loft after gettin' drunk and laid at a barn dance!

Lord, I apologize.

I do believe there should be a weight limit on piercings. My 400-pound sister got her belly pierced. Ya know I love my sister but if you're 400 pounds I don't think a belly ring is gonna make ya look any sexier. Instead of a belly ring, she oughta be getting onion rings. I'm not sayin' that to be nasty. I just don't think you should get a body piercing if ya have to lift up a roll of fat every time you want to show the thing off.

I mean I love my sister, but the bolt ring she got in her stomach looks like a damn hitch. One day, my truck got stuck in a mud hole. I actually wanted her to run over and hook her stomach up to the bumper so she could pull me out.

I never got the tongue thing either. I once sat next to this girl in church and right away noticed somethin' funny about her mouth. I leaned over and whispered, "Sister Marion, why do you have a bolt in your tongue?" She smiled and said that it made oral sex more pleasurable. I don't know about y'all, but every time I pop a boner I don't want some girl hittin' it with a steel rod! Call me a prude.

However, I did once pay for an oriental whore to slap my ass with a Hot Wheels track to celebrate my first gold record!

Lord, I apologize.

Before we reach the end of this chapter, I'd like to list some examples of other things I've done that have merited apologies:

1. I actually wrecked my truck to get the insurance money to make my truck payment. This usually works only twice, until they catch on that you might be a deadbeat.
2. If ya ever rent a car and try and cheat on the mileage, don't use Wite-Out. They got that deal figured out.
3. No matter how hard ya try, it's impossible to baptize cats. Not only do they not have a cat heaven, they scratch the hell out of ya because they hate water. I do, however, know of a Pussy Heaven just up the road that has a 15 dollar cover and a great buffet on Fridays!
4. A strip mall is not a mall full of strippers. I learned this real quick when I asked the girl working at the Orange Julius to show me her titties and got banned from the place for four months.
5. Going into Bath and Body Works and asking if they have any cinnamon-flavored butthole scrub is apparently not funny to any of those uptight chicks working there.
6. Don't ever get a vasectomy at a kiosk.
7. If you take your girlfriend or wife hunting, make sure she isn't alone for too long. The first time my girlfriend came on a hunting trip, I had to leave her while I scouted the terrain around a hill. I told her if she shot a deer while I was gone, she had to guard it with her life so nobody else could claim

it. So what happens? I'm not gone two minutes before she blasts some beautiful creature. Right away this hunter came runnin' from around the corner. She aimed her rifle and told him if he got any closer to the animal, she'd shoot him dead. He said "OK, sweetheart calm down. You can keep the body, but can I at least get my saddle off of it? (This story really has nothing to do with "Lord, I apologize" or any of its uses. Fact is, there's really no point to it at all, other than it bein' a joke my grandpa told me just before he died. We were bringin' him to the hospital after he had fallen from the roof of his RV while trying to moon Jeff Gordon coming around Turn Two at Talladega. It has great sentimental value so I included it here.)

8. Have ya ever gotten so drunk, ya dreamt that ya drank the world's largest margarita? Then when you woke up the next morning, there was all this salt on the toilet seat? This I did do and Lord, I apologize! Thank God I didn't eat the giant worm that was floatin' in there.

I will do only eight of these because everybody does a Top Ten list and I want to be different. Besides, I can only think of eight of these stupid things. All of them are true and all of them worth apologizing over.

Now do I really think this is a good way to earn forgiveness? Obviously not. My act ain't a revival meetin', it's a comedy show. I like to think the Lord has more important things to do than come to my eight o'clock performance in Birmingham on a Friday night.

When I say "Lord, I apologize," I'm not truly prayin' or apologizin'. And anybody who thinks I am needs to get the retard bus started up and pulled around front to take 'em to Chuck E. Cheese. It's just a silly mindless phrase that started as an inside joke between me and my brother.

People need to quit taking things so seriously. I don't think sayin' "Lord, I apologize" matters much in the grand scheme of things (now, there's a phrase I'll never understand, "the grand scheme of things"). But I have caught some flack from church people for usin' it in my act. That's amazing. I get all these angry letters about that one phrase but if I do a joke about eatin' pudding out of Michelle Pfeiffer's crack, no one says a word. Go figure.

I'll tell you what irritates me, though: hearin' people invoke the Lord's name in the dumbest ways possible. For instance, whenever I hear football players say, "The Lord was with us today and gave us the victory."

The Lord gave them the victory?

What was the other team, a bunch of devil worshipers?

Look, I don't think the Lord gives two cents about a football game. He cares about each individual person. He cares about things that matter in the grand scheme of things (there's that fricken phrase again). But I doubt he's in heaven with a bowl of chips watchin' the NFL package on DIRECTV, okay?

Well, I hope ya enjoyed Chapter 3. If you're still reading the book after this, than you're either a true fan or you have no friends and probably haven't been laid since Eisenhower left office. But, either way, you're still turnin' pages and I'm grateful. If ya think that I am retarded and that what I have written is way out there and ridiculous, then wait till ya read the next chapter. It's about to get worse. On the other hand, if ya think what you've read so far is fascinating and ya can't wait to dig into the next chapter, you should get professional counseling as quickly as possible.

Chapter 4

LAWRENCE THE TELEGRAPH GUY

AFTER THE RADIO COMMENTARIES got rollin' in the mid-'90s, I started lookin' for other bits to do on the air just to keep things interesting. I didn't want my listeners to get tired of hearin' the same act over and over again.

The commentaries were fun, but before long even Bill Clinton got boring. Unless he was humpin' a whore or givin' away secrets to the Chinese, there wasn't much to write about. So I decided to create a goofy long-running story that I could turn to in a pinch whenever pokin' fun at the government got tedious. That's when my great-great-grandpa "Lawrence the Telegraph Guy" was born. This chapter will tell ya all about him, as if anybody cares. However, I think it will still be funnier than anything Margaret Cho has ever done.

But first: a funny thing happened on the way to writing this section. I discovered a cyst on my ass. This sumbitch is drivin' me nuts. Every time I try and type it feels like I'm sittin' on George Costanza's big wallet!

Do I get bonus points for the *Seinfeld* reference?

Anyway, this cyst on my ass is quite troubling, but just because I love y'all so much, I'm writing this whole chapter while sitting on a hemorrhoid pad.

One day I was workin' around the house, hanging a new rebel flag and checking my girlfriend for ticks. I sat down to write a radio commentary on Jane Fonda, but then I started thinkin' about a completely different radio bit.

I had just finished doing a crap load of social commentaries about Janet Reno that went into how she looked like Peppermint Patty on steroids, plus some other hilarious stuff about her testicles.

But Janet was getting overdone. I mean there was a time you could always nail Reno for something when nothin' else was happenin' in the world. She was a great comedy target. However, after five days in a row ya gotta switch to somebody else. Besides, I had talked about her so much I was startin' to wear big thick glasses and burn down buildings. I needed to move on! So I had to come up with some radio time fillers, but I wanted them to be about something I really knew.

When I was growing up, there were only two subjects my dad and I enjoyed talkin' over with each other. One of them was Farrah Fawcett. Farrah was actually my first wet dream; I never had another one until I saw Marty McFly's badass truck in *Back to the Future*. I musta played with myself a hundred times to romantic thoughts of that vehicle. But Farrah has a special place all by herself as wet dream number one.

I'll tell ya who else had me goin' back then: Daphne from *Scooby-Doo*! Every morning I'd lay in front of the TV with a bowl of Sugar Smacks wishin' I was rockin' that van with that Hanna Barbera piece of cartoon ass.

Somehow, though, I just didn't think Farrah or Daphne could supply me with the material I needed.

So I started thinkin' about the other subject Dad and I often discussed. Our family history. Long as I could remember, I've been interested in my family's past and how grasshoppers made love. I spent hours researchin' ancestors and all the things they did.

No one fascinated me more than my great-great-grandpa. At the start of the Civil War, he was what they called a copperhead, someone who was sympathetic to the South even though he lived in a neutral state.

My great-great-grandfather actually gave horses and guns to the Confederate army until some Union officers told him to either stop or face the consequences. We're talkin' about the harshest of punishments too, like being forced to watch *The Tony Danza Show* for hours on end. He stopped supplying the Confederates (who wouldn't, with that threat hanging over him?) but then he went to Oklahoma and did the same thing down there.

(This, by the way, is a true story other than the part about *The Tony Danza Show*. However, I understand they torture captured terrorists in Iraq by making 'em watch that program on top of Whoopie Goldberg's most recent HBO special.)

I got to thinking how awesome it would be to read something my great-great-grandpa actually wrote about his experiences. I searched for any journals or correspondences he might have kept among all the pictures and letters in our attic. The only thing I found was a box of *Hustlers* and some old church bulletins. I never really learned anything more about him in that attic. However, I had fun trying to find the hidden Playboy bunny on the cover of all them *Hustlers*.

So there I was, back to checkin' my girl for ticks (four in all by the way) when this great idea popped into my head: why not make up some letters and say my great-great-grandpa wrote them during the Civil War? I figured since I actually had this ancestor that had participated in this historic event, it would be a great radio bit to read some letters describin' his experiences. Who cares if I made the whole thing up? It for sure would give us a break from all those tedious commentaries and Janet Reno references I was doin' everyday.

The next night I sat down with some Jim Beam to write the first installment of Great-Great-Grandpa's Civil War letters. That's when I remembered the first rule about writing anything: never write while hammered. I did that once in Bible college and wrote a made-up story about a fake bible character. It ended up being chockfull of titty references and dick jokes which garnered me a suspension and several closed-door meetings with our pastor.

I hadn't been in that much trouble since I penciled in the words "Who farted?" on the robes of all the disciples in a picture of the Last Supper in our church foyer!

I wanted the Civil War letters to be a running story, kinda like a retarded version of *Lonesome Dove*. That way I could create other characters throughout so people could get into a buncha people besides my great-great-grandpa. My character creations, however, tend to appeal only to 14-year-olds, folks with brain damage, and my brother who once wrote a book called *The Retard and the Kitty*.

At first I didn't know if people would enjoy the letters, being as how I was totally in another world when I wrote them. But they actually turned out to be one of the most requested things I've ever done other than the commentaries. Since it was radio and you could play with listeners' minds, they all thought these were my great-great-grandpa's actual Civil War letters.

When ya read them, though, remember to keep an open mind, because I was either really hammered or high after sniffing the plastic crotch on a Britney Spears doll when I wrote 'em. Even though I did these over 13 years ago, I still find it very disturbin' that my mind ever thought this way.

But what's even more disturbin' is the fact that these are so ridiculously stupid yet still way more entertainin' than an evening with Janeane Garofalo.

The first time I called these into the station, I thought they were gonna end my radio career; I actually applied for a position at Home Depot after they aired. Luckily for me, a lot of people like the same kinda goofy stuff that I do. God bless 'em. There's nothing wrong with laughing at goofy stuff; even Harvard-educated people laugh at fart jokes. If your life is so uptight that you can't get a chuckle over somethin' goofy, then hang yourself and end your misery!

I actually patterned these after letters I saw in a Civil War diary book I had read many years ago when I thought reading was cool: I got over that fad real quick. So here we go. I present to you letters from my great-great-grandpa Lawrence the Telegraph Guy to his wife, Evelyn, exactly as he wrote them during the time he spent fightin' the Civil War.

DEAREST EVELYN.

Today it's colder than a witch's tit. My horse was shot today in a brief skirmish with Union cavalry. Last night it was so cold we degutted ole Blackie and slept inside his carcass for warmth. It reminded me of the time during the great blizzard when your fat cousin Artie died and we degutted his body and slept inside him and made love for the first time. I heard a noise and popped my head out of the butthole of the horse carcass and almost strangled myself tryin' to wiggle back in. Today we're on our way to Lexington to meet with General Boragaurd about getting fresh blankets and titty books.

I'll write more later,

Lawrence

So that was the first letter I ever did. You probably had the same reaction to it as my friends when I read it to them: "Dude, you're f-d up." Well, whatever the case, I laughed the whole time I wrote it and I was way more entertained in those three minutes than I ever was in an entire half hour of *Who's the Boss*. I do, however, have a few observations about this story, as when I wrote it, the radio and the world weren't as politically correct as they are now.

For example I could never say "titty" on the radio anymore unless I was on Oprah. Oprah can do anything she wants as long as she does it in a medical way. She could actually have strippers spread-eagled with bananas up their cranks on her show. But if Oprah said they were just demonstrating the dangers of putting bananas up your crank, people would call that an educational experience.

However, if I were to say "titty" on the radio, all hell would break loose. It's unbelievable!

Also, I would never be able to name my horse Blackie. Even though it has nothing to do with race, the word *Blackie* offends the uptight PC crowd; I would have to change the name of the horse to African Americanie.

People are retarded about that crap. In *True Grit*, that girl that teams up with Rooster Cogburn has a horse named Blackie. No big deal, but say "Blackie" in today's PC world and all hell breaks loose.

About that part where I had to stick my head out of a dead horse's butthole, I know that could actually happen because I seen Jim Carrey do just that in *Ace Ventura*. The only fake part of this first letter that troubles me is the saying "colder than a witch's tit." I personally have never felt a witch's tit. I've never seen a witch whose tits were worth touching, unless it was the good witch from *The Wizard of Oz*; and I doubt she was giving anything up.

However, witches' tits are apparently really cold because everybody says it. We'll never really know unless Oprah has a panel of topless witches and fondles their tits in a scientific way. God knows if anybody could get away with fondlin' witches' tits on TV it would be Oprah.

OK, lets get back to the letters.

I did this one back in 1994. I had just walked in after gettin' hammered at a country bar while hosting a bikini contest and only had two hours to come up with somethin'. So this next letter is the brainchild of many beers and shots of hard liquor.

DEAREST EVELYN,

Last night I was stung by bees bathin' in Salt Creek. My wiener had swollen so bad that I had to march 5 miles while 6 soldiers held it like a rammin' log. It was very awkward and painful however we did come to a burning southern city and the men aimed my yanker toward the fire and I peed out 2 sheds and a saloon.

At night when I sleep a man stands guard on the tip of my swollen wiener and is up there a good 35-40 ft. It makes a great lookout. However 2 nights ago my buddy Fritz was standin' guard on my wiener and I got to thinkin' about you in them bloomers bent over the fence sloppin' hogs and I got so excited I let loose and sent ole Fritz half way to Gettysburg. Boy was he pissed. The good new is that the doctor said that my swellin' would go down in a few days so we're tryin' to make it to Ft. Pierson which is a Yankee stronghold. He's hoping however that I stay swollen enough to ram down the fort doors. I hope the swelling goes down though because I don't want to scuff the sumbitch.

The food here sucks so bad we pray after we eat! I'm

not kiddin' Evelyn it sucks! Corporal punishment is a plate of seconds. Tomorrow we are headed to Ft. Waterhead. It's a special Yankee fort full of midgets with big heads that wanted to fight but couldn't because they made people laugh more than fight.

Pray for us because no one's ever taken that fort. It's not that they're good fighters it's just that watchin' those goofy lookin' little bastards run around yellin' soundin' like toy dolls with guns twice their size always make the enemy laugh so hard they get stomach aches and end up leavin'. Hopefully we can kill all them little sumbitches this time before we get too tickled. I have to go now they need my wiener to pick some oranges.

Lawrence

ED NOTE: I thought this was genius. Weiners being used as battering rams. Come on! you can't get this kinda dialogue in Hollywood anymore. Trust me, if the last Alamo remake woulda had somethin' like that in it, Billy Bob Thorton would have been labeled the next Scorsese!

DEAREST EVELYN,

We was down by the creek last Thursday collectin' grub worms and shootin' beavers when we seen what looked like Orvill Kiper, your brother's sister's uncle's cousin. I called out for him but I guess we accidentally shot him because he never called back. I felt bad because it wasn't a beaver and nobody is buyin' Orvill Kiper pelts.

However good news, when I got there we had shot an

old oriental gypsy sellin' wood statues. I'm so glad it wasn't Orvil. I don't know what I hate worst, oriental gypsies or beavers. After we scalped the sumbitch and took his statues we headed back to camp for dinner.

Captain Bisby was there. He has quite a story, Evelyn. He went to take a shit in the woods one day and was attacked by coyotes so for 5 weeks he was scared to poop. He walked around all the time squeezin' his ass cheeks together tryin' to always hold them back. He gained 52 pounds in 5 weeks and we were worried about him.

Then 2 days ago a Yankee sniper shot him in the ass cheeks as he was patrolin' the woods and his ass let loose a fury of turds like a damn cannonball thunderstorm killin' 37 Yankees, wounding 65 and forced the rest to beg for surrender and soap. He was given the medal for bravery and honor and sent home to heal. His ass however was totally exploded off so we have collected money and we bought him a wooden ass from the ass cobbler up the road. He has to lay on his stomach for 5 days while we borate his ass, treat it for termites and then varnish it. The good news is that he'll be home soon with a beautiful new hand-carved ass.

He's one of the lucky ones.

Lawrence.

ED NOTE: For some reason everything was made out of wood in the old days. Teeth, asses, fake legs. If you had a bad body part, they had a cobbler for it. I used to date a girl with a wooden leg. We went dancin' one time and when I spun her in the wrong direction, she got taller!

In the next group of letters I wanted to execute a delicious blend of suspense, drama, and comedy by thinking of a trilogy of exciting letters that would keep the listener intrigued and wanting more. After several days of thought I came up with these gems. Tell me they don't actually have a better story line than *Coyote Ugly*:

DEAREST EVELYN,
    Today my penis finally got down to regular size. The bad news is I got in a skirmish with some Yankee sumbitch and to make a long story short my wiener was blown off.
    Not a good day. I'll write more later.
                                                        Lawrence

DEAREST EVELYN,
    Thank you very much for the wooden penis that Uncle Ray cobbled for me out of birchwood. Its better than nothing and I'll for sure use it. I hope the other troops don't catch me widdlin' to your picture.
    Love,
                                                        Lawrence

DEAREST EVELYN,
    Damn termites!
                                                        Lawrence

That was all for the wooden termite trilogy. J.R.R. Tolkien and his *Lord of the Rings* can kiss my ass.

Now on to some real touching letters that show the ferocity of battle, the drama of war, the sense of humor of a 33-year-old that still finds retards and deformed midgets a major source of comedy:

DEAREST EVELYN.

Today we exchanged gunfire with Union cavalry. Our lieutenant is a Siamese twin that joined up from the carnival. He's a hell of a fighter. He has two huge heads and he leads all our charges because he scares the enemy with his deformity.

Today however there was tragedy. Herbert, the bearded head on the left was shot, leaving only the right-headed Darrel to fend for himself and try and march with his dead brother's dead head heading.

I feel real bad Evelyn because Herbert who was killed had the twins' only workable nose so Darrel has to now breath through only the mouth which is located on his shoulder blade.

I'll write more later,

Lawrence

ED NOTE: Right now you're probably putting this book down and saying "What the f###!" Believe me, I think the same thing when I read anything that Al Gore's ever written. Let's go back to the attic . . .

ED NOTE: I started adding dates to make the letters more believable, as if a double-headed cripple and me sticking my head out of the butthole of a dead horse wasn't believable enough for people, but whatever.

June 14th 1862.

DEAREST EVELYN

Today my back is sore I can't move. Last night at the battle of Moon Creek me and my buddy de-Wayne faked being dead to avoid battle. I was lyin' awkward over some hickory logs for 6 and a half hours. De-Wayne wasn't as lucky as he faked bein' dead down by the creek bank and got trampled by the Unions' 153 cavalry.

The doctor said de-Wayne will probably lose his legs and be a retard.

I'll write more later,

Lawrence

June 21st 1862

DEAREST EVELYN,

Today to help morale a young fellow named Bob Hope came into camp to cheer us up. He was funny and I believe has a bright future ahead of him. I hope he lives forever.

Lawrence

ED NOTE: I loved Bob Hope. I really thought he would live forever and it really isn't a stretch to think he performed during the Civil War. That was what puzzled me when the Pope died. Everybody thinks popes are like a god but every one of 'em dies in his mid-80s. You'd think if someone was so blessed, the Lord would let him live a lot longer than that. I mean you'd think the Pope would be more like George Burns or Bob Hope or Dick Clark. Hell Dick Clark never ages; he would be a great pope.

I remember when they were tryin' to pick a new pope and the first day black smoke came flyin' out of the chimney, I thought, good heavens, they've either elected the first black pope or else Father Mahoney burnt the toast again.

Let's get back to the letters.

July 1st 1862

DEAREST EVELYN,

Today all the Yankees took over all the titty bars in
Baltimore. Those bastards! They fired all the southern strippers and replaced them with flat-chested
Yankee whores. The Yankee dancers wore pasties
while the southern strippers were totally nude.

Love,

Lawrence

P.S. War is HELL!!

**ED NOTE: This shows how political correctness was seeping into
America even back then and why the South should have won the
war. The North couldn't handle totally nude dancers because the
PC women's rights groups up there thought they were degrading.
This proves that the Civil War was not about slavery, but covering
up tits.**

I actually felt for my great-great-grandpa and all the other troops
in this. Here they have a hard day of killing each other and, God
forbid, they go see some naked titties. If the South would have
won, all titty bars would now be totally nude. Thanks a lot, North-
erners!

And that brings me to somethin' that always irritated me about
titty clubs. Ya got all these women's rights groups that scream pro-
abortion and say it's wrong to tell woman what to do with their
bodies. According to them, a woman has the right to choose
because it's her body and she can do what she wants with it.

This I totally agree with.

However, these same women's rights groups try to ban titty clubs by saying these places demoralize woman. Wait a second! What happened all of a sudden to a woman's right to choose? If a woman wants to dance naked, ain't it her right to do so? Ya can't preach in support of women's right to choose one minute and then the next minute try to control what they do with their bodies.

That's what we've come to in America. A woman can kill her unborn kid if she wants to. However, she catches holy hell if she decides to dance with her nipples showing.

And you didn't think that Civil War letter had any deep meaning (I really do need counseling).

I still hadn't created any characters that people could follow weekly, so enter "The Human Turd" and "Chief Many Farts!"

This is getting really exciting, ain't it? It's almost as if Louis L'Amour himself is guiding me in this retarded romp through history:

July 3rd 1862

DEAREST EVELYN,

Today we raided a Yankee travelin' circus train. Me and my Indian guide buddy Chief Many Farts raided the freak show car where we got in a gun battle with four freaks of nature. I shot and killed two freak show waterhead midgets and Chief Many Farts gunned down an oriental humpback with deformed ears.

The Human Turd got away!!

I'll write more later,

Lawrence

ED NOTE: The Human Turd actually became so popular I put out "Human Turd Wanted" T-shirts and sold tons of 'em. You have no idea how proud I was going to the local mall and seeing a young child wearing his "Human Turd" shirt.

It's these things that restore my faith in America's future!

Back to the letter: notice how I've created a wonderful story line. Chief Many Farts, the strong hero, the Human Turd, the wily enemy. It's a wonder Hollywood wasn't knockin' on my door over this one.

People may think I'm crazy, but when I was a kid one of the networks actually had a show called *Manimal* where a guy turned into animals and solved crimes. Now if some sumbitch sold that stupid idea to Hollywood, this one ain't so far-fetched!

After all, it can't be any dumber than *The Apprentice*. Here's a show that's basically a game show where the first prize is a job! Who the hell wants to win a job on a TV game show? What's second place, jury duty?

American Idol sucks, too. I seen the first week of that ridiculous show and thought I was watchin' the Special Olympics. You think I'm kiddin'? After the second singer I had my checkbook out!

Here's another dumbass show, *Cold Case*. What a ripoff, the whole show there wasn't one person drinkin' a beer!

I got an idea for a show: how about puttin' a bunch of television executives on a desert island and nobody can get off the island until one of 'em comes up with an idea for a TV show that doesn't suck! I'm tellin' ya right now for the record, Chief Many Farts, if given a chance, would have been one of the most adorable TV characters since Lassie.

I know you're excited to hear the further adventures of my Civil War ancestor, so let's continue . . .

July 12th 1862

DEAREST EVELYN,

Today we're on a massive man hunt for the Human Turd. I hope you remember him from my last letter, he's the freak of nature that escaped from the freak show circus train during our gun battle. Chief Many Farts has picked up his scent and we are tracking him in the hills.

The Chief is worried that the Human Turd is headed toward the town of Belfry. It is basically abandoned except for a brothel full of rejected whores. They are either full of dysentery, retarded or invalids. The invalid whores are usually half price. however ya need a spotter to hold them up for you (not that I would ever cheat, I'm just sayin').

Evelyn, I hate the Human Turd and I will stop at nothing until he's stuffed, shellacked, deodorized and hung on our wall! I'll write to ya later,

Lawrence

P.S. Chief Many Farts says hey!

ED NOTE: Notice how I have radio listeners on the edge of their seats with this story. Ya know what, screw the networks! I'm takin' this fricken thing to Disney!

July 24th 1862

DEAREST EVELYN

I miss you. I got attacked and leg humped by 4 coyotes last night. I shot a one of the horny beasts but it was dark and I accidentally shot Billy Woo our oriental cook. I blamed the whole thing on the Human Turd. Nobody really gave a damn because the little goofy sumbitch always put pea pods in the food and everybody hated him.

Lawrence

P.S. Chief Many Farts says hey!

ED NOTE: The coyote thing brings to mind something I once experienced. I gotta tell ya when a dog humps a leg it's funny. But when a dog humps *your* leg at a party with 40 other people around, it's somethin' else again. I once had a dog hump my leg at a birthday party. People just laughed and laughed. But I took it as an insult and I'll tell ya why. Just think, out of all the people that were at that party the dog looked at me and said, "Hey, I got a shot with that guy!"

Aug 5th 1862

DEAREST EVELYN,

Today our new cook started and the sergeant got sick and threw up which caused a chain reaction among the soldiers. People were throwin' up left and right. The road was eventually covered with beanie weenies. I tried to throw up a rancid Polish sausage but nothin' came out but watermelon.

Love,

Lawrence

PS: Chief Many Farts said hey.

ED NOTE: I took this from another actual experience. My friend Donna threw up on my friend Marty at a party. Then my buddy Jay tossed and soon the whole room was gagging and heavin' as part of a chain reaction. That's a lot of puke! It was worse than when Air America realized George Bush was getting re-elected.

Sept. 6th 1862

DEAREST EVELYN,

Today there was a small tragedy. A stubborn donkey kicked my Indian buddy Chief Many Farts in the nuts.

While he was rolling around on the ground, the Human Turd came charging around the corner on a pale white horse guns a blazin'. He now travels with a small gang of freak of natures he met while playing poker.

We have identified the other gang members with some help of some Texas Rangers. They are the Uribe Twins, they are, or it is, a muscular double headed Mexican with one big body and 7 penises. Them and the Human Turd is the brains of the whole operation.

There's also Stumpy Jackson, he's an ex-Confederate sergeant and lost his arms and legs when he got drunk and crawled inside a cannon. He defected one night after disguising himself as a tumbleweed and rolled out of camp down a hill where he joined up with the Human Turd and his gang. We think what they use him for is they tie a rope around Stumpy's armpits and drag him behind their horses to cover up their tracks.

The final member is Watersack Jack and his deformed girlfriend Five Boob Myrtle. He's a midget with bad gout in his nuts. They are so swollen and waterlogged that at night his nuts can fold out into a water bed comfortably sleeping 9 soldiers. I must go, Chief Many Farts says hey!

                                                    Lawrence.

ED NOTE: Nothing at this time.

Nov. 29th 1862

DEAREST EVELYN

Tonight it's very cold out. We are keeping warm by burning horse turds and taking turns sleeping next to fat guys. Two nights ago we had quite a scare. We had all had beans for dinner and since it was 17 below zero all our farts had frozen in limbo in the middle of the frozen air.

The next morning when the sun came out our farts, which were in nighttime hibernation, began to thaw and explode rapidly throughout the camp. We had all jumped to our bunkers thinking we were being ambushed by Yankees with gatlin guns. Evelyn I was so scared. We then realized we were in no danger when we smelled no gunpowder only a strong odor of beanie weenies [that was a very popular soldier dish] and salt pork.

Tomorrow me and Chief Many Farts will continue to track the Human Turd. We think he is hiding out in the town of Big Nipple with his wife who is pregnant with turdletts. We have contacted the sheriff of Big Nipple and told him to be on the look out for the tapered headed outlaw. Sunday Chief Many Farts' brother Chief Occasional Farts will be getting married in the town of Wiener Lick I've never been to a tribal wedding but they say it's a lot of fun and there'll be a lot of drinkin' and shootin' arrows at stop signs.

I gotta run, take care of those boils.

Lawrence!

ED NOTE: Anytime you can write a story and include the word "turdletts," you have something. Make fun if ya want, but this stuff sells. How else can you explain the popularity of *South Park*, which is nothing but fart and retard jokes? I never miss an episode. If the president told fart jokes and had a retard choir sing a Christian hymn before he gave the State of the Union speech, he'd always get high marks. And if anyone in Hollywood says it ain't true then don't make me pull out the movie *There's Something About Mary* on ya, 'cause that was chockfull of farts and retards and the critics loved it!

Dec 4th 1862

DEAREST EVELYN,

Today Bob Hope came out again. Great show!

Lawrence

ED NOTE: Sorry, I had to do it. Love the Bobster.

March 5th 1863

DEAREST EVELYN,

Yesterday the town of Big Nipple was burnt to the ground by Union soldiers. I don't know why they have such a hatred toward anything to do with nipple or tits. First they make strippers wear pasties now they burn down Big Nipple.

It was a lovely town founded by the late Dorothy "Big Nipple" Harrington. She was a large 350 lb prostitute with mammoth titties and legend has it that during the cholera epidemic all the milk was tainted and Dorothy "Big Nipple" Harrington single handedly titty fed over 700 hungry toddlers 12 hours a day for 5 straight weeks.

One night when she was sleepin' a runt toddler got pinned under her left breast and smothered to death. She never realized what had happened until 2 days later she discovered a lump under her life giving boobs and found the hungry dead runt. She became so depressed she hung herself in the saloon. Her tits are preserved in a pickle barrel at the Big Nipple court house.

All this wonderful history was destroyed by the Union Army, sorry bastards! We've been marching for miles, our shoes have worn out so we have made shoes out of dried out cow pies. I have a beautiful pair of charolai cow pie sandals. I also made a nice pair of horse poop loafers; however, the lieutenant's dog ate the heel so I threw them out.

Chief Many Farts is still tracking the Human Turd. He said the Human Turd had gone to the doctor to get some corn removed from his foot. His wife has given birth to twin turdletts. Evelyn, this is getting serious, We must find this tapered headed outlaw before he gives birth to any more brown growlers. We have picked up his scent again and we think he may be on his way to the town of Camel Toe. It's a town full of saloon girls with really tight jeans. It's a very popular stop for minors and talcum powder salesmen.

Love ya,

Lawrence

ED NOTE: I threw in the part about the town of Camel Toe because I've always been infatuated with the way some woman wear their pants so they have a buttcrack in the front of their jeans. This is actually disgusting only if the person is over a certain weight. For instance, Heidi Klum with camel toe is way more tolerable than, say, Kirstie Alley with it.

Speakin' of camel toe, they say that you can actually see Dwight Yoakum's camel toe from space. Rosie O'Donnell, thank God, never has camel toe because she always wears baggy slacks. However, her problem then becomes that she always gets mistaken for Dan Deirdorf when she goes out.

March 10th 1863

DEAREST EVELYN,

I hope this letter finds you well. I however have dysentery and cold sores and am in really bad shape. Last night we were ambushed by a Yankee regiment and Chief Many Farts tried to send out smoke signals but spelled "send posse" wrong and a bunch of Apache squaws showed up totally naked. He always gets his "u"s and "o"s mixed up.

No matter how ya spell it though it saved our life.

More later,

Lawrence

ED NOTE: That "posse" joke was actually one I had heard backstage at a Lee Greenwood concert the night before, so I figured I'd add it here. I like Lee Greenwood, but he only sings that one song, "God Bless the USA" (which *is* a great song) and he tours only when there's a tragedy or a war. Every time I see Lee Greenwood is singing somewhere, I hurry up and turn on Fox News to see what the hell just happened. I really think he goes to foreign countries and tries to start trouble just so he can fill his summer calendar with work. I love him, though!

March 21st 1863

DEAREST EVELYN,

Tonight we're gonna have a barn dance to help boost morale. I hope ya don't mind but I'm gonna take a legless armless crippled Indian named Weeble. The general has been using her in his office as a door stop. I'm gonna strap her to my back like a book bag and go to the dance.

The lieutenant is mad because we took the wagons out muddin' and got them stuck. We ended up hitchin' 'em to a fat Indian woman and we dangled some coyote meat in front of her and she pulled them right out. Write more later,

Lawrence

ED NOTE: These are still funnier than Margaret Cho, I don't care what ya say.

April 4th 1863

DEAREST EVELYN,

I hope this letter finds you in good health as of your last letter you were getting strange warts. I hope you put ointment on them instead of cutting them off with fingernail clippers. It has been a rough month Corporal Winchester got kicked in the nuts by a horse and they swelled up so bad that he had to bounce in formation off his nuts like a hippity hop for 13 miles. We ended up putting him in the river and he floated himself to Ft. Briggs and they popped his scrotum with a pin, and the explosion took his legs.

Lucky fellow, now he can go home and be outta this damn war. He rolled into my tent today and said his good-byes and then stood on his hands and ran to the stagecoach. He sure is a ball of fire.

Today was the annual baseball game between us and some Yankee prisoners. We used a ball made out of dried horse turds and boy was it juiced! I hit 2 home-runs and one was hit so hard it split the turd ball and some grain flew out of it and went in some Yan-kee's eye and he was blinded for 30 minutes so we called the game.

We ended up winning 24-0. They actually could have scored more but since they were the visiting team and prisoners we had a guy on a horse that would rope them every time they got a hit and headed for second and he would drag them around the bases until we tagged 'em. It may not have been fair but screw 'em, they ruined all the titty bars.

On Sunday we had chapel and the preacher talked about "patience". I wanted to stay for the whole ser-vice but I had to go to the bathroom and any more "patience" woulda had me shittin' my pants. By the way I made ya a nice bracelet made out of pig innards. I'll send it to ya as soon as it dries out.

Love you,

Lawrence

ED NOTE: How can I do any Editor's Notes on perfection? Alright, almost perfection. I gave this an A–, the minus comin' only for punctuation.

April 15th 1862

DEAREST EVELYN.

Today Evelyn is a wonderful day. Chief Many Farts
has killed the Human Turd. He was shot in the head
during a poker game and it was a fitting end as he
was holding a flush. We are gonna grind up the
tapered headed bastard and sprinkle him all over a
field of tomatoes. This is a great day other than the
war.

Tell that Abraham Lincoln prick to lighten up!

Lawrence.

**ED NOTE: This was the last installment of the Civil War letters. I
would liked to have done more letters but there's only so many
retard and poop jokes and wiener and titty material that you can
do in a sketch. Besides, everyone knows how the war ends and
besides that, I had other important things to do! The elections
were starting and I had to bash Clinton for the next few months. It
didn't help. He won anyway and I'm actually kinda glad because I
then had another human turd to talk about!**

After a few weeks of people asking for more letters I thought
about putting out a CD called *The Civil War Letters*. I decided
against it, however, after hearing an actual CD a friend of mine
owned that had nothin' on it but fart sounds. I'm not kidding, it
was a CD that somebody put out with all fart stuff. I think it sold
almost 10 thousand copies statewide!

After hearing that recording, I was so upset that I hadn't thought
of the fart idea, I just forgot about doing the Civil War CD. Oh well,
sometimes ya just lose out to more creative people.

But the good news is that a lot of time has passed since I wrote these letters and I've learned a lot. I have grown older and wiser and my writing has matured enough to where HBO has hired me to direct my latest movie idea, *Freddy and Harold*. It's a documentary about adult film star Ron Jeremy as told through the eyes of his two talking cartoon testicles, Freddy and Harold.

Bring on the Emmy!

Chapter 5

MEDIA MADNESS

THIS CHAPTER IS WHERE I really want to, as they say, "stir the fires." I want to talk about an interview I did in *Rolling Stone* magazine. You've heard of *Rolling Stone,* the publication that claims to be a rock and roll magazine and then puts Britney Spears on the cover three times.

Don't get me wrong, I wouldn't mind if Britney showed up as pop-ups in the *National Review,* but three times in *Rolling Stone*! That's like havin' Bill Maher speak at the John Birch Society. Anyway, I'm gonna cover that *Rolling Stone* interview in this chapter as well as a few others I've given, plus I'll speak out against the dangers of masturbating at public functions. Here we go:

The scene: Pittsburgh, Pennsylvania.

The venue: A Wal-Mart on the outskirts of town.

The Players: Me, my tour manager, two representatives from Wal-Mart, a rep from the record label, 600 fans, and a porno star with tits the size of small utility vans.

(OK, I added the porno star part, but the vans were real.)

I was all excited that day. Not only had I just passed 600 points on my hand-held Yahtzee game, I was about to appear in *Rolling Stone* magazine! I actually showered two days before the interview and felt very good about the whole thing. As we arrived at the Wal-Mart via a beautiful Ford Focus, I saw all the fans screaming and I was smilin' bigger than the time I seen Marcia Lundford's left nipple pop out while she was doing the cheer "We got spirit, how 'bout you" at a state playoff game.

I expected the article to be fair even though *Rolling Stone* leaned left and I was a white Republican comedian that lived in the South, talked with an accent, and have been known to throw reporters a hand slap to the nuts as a "how's it goin'" kinda hello. I assumed this guy already had a pretty good idea of what he was gonna write before he even saw my great fans and ate a delicious Wal-Mart hotdog with chili. But since I get along with everyone, I figured he'd do his best to be objective.

As I signed titties, pictures, and the heads of bald drunk guys, the reporter took a few notes. Then he questioned some fans. That was cool. I figured this guy was getting a chance to see exactly how much my fans and I appreciate each other. The whole day was perfect except for the drunk guy who kept tellin' me a joke I've heard 300 times about a girl's beaver lookin' like Willie Nelson. However, I was cordial and thanked the reverend for bringing the youth department out to meet me.

The reporter didn't hear the Willie Nelson beaver joke. Lucky for me, he was busy walking through the line to check out my fans' racial diversity. Ya see, that's what makes a good comic in the eyes of some magazines, racial diversity. Never mind whether the comedian is funny, if there's not a good mix of nationalities attendin' the show, the performer is obviously a David Duke peckerhead.

The article appeared in the May 5, 2005, issue of *Rolling Stone* (#973) and I was shocked when I read it. Here this reporter had just spent a whole day watchin' the greatest fans in the world wait three hours to get my autograph or have their pictures taken with me. I even bought the sumbitch lunch and a hat from a convenience store that said, "Wine 'em, dine 'em, 69 'em."

My first beef with *Rolling Stone* comes before we even get to the words. My publicist sent the magazine 10 great recent pictures of me to run alongside the article. They didn't use any of 'em. Instead, they dug up a 10-year-old shot that had me looking like I'd just stepped out of the Broadway play *Look at All the Retards*. It just proves my point that this guy already had in his head what angle he was goin' for.

The title of the article was "Meet the Next King of Comedy?" Great title, until ya look at the picture and see that big retarded face. If the *Rolling Stone* editors had been honest, here's the title they should have used:

> *Meet Larry the Cable Guy. He's Not Our Kind of Guy. But Even Though We Don't Like Him, We Have to Accept the Fact that He's Really Popular and We Don't Know Why. So We're Gonna Show This Really Retarded-Lookin' Picture of Him . . .*

I know it's a little long, but a least it woulda been truthful. Matter of fact, it's the same title every major paper in the country should have run whenever they showed a picture of George W. during his presidential campaign.

OK, now I'll be honest and tell you why I was so upset: I had lost 30 pounds since posin' for that retarded picture that *Rolling Stone* ran. I'd had many pictures taken since then. Ya have to believe some of 'em featured me makin' another retard face. So I figured if they're gonna show me lookin' goofy, couldn't they at least make me thinner. I'd rather be a thin retard than a fat one.

By the way, I just ran outside in my underwear and shot a snake. Awesome!

Then it says, "Larry the Cable Guy Plugs into Red State Fervor."

ED NOTE: This should tell you somethin' right here. I'm already jumpin' his ass and we haven't even got past the title! This reporter seems to think that only red state Republican crowds like my act. That right there says he knows absolutely nothing about me! For the record, I do just as good in blue states as I do in red ones and I used to get laid more in the blue ones. However, I caught my only STDs in red states.

Just to set the record straight: my three biggest states are Minnesota, Wisconsin, and Pennsylvania! Those states are bluer than a 16-year-old's nuts after listenin' to Howard Stern talk a girl off over the phone! Come to think of it, I remember that show and I got a little blue myself!

I'm actually kinda sick of this red state–blue state bullshit. Is Dr. Seuss runnin' the government? My act is not just blue state or red state. It's for anyone that likes to laugh and those people live in every state. What makes this really funny, is that the guy actually interviewed me in a blue state after I had just sold out three shows with seats at $45.00 a pop.

This guy had to be sniffin' Super Glue or else he really can't see past this Dr. Seuss "red state–blue state" crap. Writing that title is like saying I only eat green eggs and ham while I'm eating red eggs and bacon!

OK, it's nothing like that so let me continue before I completely confuse myself.

In the first paragraph, the writer describes a gig I did in Pittsburgh, and rips me for my hat, my paunch, my chaw, and for a joke I tell about black folks sneakin' up behind me. Everything in the paragraph is true except I wouldn't call myself paunchy. I mean I lost 30 pounds, for God's sake, give me a little credit. If I were writing the article, I would have described myself as "a very attractive, statuesque figure with a magnificent ass of steel," but that's me.

One other important point: my baseball cap is not crappy. It was an Advantage camo and that thing is worked in good. Ya have to wear a ball cap that looks shaped-up and worked-in. The dirtier the hat, the better it is and everybody knows it. Ain't nothin' turns a girl on more than a hat that smells like eight-year-old sweat! Sorry, Mr. New York City *Rolling Stone* Big Shot, if it didn't measure up to your fag Von Dutch hat standards. Don't screw with a redneck's hat, dickweed!

I mean that in a good Christian way.

In the article, the reporter described me as havin' ". . . a mouth that seems full of chaw." Well there was no SEEMIN' to it. It was full of Skoal Long Cut Straight that night, just like it is every night. I love a dip after eatin' or if I'm constipated. I don't know what it is about dip that makes ya wanna poop but I'm tellin' ya, it works.

Now here's the real deal: I'm thankful that *Rolling Stone* decided to feature me in this article. I knew what I was getting into when they called. I knew it was a left wing magazine. But in America, ya have a right to set a few things straight, don't ya? This article mentioned that my audiences are almost entirely white, as if that's a crime in this country nowadays. Well, first off, that's not correct. There were several Mexicans working the show and the black guy from electronics asked me to sign his shirt.

OK, so maybe that's not a good example. But here's my beef. I can't control who comes to a Wal-Mart signing and who doesn't. I'm not a political candidate bussing in people of all races, colors, and creeds to make a good impression for the camera. Who cares that most of the crowd was white? Jesse Jackson spoke in Orlando not too long ago and guess what? Ninety-five percent of the crowd was black! Does that mean he's racist? No, it means that that is his demographic. And as far as I know he didn't even impregnate anyone! God knows Bill Clinton makes tons of speeches in Harlem, but I never seen him cruisin' around there on a Saturday night, chillin' with his "homies!"

At least on my way to the porno store, I drive down Martin Luther King Blvd. with my doors unlocked and my windows open! I don't see any uppity whites doin' that trick!

I would rather perform for the black audiences than the uptight politically correct white audiences any day. God bless 'em. I went on the *Steve Harvey Show* and killed with that crowd. I love 'em to death.

I like people who like to laugh and have a sense of humor. I couldn't care less what color they are. This is so ridiculous, it's actually sad. You think this writer ever counted the white people at a 50 Cent or a Ludacris concert? Of course not, but I'm a white guy from the South and my crowd is mostly white. So I'm gonna get labeled by uptight PC reporters who still think we're living in 1864.

Sure, most of my audience is white. In business, they call that your demographic. Hello! It's obvious that *Rolling Stone* magazine caters to its own demographic: young white hipsters. Isn't that age discrimination? *Rolling Stone* ignores a lot of music old people like. If I was old, I'd be offended by all the Weezer articles. Everyone in the entertainment field—whether it be movies, radio, television, or publishing—attracts a certain demographic.

Mine just happens to be white folks, so suck on that, poop faces!

In the article, the reporter quoted a joke I do in which I look at my shadow and say, "I thought a couple of black guys were sneakin' up behind me." I've been deliverin' that punchline for years in front of all kinds of audiences, including blacks, and they all laughed their asses off over it. They thought it was funny as hell!

You have to wonder if this reporter ever goes to a show featurin' Chris Rock or Dave Chappelle and writes about their honky jokes (which, by the way, are downright hilarious). It's apparently OK for Chris Rock to tell jokes about white people. However, if I make one joke about my shadow that mentions blacks, I'm a racist and my audience isn't diverse enough.

My crowd comes from every walk of life, from rich to poor to middle class to drunk and naked vomiting in the back row. They're all good, honest, hardworking Americans who just want to laugh and have a great time. The last thing they need is some PC *Rolling Stone* reporter telling them they're racists because my show doesn't meet his audience diversity quota!

Oh, by the way, both Dave and Chris, who are two of the best comedians on the planet, happen to be friends of mine. Well, I worked with Dave once at a Florida Gator pep rally, but I'm sure if I said hi he'd give me that familiar "hey you" look. I've met Chris three times in New York City. We got along great and actually held hands during a Paul Mooney concert!

Oh, I'm sorry. That was Lewis Black.

The *Rolling Stone* article actually made me laugh harder than when that Canadian chick slipped on the ice while screwin' up the American National Anthem. Can't anybody even go to a comedy show anymore without havin' to worry about the PC police attackin' ya for doin' nothin' except drinkin' a few beers with some friends and havin' a few laughs?

I swear this world is nuttier than squirrel shit!

If ya want to read the article, I told ya what issue it was. The point I'm tryin' to make is that some reporters just don't try to get it. After hearing a joke, they have to analyze it to find some political or social significance before they can decide whether it's funny. That's nonsense. A joke is funny because it's funny and there's no explainin' why.

Writers like this guy'll never understand that some people just like to be entertained. My fans come out to laugh over nonsensical bullshit and have a good time. Comedians don't have to make deep political points or talk over anyone's head. But there are some comedians who go out of their way to treat their fans as if they're stupid.

Case in point, David Cross. I've never met this guy in my life, but he appeared in my article blasting me and my crowds. He said my humor was anti-gay and racist. That's garbage, but according to Cross and the politically correct police, any white comedians who mention the word *black* or say somethin' humorous but faintly negative about any race are racists.

And if ya do a gay joke and you're a heterosexual white from the South? Oh shit, run for the hills! Now you're a homophobe and a gay basher. These are the rules of comedy in the PC world. However, these rules don't apply to all comedians. Ya see, when PC people make the rules, they allow certain exemptions.

For example, if you're a gay comic, you can basically say or do anything you want onstage. I mean you could even kill and gut Christians and Republicans as an encore and it would be perfectly legal in 21 cities!

When a gay comic or a comic who isn't white does retard jokes, fart jokes, gay jokes, or even racial jokes, it's a riot. I do the same stuff and I become the asshole with the crowd that thinks "the comedian ant" is groundbreaking. It makes about as much sense as a harelip ordering biggie fries! I just don't understand it.

That brings me to somethin' else about that article that made me madder than a prostitute tryin' to put a rubber on an epileptic. *Rolling Stone* printed one of my jokes to demonstrate that my act was somehow homophobic. The line the reporter quoted was "madder than a queer with lockjaw on Valentine's Day." C'mon, that's a fricken hoot. And not only is that funny, it's kinda true. If I were gay and had lockjaw on Valentine's Day, I'd be pissed.

Despite what *Rolling Stone* thinks, gay folks come to my shows and they laugh their asses off. I asked a lesbian fan who loves my act why some lesbians hated me. She said "because there's some lesbians that are uptight bitches and they hate themselves just as much as you!"

That's a direct quote.

I have a good buddy of mine that's gay. I love him like a brother . . . sister . . . whatever. We were drinking Mogen David wine and dancing to Seal one night when he told me that the only people that get offended by gay jokes are people that aren't gay.

OK, I never danced or drank Mogen David with my gay buddy. However, I did attend a dwarf toss and a dwarf said that the only people that get mad at dwarf tossing are people that aren't dwarfs.

Now that's funny to me. But I guess I'm not as intellectual as David Cross. In that *Rolling Stone* article, he sure showed us what a deep thinker he is by sayin', "America is in a stage of vague intellectual pride."

No it's not, David. America's in a stage of boredom from watchin' humorless comedians act like they're better than everyone else. America's sick of payin' good money for a comedy show that only earns one laugh every 12 minutes because the comedian onstage is too busy demonstratin' how much smarter he is than his audience

Here's another comment from David Cross. He complained that I'm pullin' the wool over my audience's head by claiming that I'm this "gee shucks" redneck while I'm actually making millions. See, to his mind, bein' well paid means I'm no longer real and I can't be a country boy anymore. It's just an act.

Ya pegged me, David, ya got me! I've really pulled the wool over people's eyes—I give up! The secret's out! I'm really a Jewish lawyer named Hyman from the Upper West Side. Of all the stupid statements, this has to get the blue ribbon in the stupid statement contest.

I can assure everyone that I'm not pulling any wool and I haven't changed and never will. I'm the same country boy today I was 20 years ago, except I have a bigger lift on my truck. I was taught that every moment's a blessing, kindness comes back ten-fold, and a strong work ethic is a great thing to have.

Maybe that's why my fans relate to me so well. They were raised the same way I was. If I found out my neighbor had a broken arm, you bet your sweet ass I'd be over to his place to help him feed his pigs. A few coins in the bank don't change who I am.

For instance, just because I have made some money doesn't mean I have to dress in jeans or shirts that cost more than most people's monthly grocery bills. Normal people don't wear 200-dollar jeans! And making Hollywood's "best dressed" list is not why I got into comedy. I still buy Wranglers at the Wal-Mart because they're comfortable, not because I'm trying to be something I'm not.

Perhaps David Cross should bitch out my parents for the money I've earned. They're the ones who woke me up early every morning to do farm chores.

Their good parenting taught me that a little hard work never hurts anyone. I wasn't selling tickets overnight; it's been 20 years of hard work, personal sacrifice, endless Sky Miles, and living on Waffle House grilled cheese sandwiches that got me where I am.

Look, I don't have to justify myself. My friends and family know the kinda person I am. I actually struggled with writing these comments about David Cross for a full 10 seconds. I have a great relationship with all the comics of my generation (Lewis Black, Colin Quinn, Nick Di Paolo, that generation) and I've never said a bad word about any other comedian.

This was different, because David basically hammered my fans in that *Rolling Stone* article by implying that they were ignorant. He crossed the line when he railed against them, so I had to tell ya what I felt about that. He can hammer me all he wants, but when he screwed with my fans, it was time for me to say something.

Ya see, David, here's the deal: we're comedians and that's all. We do not influence the outcome of world events. We exist to help people enjoy themselves for a few hours after they've had a bull-shit day. We make no policy decisions. I repeat, WE MAKE NO POL-ICY DECISIONS! I know you wish we did, but trust me, no president has ever made a decision based on something Bob Newhart or Steve Martin said. So quit taking yourself so seriously. Go write a fart joke and lighten up! Other than that, God bless ya, I am honestly happy for all your successes. I thought *Mr. Show* was hilarious and I wish you even more continued happiness; other than that, leave my fans alone and kiss my ass.

I'm not going to bore you with the rest of the article. I just wanted to straighten the record on some of that bullshit. I called my buddy Lewis Black after I read the article. I wanted to thank him for sayin' some cool stuff about me. Lewis is hilarious. We gen-erally disagree about politics, but we're still great friends and he is one of my favorite acts and dad gum hilarious!

The PC police got on his case when he offered to change his name from Lewis Black to Lewis African-American. Lewis told them to blow it out their asses in a way that only Lewis could make funny, with a lot of yelling topped off with an f-word at the end for punctuation!

That *Rolling Stone* reporter called Lewis and asked for his opin-ion of my act. Lewis said that the guy kept pumping him for nega-tive comments, and he was kinda taken aback when he learned that Lewis liked me. Basically the guy was calling comedians hoping they would say something negative about me. He didn't realize that I had started out with a lot of those guys and we're all pretty good friends.

The only bad thing Lewis could come up with was actually funny. He told him about the time he caught me masturbating to an Atlanta Braves playoff game. That was the one where Sid Bream slid across home plate to beat the Pittsburgh Pirates for the 1992 National League championship. That was awesome!

It was also awesome seeing my name in *Rolling Stone* magazine even if they did print that picture of my fat retarded face and made me out to be the Antichrist of America's intellectuals. They did, however, say that my fans love me and that I love my fans, which is true.

Especially the one who had me sign her tits next to the batteries.

So let me say thank you to *Rolling Stone* for the article; I enjoyed hanging out with your reporter. Since doing that interview, however, I've looked at some of your past issues and guess what? Ninety percent of the people you have featured in your magazine have been white. Was I outraged! I can't believe I appeared in such a racist publication. Sure, there was an occasional rapper, but c'mon, let's have more diversity!

Recently I've been doing Internet interviews for colleges and different websites. I enjoyed the Net when I first went online to check out the sports and porno stuff. Now I hate the Internet. The porno just isn't fun anymore because of all those viruses that can come across cyberspace.

Then there's the pop-ups. When ya finally do get the perfect crotch shot of some gal on orientalwhore.com, the next thing ya know some weird window pops open. Now ya got a picture of a donkey and some 14-year-old jailbait slut lookin' back at ya and you're scared to stay online for fear that the FBI got ya in some kinda sting. And you didn't do nothin' wrong except browse orientalwhore.com while your girlfriend ran to the store! Fricken perverts. Ya can't even look at a Japanese girl's ass crack without some idiot shovin' underage filth down your throat. I tell ya, the whole Internet sucks.

But I still have to do these college interviews. I don't mind them. However, if there was ever a breeding ground for political correctness, it's a college campus. Well, there and Barbra Streisand's vagina.

These students just don't seem to understand what I do. They're always askin' why I tell certain jokes.

Because I'm a comedian! I mean, how hard is that to figure out?

Then you have some college students who think their shit don't stink and they're out to change the world. Most of them ask me heavy political questions, like this one kid who said, "I see where your dad was a preacher. Do you think it's possible to do your act and still be a good Christian, and how does fundamentalists trying to put restrictions on the FCC affect you?"

In response to that, let me share two observations:

1. The kid's an idiot; and
2. I could care less about the FCC. I think they've overstepped their bounds and have no common sense about them. But what am I gonna do? I'm not a politician. . . .

I'm a comedian. I just write jokes and try to avoid saying "titty" during radio interviews. I comment on something like FCC policy only if I can get a laugh in the first eight seconds. Otherwise, who cares. Why is that? 'Cause getting laughs is my job.

Askin' whether I can be a good Christian and still do my act is a retarded blast of crap. There's no sign on any of my shows that says "Revival meeting, 8 p.m. tonight!" I go to church and worship the Lord. I go to a comedy show and laugh at the jokes. God has more important things to do than go to my Friday late show to make sure I'm not doing something offensive.

The people attendin' my shows aren't expecting me to witness to them either. They come to laugh, not learn bible verses. So I leave my spiritual life completely out of my stage life. Well, except for the part in my act when I talk about playing with my church camp counselor Sheila Stark's tits ! But it's a really funny story and a great closer.

Now I've got a religious question. Does a gay priest find it hard to talk about the bible on Sunday after hacking up pubic hairs from his boyfriend's nutsack on Saturday night! Compared to that spiritual dilemma, my little jokes somehow seem insignificant.

Other than being interviewed by our local paper after winning a greased pig contest at the fair, I never had done anything worth writing about until I became a comedian. I remember my first brush with the national media. I was in Los Angeles trying to per- saude Buddy Ebsen (who was alive at the time) to read a screen- play I had written called *The Life and Times of Larry the Cable Guy Starring Buddy Ebsen.*

While I was in L.A., I hung out with Drew Carey. I knew Drew way before he became famous and we were great friends. Right after he had landed the *Drew Carey Show* I actually wrote a movie for him called *The Life and Times of Larry the Cable Guy Starring Drew Carey.* He was interested until his sitcom became a big hit.

Which is why I was in Los Angeles talkin' to Buddy Ebsen.

At the time, a writer for *Esquire* magazine was doin' a story about Drew. Seems like he was around whenever Drew and I got together. I thought this was great, since it gave me the chance to get this dude interested in my Larry/Buddy Ebsen screenplay. I gladly put in my own two cents about Drew, how he was a great comic and so down to earth, and that I was proud to call him a friend.

I was also proud of myself. Here I was about to be quoted in a big magazine. It was so exciting, I forgot to mention that movie I wanted to do with Buddy Ebsen. I couldn't wait for that article to appear so Drew would call and say something like "Thanks for the nice words."

After my Buddy Ebsen search came up empty, I returned home. One afternoon I was strolling through the mall, checking out the buns on the girl ordering bourbon chicken, when I remembered *Esquire* was due out that very day. Nice buns or not, this was my interview debut. I hauled ass like that little dude in *The Incredibles* and grabbed a copy.

Boy, was I in for a shock! There, right next to *Esquire,* was a *People* magazine with a headline that read, "Buddy Ebsen Dead!" There went my movie. But I got an even bigger jolt when I opened the *Esquire.* What I read was the biggest butcher job since Jeffrey Dahmer moved to Milwaukee.

The writer basically ignored all the nice things I had said about Drew. He had me trashing my friend and calling him an asshole. I've heard about takin' things out of context. However, this dude either shot heroin into his toes or else he heard me commenting on Sammy Kershaw for a *Country Weekly* interview on the same night we discussed Drew and he mixed up my words. The guy totally twisted everything I said and took other liberties to portray me as the villain in the article.

Drew knew it was all a bunch of crap. The next time we met, he said that the guy had totally hosed me. He knew I never said any of those things. But this is the point I'm getting at about interviews. I avoid 'em whenever possible because the writers will misquote you and make up stuff in 65 percent of 'em. Ya might get an apology if you hound 'em, but they'll bury it somewhere in the back of the magazine or book. These writers don't care about the damage their false reporting can inflict on people. They're the media, and, by God, they're holier than Christ himself!

So that's it. I know I did some pretty good bitchin' here, but I just wanted to show ya what reporters can do when they have an agenda. Not all of them, mind you. I've done tons of great interviews. However, whenever you read an interview or an article with a celebrity, ya should take some things with a grain of salt.

Now on a more serious note, after several phone calls and some extreme diligence on my part, I think we finally will be able to do that movie. It's now called *The Life and Times of Larry the Cable Guy Starring Craig T. Nelson!* I can't wait.

Chapter 6

RODEO RIDERS NOT
NAMED CODY

Chapter 7

NASCAR

FINALLY, I AM GONNA WRITE about something I know about: how to find free porn on the Internet!

Wait a second, that's a pamphlet I'm doing for kids who get bored while visitin' their grandparents. Let me go back over my notes. Oh, NASCAR is what this chapter will be on! Great.

I love the sport of NASCAR about as much as I love watching oriental gymnasts do flying camel toes. Bein' from football country, I didn't start off a big NASCAR fan when I was growing up. In my town, if ya weren't a Nebraska football fan, you were either a pussy or a communist. I didn't want to be a pussy or a communist, so I became a big Huskers fan. I did, however, feel a girl from Russia's titties on a Disney trip when I was 15.

Don't ask.

I became a NASCAR fan after my cousin started racing cars up in Wisconsin. Since he was in a wheelchair at the time, he was an inspiration to the whole family. He was at such a loss without his wheelchair, though, he actually sat in it while he raced. His pit crew actually cut out the regular seat in his car and made special peddles so he could drive while remainin' in his wheelchair. It was crazy.

My cousin was in a bad accident one afternoon. He hit a wall and flew out through the car's front windshield. Luckily, he landed upright in his chair on its wheels. He rolled all the way around to the finish line and finished a solid fourth.

That brings me to Dick Trickle. My cousin actually raced against him on occasion. At the time, Trickle had won about everything a driver could win at short track racing. I became a huge Trickle fan when I learned he was the only NASCAR driver who still kept a cigarette lighter in his car. I love those guys that do what they want and tell the PC crowd to kiss their asses.

In fact, I like all the NASCAR boys because they're as regular American as you can get. They have a talent for racing cars and they're not into all that Hollywood flashy stuff. Anyway, most of the older drivers like Trickle aren't.

Dick never won many NASCAR events, but just the fact that I got to put a bumper sticker on my truck that said "Racing makes my Dick Trickle" made being his fan worthwhile. I also had a Dick Trickle mailbox until the night my grandma came home hammered from playing canasta and backed into it. She knocked the Dick right off the Trickle. Those canasta games can get so damn outta hand!

After spending many nights watching my cousin race at the local tracks, I got hooked on NASCAR and elephant ears. If you don't know about elephant ears, they're fried dough with powdered sugar on them. When ya really wanna commit suicide without all the pain of shooting yourself, eat those damn things. They're tastier than 18-year-old titties but, believe me, two of 'em will require you to get a C-section just to poop. I was backed up like a urinal after the St. Patrick's Day parade after eatin' some. I actually read where elephant ears are the biggest cause of death next to heroin and any TV show with Valerie Bertinelli in it.

Elephant ears weren't the only thing I loved about NASCAR. The atmosphere at a race is magical. It's the last truly American thing that political correctness hasn't damaged too much. It's a lotta good old-fashioned fun started by a buncha moonshiners. Just see-ing all the ZZ Top–looking folks drinking beer, havin' a good time, and not giving a damn is awesome.

And that's just the women!

NASCAR fans are honest, hardworking Americans who love rac-ing. Some people save the whole year just to make it to Daytona or Charlotte or Talladega. They'll plan vacations around their favorite races. They like nothin' more than spendin' the weekend with friends and havin' a party.

That's why all the uptight morons that diss the sport and its fans piss me off. I remember goin' to a sports bar one night after egging some street whores after church. There was this snobby couple watching soccer on the main big screen and everyone was pissed because one of the few NASCAR night races was scheduled and we all wanted to watch it. We asked very politely (as politely as you can, I guess, while usin' the f-word) if we could switch the channel.

They said they didn't want to watch a sport where a bunch of drunken rednecks do nothing but drink Busch beer all day, get into fights, and watch cars go around in circles. That got me goin'. I told the dude that he just didn't understand the sport. NASCAR has much more to offer fans than that.

For instance, we also got Budweiser!

But honestly, I hate those snooty-assed people. Correction, I don't hate them. I don't hate anybody except Satan and the net-work that canceled *Hee Haw*. But these uppity soccer fans can kiss my ass. Soccer, please! I'd rather stick my nuts in a meat grinder than watch soccer.

And look who's calling the kettle African-American (that's for the PC crowd). I've been to 40 NASCAR races and about 200 short track races as well as watching countless events on TV and I've seen maybe five fights total. You can't watch a soccer game any-more without a fricken riot breakin' out.

Now tell me who the rednecks are.

Believe me, your average NASCAR fan is more well behaved then any soccer fan. Unless, of course, somebody makes fun of the late Dale Earnhardt Sr. in front of a NASCAR follower. Then somebody's getting their ass kicked.

Sorry, but that's in the rule book. My buddy Ray once twisted his ankle at a NASCAR race and I asked an official for the fastest way to get to the hospital.

He said "Just say somethin' bad about Dale Earnhardt!"

I love NASCAR and I'm glad it's so popular that everyone wants to attend the races. That is if ya can fork over about 600 bucks along with your firstborn. I mean, good God, what's a T-shirt go for now, 75 bucks? I got a couple of Michael Waltrip coolies and a flag on layaway down at the mall. But that's the cool thing about NASCAR fans; they're so dedicated to the sport. They'll pay about anything to hear the roar of them engines (havin' a lot of women walkin' around with their titties hanging out doesn't hurt either).

But with any growth comes change. I'm all for anything that makes NASCAR better and more exciting. But I don't believe in changing just because the PC crowd demands it. Political correctness is already killing the country, not to mention strip clubs across Florida and Georgia. Can't we at least leave it out of NASCAR?

For pete's sake, God himself follows NASCAR! Why do ya think we race on Sundays? That's the Lord's day off and it gives him a chance to watch his favorite sport. He needs a little rest and relaxation after a hard week of trying to find ways to feed starving pygmies and dealin' with the Middle East and their backass bullshit all week. After dealing with the complexities of the Third World, I'm sure God enjoys the simplicity of the oval on a Sunday afternoon.

This is why I brought up Dick Trickle and the cigarette lighter in his car. That's the appeal of NASCAR to me. It's about regular guys that haven't lost their connection to the rest of us. That's why this so-called new NASCAR is pissing me off. The sport is losing that bond with the people that have supported it all these years

For example, changing the name of the Winston Cup race to the Nextel Cup. In the words of the Reverend Billy Graham, "You gotta be shittin' me!"

OK, I don't think that was him that said that, but I'm sure he may have swore once in his life, so I'm not far off.

I don't smoke cigarettes, but I really doubt that having Winston sponsorin' a NASCAR event has anything to do with kids adoptin' the habit. More kids smoke pot than cigs and I have yet to see a car drivin' around the track with pot leaves sproutin' from it or carryin' Cheech and Chong head shots for bumper stickers.

If I was in charge of NASCAR I woulda told them non-smokin' pussies to kiss my rock-hard, eye-watering ass. You really think a NASCAR fan gives a rat's ass about cigarettes? I doubt there are many people attendin' these events on big health kicks. Hell, as long as the race don't get rained out, most fans couldn't care less if ya stood up and dropped a load in your pants in the stands. It's a car race, not a church banquet.

OK, perhaps standin' up and crappin' your pants at a race isn't a good thing, but I'm just stickin' up for my brother.

All right. I confess. I was the one that did that. So sue me.

Damned elephant ears.

I was watchin' the Twin-125s last year while an oriental rub-down girl gave me a massage and I was appalled! Not at the race. At the big white pimple on the rub-down girl's right thigh.

Anyway, I switched to CNN Headline News for a second and saw where a tribe of Indians—sorry, I meant Native Americans—and they . . .

Hold on, I have two ED NOTES to add here. First: I seldom watch CNN because Ted Turner is one step below a maggot-infested trash can in my book of favorite things. But I kinda feel sorry for his old network sucking so bad, so I figured I'd help out by doubling their viewership all the way to two.

Second: I used to date a "Native American" and she couldn't care less if people referred to her as an Indian. She thought the whole debate was ridiculous. Our country has become so damn uptight about labels. I think it's hypocritical for the PC crowd to preach that we're all Americans and that we need to unite as brothers and sisters in one country. Then in the next sentence they label everyone into different groups. I love Indians, Native Americans, whatever. Just because I say "Indian" don't mean I'm a bad person. I go to their casinos and spend money. What do they care? If I hated Indians I wouldn't be crying over a roulette table down at the Kickapoo Casino Palace after losing my rent money on green double zero.

By the way, that girlfriend of mine was awesome. I met her at a strip club and she was half-Cherokee. Her Indian name was Pork-a-hontas!

Anyway, to make a long story even more boring and longer, that CNN report said that a group of Indians were gonna sue tobacco companies. *Here we go again*, I thought. Everybody lookin' for a free buck wants to sue the tobacco companies. Let me tell ya, if you don't know by now that cigarettes are bad for ya, then you really need to end your existence because you're way too stupid to maneuver your way through life.

I mean, it says right on the box that smoking might cause cancer. I might as well sue *Hustler* magazine for giving my wrists carpel tunnel syndrome. I oughta sue Indians for selling those stupid ugly damn dream catchers in flea markets. I once bought a dream catcher for $17 and didn't catch a damn thing. They oughta call 'em dust catchers. That's false advertising and these Native Americans know it! They're rippin' me off!

I'll tell ya what a good dream catcher is. My underwear! I caught three Heidi Klum dreams in them dad gum things last week. Enough of suing tobacco companies for free cash. It's ridiculous!

I always thought Stayfree mini pads oughta sponsor NASCAR. That would make for some good announcing:

Announcer 1: "It's a beautiful summer's eve here. We're only one lap into the race and we already got a red flag!"

Announcer 2: "There's Jeff Gordon in the #24 strawberry douche Chevy Monte Carlo!"

Announcer 1: "This is sure a popular race, I wonder how those folks in the front row got tickets to this Tampon 200?"

Announcer 2: "Bet they pulled some strings!"

Announcer 1: "The K-Y jelly car has just accelerated and easily slipped into the Number Two hole. The Vagisil car has been itchin' and burnin' rubber all season out there and remains Number One in the Bush Standings!"

Announcer 2: "Hey Jim, did ya know that the Viagra car is the only car that has windshield wipers on the inside?"

Announcer 1: "Hey that's Larry the Cable Guy's joke. That guys a riot! I don't know what the hell *Rolling Stone* magazine was talking about when it said he was only popular in the red states. I'm from New York and I find him hysterical!"

Announcer 2: "Ya read his new book yet?"

Announcer 1: "Yeah. What the f##k was that all about?"

Announcer 2: "I don't know. It was funny as hell though. I loved the NASCAR chapter."

Larry the Cable Guy: "Hey boys, I know you're really having a blast being in my Tampon 200 routine and I 'preciate the fact that you think the book is funny, but I really need to move on here. I got six more chapters to write and you're really drawing this bit out too much!"

Announcer 1: "You created me, jackass, do what ya want. I just wish you would have givin' me a name though instead of just calling me Announcer 1. It's so distant, so impersonal."

Announcer 2: "Yeah, me too! What the f##k! How do ya expect me to pick up chicks saying, 'Hi, my name's Announcer 2?'"

Larry the Cable Guy: "Alright, I'll call ya Jim and Lance."

Announcer 2: "Lance! That's a fag name! Gimme a break. How 'bout Rikki. Yeah, Rikki. I like that one."

Larry the Cable Guy: "Okay, I'll call ya Rikki if ya quit cursing. At least don't use the f-word."

Jim: "Okay."

Rikki: "Cool. "

Larry the Cable Guy: "Glad we settled that. Okay, see ya. I'm moving on with the rest of the book."

Rikki: "Don't forget to use us again when ya talk about what it'll be like when NASCAR has an all-hard-liquor-sponsored race. Remember we're under contract for this whole chapter."

Sorry about the conversation with myself back there. My split personalities really get pissy sometimes if I don't name them. And I must admit, that while I think we're a long way from an all-tampon sponsored race, it still would be awesome.

Do you get the feeling I may need some sort of professional help?

Now to get back to my original point. Those uppity non-smokers who persuaded NASCAR to drop the Winston Cup really chap my ass. Here's a great example of their hypocrisy. One night, my buddy Brad and I visited a fast-food joint called the Steak and Shake after throwing eggs at street whores.

Yeah, we do that a lot. We actually competed in a league one year and took second place.

Anyway, it's about three in the morning and Brad's smoking a cigarette. Sitting next to us was some girl who was about 4' 8" and

275 lbs. She turns to us and says in this loud voice, "Ya know smoking is bad for ya." I look at her plate and whattya thinks she's eatin?

Chili cheese fries!

I thought, *This is typical.* Here we are getting health advice from a girl that looked like the fat purple chick in Willy Wonka's chocolate factory. She's downing those chili cheese fries like she's on death row and it's her last meal. So I said to her, "What are you, on a health kick?" And her response was, "At least I'm not affecting other people."

I was like, "Not affecting other people! I've been smelling your nasty chili cheese ass for about forty-six minutes and ya done already cleared out four booths! Now can you please leave or do ya need me to drive my pickup to the door and hook a winch to your politically correct, non-smoking fat ass to help pull ya out!"

These people are unbelievable. I can't believe that NASCAR bowed to their shenanigans. Even though King Richard Petty fought hard to stop the higher-ups from dropping the Winston Cup, they did it anyway.

Which made the score: Political correctness 1, NASCAR fans 0.

If I wanted to be involved in uppity racing, I'd watch Formula cars. That's racing for the wine and cheese crowd. Anyway, that's the impression they give. Ya got drivers with French names and they drink milk after winning a race. That's why Formula racing will always play second fiddle to NASCAR. NASCAR drivers drink beer and that's *before* the race! The majority of Americans watch NASCAR because they identify better with the drivers. Them French, milk drinkin', politically correct, white-collared, Formula-drivin' pussies can keep all that uppity wine crap. Ya know what built NASCAR? Beer bellies, moonshine runnin', tobacco spittin', axel grease–stained, rebel flag–flyin' rednecks!

God bless 'em!

Give me beer, loud cars, Beef Jerky, camo clad woman with shorty shorts and you got yourself a nice Sunday afternoon. That's the way God intended it. NASCAR, I love ya to death, You're the last true American sport that the commie, PC Hollywood fat cats still haven't changed much. So I'm beggin' ya, stop cavin' in!

I do see some things in the new NASCAR that are encouragin'. For instance, they've started signing hard liquor sponsorships. Now that's America. I can't wait to see the first all-hard-liquor-sponsored race. Let's return to our announcers:

Jim: "Welcome to the Grand Marnier 500. We're only one lap in and the #7 Jack Daniels car has already swerved off the track."

Rikki: "Followed closely by the Coca-Cola chaser car, Jim."

Jim: "That right, Rikki. Hey it looks like all 15 passengers in the Jose Cuervo car are still waiting on a jump start."

Rikki: "I think the officials are gonna also make them unhook the lawn maintenance trailer from the back of the car."

Jim: "Well they should, Rikki, they threw a shovel and a weed blower around turn two."

Rikki: "You know, I really like the name Larry gave me. I'm glad he didn't use Lance or I would have had a fag name for another eight pages."

Jim: "I probably should have went with something less common, but Jim is pretty standard for an announcer."

Rikki: "Larry, just to let you know, I haven't used the f-word since you last gave me dialogue."

Larry the Cable Guy: "I'm proud of ya. I just don't think we should use that word too much. I don't know who may read this book. I don't use it in real life unless I hit my finger with a hammer or if the Braves lose. So I don't think we should use it here unless in the most extreme cases."

Jim: "Like if someone mentions Barbra Streisand!"

Rikki: "I can't stand that f###in' bitch! Oops, sorry!"

Larry the Cable Guy: "Don't apologize, that was an extreme case. OK, I gotta go finish this chapter. By the way, I think that's it for y'all. I don't have anymore announcer bits."

Jim: "Well we sure enjoyed bein' a part of it. The book is very funny."

Rikki: "Yeah, it's a riot! Especially my part. See ya, you f###er!"

Larry the Cable Guy: "Watch your language or I'll invent another announcer bit and give you the name Lance!"

Rikki: "Damn, I thought you were a comedian. Can't you take a joke?"

Larry the Cable Guy:: "Sure, Rikki, say knock knock."

Rikki: "Knock knock."

Larry the Cable Guy: "Who's there?"

Rikki: "Uh . . . I don't know . . . Jackass . . . I can't believe I fell for that stupid joke!

OK, it's time for me to admit somethin'. Much as I hate it, I can live with NASCAR dumping Winston like the plague. If the officials who run NASCAR want to let political correctness seep in and drop a company that has stuck by their association from the beginning, that's their business. In my mind, it'll always be the Winston Cup. However, if they want Nextel to sponsor the event, it's fine.

And in 20 years, when people start getting brain cancer from cell phones, they can go back to cigarettes.

But here's something that really gets me going. NASCAR now puts on a race in Mexico. Good Lord, Jesus, and Cale Yarborough! You gotta be shittin' me! That's crossing the line! NASCAR, the all-American sport, in Mexico! This has to be a bad dream. You got a country that gets most of its gross national product from illegal immigration into the United States. We're gonna reward 'em for that with a race?

Please tell me we didn't do that. Is nothing in this country sacred anymore? Next we're gonna have the Slim Fast 500 coming from Ethiopia. Can anyone say "sellout"? I'm all for free enterprise and get it while its good, but can't we at least keep something this American from going to Mexico? That was the only auto race I've ever seen that was red flagged because a chicken came running across turn three and got stuck in a car's grille!

C'mon, NASCAR, enough is enough. Every day the Americans watching your races are seein' their jobs shipped to Mexico. Now you wanna send a race there, too? Don't bite the hand that feeds ya! You've already started banning rebel flags at your events. Next you'll have us wearing ties and bowing to Allah whenever we attend races.

Good Lord, Jesus, and Morgan Shepherd!

And another thing while I'm on the subject: a race in Mexico is unfair to our drivers. Everybody knows a Mexican pit crew can rip four tires off a car, sand the body, and re-paint it before we even get gas into ours! You know it, I know it, and the American people know it!

I just don't get it. Here ya have one of the greatest all-American sports in history, started by moonshiners, and the folks in charge are letting political correctness change it at every level. I'm sure we'll see women drivers next. Obviously I'm kidding. I couldn't care less who races as long as they can do the job.

I know several girls that can race good. I just hope it doesn't get so politically correct that they let in people that can't really drive, just because they want diversity in the starting lineup. I personally think NASCAR should have a married couples race once a year. Here's how that would sound in a nutshell:

Liz: "You don't know where the hell you're going, do ya? We've been going around in circles for two hours! Pull over, I gotta pee!"

I'd hate to hear that Michael Waltrip didn't win Bristol because his wife, Buffy, had to stop by the Albertsons to get a veggie tray for the bus!

Here's another thing that made me madder than a one-legged Ethiopian watchin' a donut roll down a hill. NASCAR recently fined Dale Earnhardt Jr. for cursing. Now I understand ya can't cuss on TV. However, cussin' just to cuss is one thing. It's entirely different when you cuss during the heat of competition.

If you're going to fine someone for cursing on TV, at least use a little common sense and consider how it happened. For example:

Jim: "Well, Dale, ya just won the Daytona 500; how do ya feel?"
Dale: "Ah shit it's great! I'm just so excited, I wanna thank my sponsors and Larry the Cable Guy for all the laughs!"

ED NOTE: I actually thought I was done using Jim and Rikki and was ready to put another announcer in this spot. But, as you read earlier, these guys are under contract for the whole NASCAR chapter.

OK, here we see Dale saying "shit" and not even realizing he said it. I think in this situation, a simple apology is acceptable. It was clearly a slip of the tongue and not enough for anyone to get too upset over. It happens. I even heard Billy Graham say "You gotta be shittin' me" one time.

OK, maybe not, but, to rehash what I wrote earlier, he might have. I'm still not sure.

Now here's another example of cursing on TV.

Rikki: "Wow! Dale Jr. ya just won Daytona. How do ya feel?"

Dale: "How the F### you think I feel ya F##### C### S####! You obviously saw me F##### jumpin' up and F##### down. Ya stupid A#####e!"

OK, common sense says this is probably a good case for fining someone. Sure, it occurred during the heat of the moment. But, unlike the first example where the word "shit" slipped out quickly, in this second imaginary interview, Dale sounds like "Scarface" Tony Montana after he took over the business.

In the world of political correctness, though, there is no common sense; both of these interviews are treated as equal violations. Instead of letting Dale off with a reprimand, NASCAR bowed to the PC factions and fined him for an honest mistake.

Who'da thunk it. Ya can't cuss in NASCAR? Next they'll tell us you can't pee in the pool during synchronized swimming. The worst part of this is that it actually affected Dale's point totals. That makes the entire episode as disgusting as Oprah in leotards spread-eagled on a floor mat.

I'm talkin' about the fat Oprah now. Oprah's a lot like Elvis, only fatter and darker. There was the fat Elvis and there's the fat Oprah. Then there was the skinny Elvis and the not-quite-as-fat Oprah. Oprah needs to pick a weight and stick with it! She goes up and down more than Barney Frank at a Village People meet-and-greet. One minute ya see Oprah lookin' like she just got done pulling trucks outta the mud with her ass crack. The next minute she looks like supermodel Oprah.

Actually, I got no problem with Oprah; I think she does some great things. I just can't get past this Dr. Jekyll and Mr. Hyde shenanigans. It's almost like she has a valve stem in her hind end that adjusts the air in her body depending on the month.

I know. This has nothing to do with NASCAR. But honestly does any of this book make any sense?

I really don't watch Oprah that much. After Jerry Springer hosted a show called "Little People Klan" that featured skinhead midgets who were KKK members, I figured that was it; no one could top that for entertainment. I must admit that Gordon Elliot came close with a show about crippled women who prostituted themselves. The redhead burn victim was a riot!

But Oprah can piss ya off sometimes. A few weeks ago I was so damn mad at Oprah and I don't even know her.

I had come home in a great mood because our Mexican neighbor that blared Los Lobos from speakers the size of a 10th grader every night at midnight just moved out. Little did I know that Oprah had presented a relationship show that afternoon. I walked in to find my girl crying and screaming about Oprah sayin' I needed to buy her more flowers.

I was like, then maybe you oughta start humpin' Oprah!

Here I'd already bought my girlfriend some vacuum cleaner bags and a poopin' pig key chain from the local convenience store. Now I gotta sit back on a Friday night and listen to Oprah ream me a new butthole! Somebody should stick a corn dog in Oprah's fat mouth before a person gets shot over one of her intimate relationship shows.

And what does she know about being intimate anyway? The last thing she got cuddly with was a box of Hungry Man Sloppy Joe mix! Boy was I pissed at Oprah that night. But, like I said, she does a lot of good things. It's just that the woman needs to mind her own damn business or I'm gonna go broke buyin' flowers!

ED NOTE: If Oprah is skinny again then disregard the fat jokes. You can never tell with her. Weightwise you can only pick on Oprah seasonally. Six months outta the year I'd love to bang her, and the other six months she looks like a spokesman for Fiddle Faddle! I don't get it!

Ya know, it just occurred to me that I might be the only guy that can write a book with a whole chapter dedicated to NASCAR and work Oprah into it somehow.

Be that as it may. . . .

Why do people say that? Be that as it may. I don't even know what the hell that means.

Anyway, I have another experience to tell ya about. A few years ago, I went to the Talladega 500 with a girl I had just met. She was sweet with very childlike qualities. No titties! (I could do this all day.)

She didn't understand NASCAR, so I took her to the race to step up her education. She was nice enough to buy me a NASCAR shirt for the occasion.

Of course, bein' unfamiliar with the sport, she didn't realize at the time that the shirt actually said "NASDAQ." Be that as it may (huh?), I wore the shirt and got into a conversation with a guy from Palm Beach about low-yield junk bonds.

About an hour into the race, the girl went back to my car to change her pants. Some Rikki Craven fan had puked all over 'em. While she was gone, I noticed some girls in the infield sitting on the shoulders of their boyfriends.

Now if I'm with a girl at a race and she wants to show off her assets by sitting on my shoulders, I say go for it. But I felt sorry for these guys. I'm not saying those women were huge, but if they were guys they'd be named Tiny and drive mini bikes.

And here's the worst part: not only were these women the size of newborn pachyderms; they never flashed their boobs! I mean c'mon, if you're on some dude's shoulders at a NASCAR race in a tube top, the rules say you must pop out the goods! Even Ronnie Milsap was yelling "Bullshit!" You either show 'em or get down and let us watch the race.

I'll tell ya what, these two girls were obnoxious, actin' like they was the hottest things on the track. It was hilarious. A pair of Two-Ton Tinas who thought they were the Olsen twins. They looked more like the Olsen twins, their cousins, and a wide range of other assorted relatives in a group photo. Those two redneck horny dudes they were sitting on were about to fall over like Stevie Wonder in a pumpkin patch. Why, their legs were buckling like they just walked in on a bean dip fart in an elevator at the Rodriquez family reunion.

The kicker came when the two girls kissed each other. They thought that was so sexy. Like we would all be excited to see 300-pound lesbians kiss at the race. Please!! It looked like they were trying to lick cake crumbs off each other's lips.

Some guy finally threw a cup of water on them two sea cows and they got the hint that they were more of a nuisance than anything else. You can bet I didn't let this pass. When I reached home, I confronted my mom and her friend about how they had embarrassed me and everybody else at the track.

My point is . . . I guess I really don't have one other than don't ever let Michael Waltrip get tickets for your relatives!

Well, that's it for the NASCAR chapter. The greatest sport ever created next to throwing eggs at street whores. I hope you all learned enough to enjoy a race in your area real soon. For you schoolteachers that intend to use my book as a reference guide for your mental health classes, I have included a few questions for the kids in case you want to throw them a pop quiz on the chapter:

1. What were the names of the contracted announcers in the Tampon 200 and the Grand Marnier 500 pieces?
2. What does "Be that as it may" mean? Use it in a sentence.
3. You can tell that a person has really let him- or herself go in the weight department when they:

   A. Have front butt
   B. Kids yell "Hey Kool-Aid!"
   C. Blind people yell "Holy S#@T!"
   D. Your last name is O'Donnell
4. What makes my Dick Trickle?
   A. Auto racing
   B. Hooters waitresses
   C. Fire ants
5. The Bonus Question: Show the rest of the class the face you
   would make if you walked in an elevator and ran into a bean
   dip fart during the Rodriquez family reunion.

I hope these come in handy and if you need anymore material I
can be reached at:

> Carmen Electra
> C/O Larry the Cable Guy's face
> 1554 Sunset Blvd.
> Los Angeles, CA 69696

I'm sorry this book doesn't have any pop-ups like the Hillary
Clinton book, but I found them very distracting. We have a few
more chapters to go so I hope you're hanging in there with me. If
you find it very entertaining and it's the best thing you've ever
read, don't be alarmed. Just get the phone book and find the near-
est counseling center for help.

If I haven't pissed off any libs or PC people yet, then continue
and I'm sure you'll find something to bitch about down at the local
moveon.org meeting.

Chapter 8

NOW WHAT DO I WRITE ABOUT?

WHEN I AGREED to do a book I thought, well, I can write about this and I can write about that. Big deal, it's easy. I mean, for God's sake, Stephen King puts out a new book every 34 hours, it can't be that hard.

Guess what? It is fricken hard!! I'm only about halfway through this thing and I'm already askin' myself, *Now what do I write about?* When ya start, the ideas in your head are unlimited. They fly around thicker then flies in front of a fat chick's crotch as she sits spread-eagled while eating watermelon at the mud bogs.

But when ya write all your unlimited ideas down on paper, they end up being pretty limited. For example, I thought to myself, *Man I could do 20 whole chapters just on NASCAR. This is gonna be cake!* As you can see, the NASCAR chapter barely covered enough for 18 pages, let alone 20 chapters, so it turned out that all those ideas were much longer in my head than on paper.

That pretty much describes my love life. I dream of Shania Twain, I end up with Mark Twain. Don't misunderstand. I think the NASCAR chapter is the funniest thing I've read since that article about those Iraqi prisoners who were piled into that big naked pyramid (and they complained even though some people pay good money for that). But Chapter 7 was still about 70 pages shorter than I had planned. That's why this chapter is entitled "Now What Do I Write About?"

Here's what I'm gonna do. I'm gonna have me a big dip, kick back, and watch me some *Andy Griffith Show*.

I love that series. I bet I could write 20 chapters on it without even tryin'!

Chapter 9

DOREEN'S DIARY

Remember earlier in the last chapter, called "Now What Do I Write About?" Think way back, it was like 35 seconds ago or however long it takes you to read maybe 400 words. Well, forget that chapter. I found my sister's diary from when we was kids and I'm gonna use it to give you a glimpse of my wacky family life.

I have two sisters, Ole Molly and, of course, Doreen. For those of you who still haven't heard of Molly, let me fill ya in real quick. My sister was covered in moles so bad she looked like a walking apple tree. It was so bad that everywhere Molly went, five Mexicans with tall ladders would closely follow.

She ended up getting saved at the church a few years ago and everyone started calling her Holy Molly. Then she married a Mexican feller and now we call her "Guacamole."

She's not the one we're focusin' on in this chapter.

My other sister, Doreen, weighs about 20 lbs. less than a stock truck full of Black Angus bulls. However, she's dieting and I know she ain't lying about it because Domino's Pizza called me recently to say they hadn't heard from her in a couple weeks and they were worried about her.

Please let me continue with the hilarity. . . .

I actually presented her diary on the radio a long time ago. Everyone kept askin' about my family since I talked about them all the time. I thought, *What a great way to give people insight into my life*. I'll read my sister's diary over the air and let people hear about things that happened to us as seen through the eyes of Doreen.

So I'd like to present a tour of my family, brought to you by way of Doreen's Diary and the folks at Kraft. Warning: since Kraft is sponsoring this, there will probably be commercials.

ED NOTE: Just like the Civil War letters, I will probably include editor's notes just like this one.

Now before we begin, the following is part of my obligation to Kraft. Sorry, but I did warn ya':

MMM. THERES NOTHING BETTER AFTER PLAYTIME THAN A NICE KRAFT SINGLES CHEESE SANDWICH. WE THE PEOPLE AT KRAFT HAVE INDIVIDUALLY SLICED KRAFT SINGLES THAT JUST BURST WITH CHEESY GOODNESS.

KRAFT SINGLES ALSO PROVIDE THAT NEEDED CAL-CIUM FOR STRONG BONES, SO YOUR CHILD WON'T SNAP HIS LEG DOING THINGS KIDS DO, LIKE POOPING ON A TEACHER'S DESK OR RUNNING FROM THE RE-TARDED KID AFTER GIVING HIM A RED BELLY.

KRAFT SINGLES: THE CHEESE JESUS HIMSELF ATE AS A YOUNGSTER, TRY 'EM FOR LUNCH, DINNER OR JUST AS A SNACK. MMM, GOOOD!

NOW BACK TO OUR PRESENTATION OF DOREEN'S DIARY.

DEAR DIARY:

Today we all got in the van after Dad jumped it and went to Easter services down at the church. Mom was mad because Dad still had those two bumper stickers on it that said, "If the vans rocking don't come knocking" and "I break for big tits." Mom thought it was a bad example being how he's a deacon and all.

My brother Larry the Cable Guy ate so many colored eggs last night while he was in the church play "The Easter Parade," he pooped his bunny suit and did the poop walk for most of the performance. My dad said he felt for him because he got the runs in the play "The Matchmaker" when he was a kid in high school, and stood in one place on stage the whole second act trying to hold back a turd.

After church we went to Uncle Ralph's and hunted Easter eggs. In his garage I found four eggs, a box of ribbed rubbers and a stack of magazines with naked black women holding plastic rockets.

We went to Stuckey's for Easter dinner. We usually don't go to those fancy joints but Dad came into some money after he won almost 30 bucks in the Scratch Off lottery. I had sausage and blueberry pancakes. Nothing says Happy Easter Jesus like Stuckey's hot cakes. Grandma was huntin' eggs and broke her hip and fell in a drain pipe. I'll write more later.

ED NOTE: I think we were around 6 or 7 here. That poop walk is common among most people. Folks'll never admit it but I don't care if you're a Harvard graduate or a high school dropout, everyone has had to squeeze them butt cheeks together while battling a brown growler every now and then, so don't lie.

I remember playing football one time and it just hit me. I couldn't go to the bathroom because there wasn't any. So after the

play, I just stood by a tree. My friends were like "lets go." I'm standing there squeezing my cheeks together, trying to buy some time
by yelling back "Hold on a minute; I'm looking at this weird bug!"
If I made 'em think I was looking at a bug, that usually bought me
a few seconds. It usually goes away but ya really need a minute
or two.

On another note: I loved Stuckey's. They had restaurants all
over the South that were known for their famous pecan rolls. If
you've never eaten at a Stuckey's, then you've missed a part of
America that has long disappeared.

The people that went to these restaurants were awesome. It
looked like the casting call for *Mad Max IV* at those tables. Two out
of every five Stuckey's customers ran a Tilt-a-Whirl at a fair somewhere. There was an old joke that went like this:

"What has two thousand legs and seven teeth?"

"The line for pecan rolls down at the Stuckey's!"

By the way, one more note regardin' Easter: How did that fag
bunny weasel his way into bible stories? When the Lord rolled that
boulder away from the cave, I don't remember one verse that
talked about him colorin' eggs and tossin' marshmallow peeps to
the apostles and the apistles. It's just another crock of commie lib
B.S. to take the Lord out of our society. Easter's about . . . uh . . .
it's about the Lord coming to this country on the *Edmund Fitzger-
ald* and baptizing non-Christian Indians.

All right, I really can't remember what it's about; I had to work
every Easter. But I'll tell ya this, I know it ain't about some floppy-
eared, carrot-eating commie *Hossenfeffer*. Don't get me wrong,
there ain't nothin' wrong with eating some chocolaty treats at
Easter. But the holiday really ain't got nothin' to do with bunnies
and eggs.

Easter's about biblical stuff like saving souls, boils and harlots, burnin' bushes, last suppers, Paul Revere, and Ronald Reagan! There ain't no queer rabbits in the bible!!

Sorry, I got a little worked up there.

OK, so where were we? Oh yeah, if you think this first diary entry was retarded, even though I did make a good point about the Easter rabbit infiltrating Easter, wait till ya read the next one. You'll be scratching your head like Mike Tyson at a spelling bee!

DEAR DIARY:

Today we went to my brother Larry the Cable Guy's T-ball game. The game was funny. Larry had to go to the bathroom in the middle of the third inning and a ball was hit to him in the outfield and he just stood their yelling "Time out! I'm looking at a bug!" Everybody knew he was squeezin' his butt cheeks together because he had to go.

That bug thing only works a couple of times.

Grandma laughed so hard she threw her hip out. Larry's team is called the "New Confederacy." They're sponsored by Uncle Jim's strip bar and they have rebel hats and jerseys that say "Show Me Your Titties." Larry didn't get any hits again this week, but his coach said he leads the league in pooping his pants.

We went to eat at Hardy's after picking Grandma up from the emergency room and Larry got on the microphone and paged Harry Balls. Grandma laughed so hard she threw her hip out again and fell down and broke her collarbone.

I'll write more later.

ED NOTE: I don't know what it is about old people but at a certain age it's almost like their hips become papier-mâché. Everything snaps their damned hip, showerin', playin' cards, bingo, readin' a book.

It sure sucks getting old. I'm so depressed thinkin' about it, I want to go right to another diary entry to cheer me up:

DEAR DIARY:

Today we left for family vacation. Dad got mad at Larry because he left his "muff diver" ball cap at Stuckey's. Mom said that he should be more responsible and that that's why we can't have nice things.

I met a nice fellow at Stuck's that ran a Tilt-a-Whirl at a local fair. He said anytime I wanted to come ride he would let me go for free. He was a nice man other than he was talking real fast and sweating and not wearing any pants.

Larry is gonna get grounded when we get home because Mom and Dad and I were singing "row row row your boat" and Larry kept singing, "scratch scratch scratch your nuts."

Guys are so juvenile.

Larry taped three Hustler centerfolds to the back window and we watched truckers wreck for 16 miles. Then Larry fed our dog Waylon a whole bag of saltwater taffy and he pooped rainbow-colored turds in the parking lot of Howard Johnson's. It was cool, we each took our picture with the rainbow-colored dog turds and then went to eat dinner. We called for Waylon, but he just stood there like he was looking at a bug.

The hotel Dad picked is nice, but the sign next door that says "All Nude" is really bright and it's hard to sleep. Mom's worried about Dad. He said he was just gonna quick run to the store, took his ATM card, and has been gone almost three hours.

ED NOTE: I loved that ball cap.

DEAR DIARY:

We're now in Vegas. Dad went to a feller at the Tropicana and said he needed some money for a place to stay and eat because we went through all our money on the way out. The guy told Dad he wasn't gonna give him any because he would just gamble it away. Dad said he wouldn't and that he had gamblin' money!

BADADOOM!

ED NOTE: OK, its an old joke but, c'mon, ya never saw it coming.

DEAR DIARY:

We're now in Vegas staying at a hotel called the Happy Mexican. We wanted to go to the Hoover Dam, but Dad said we really didn't have any time but when we got home and if we still wanted to see a big dike, he'd take us over to Aunt Donna's house.

There's nothin' to do here but gamble. It sucks. Dad lost all our college money he'd been saving for two years playing black jack. Ninety-five bucks gone just like that! Larry found out when all the topless girls that dance in the shows here work out in the gym, and now he sneaks from his room at 7:30 every morning to get pictures of 'em doing leg lifts and squats.

Grandpa and Grandma are with us. Grandpa got drunk at the Wayne Newton show and stood up in the middle of the show and called Wayne Newton a pussy. Security wheeled him out of the showroom. Grandma tried to calm everyone down, but she broke her hip in all the excitement.

Dad said Sandy Duncan was at the roulette table and he said they were both betting and Sandy leaned over so far, her eye popped out on the table and landed on black 7 and won him forty bucks. She invited him to another table, but he'd just downed a corn dog earlier and he just stood there squeezin' his cheeks together like he was looking at a bug as she disappeared into the crowd.

More later.

And now an important message from our sponsors at Kraft:

KRAFT SINGLES ARE GREAT IN ALL RECIPES. IF YA WANT TO CHEESY SOMETHING UP FOR GUESTS, THE RICH FRESHNESS OF KRAFT CHEESES WILL HIT THE SPOT EVERY TIME. WHETHER IT BE MACARONI OR CAULIFLOWER OR JUST PLAIN BREAD, KRAFT IS YOUR ONE-STOP SHOP FOR GOOEY, CHEESY GOODNESS. FOR EVERY PACK OF KRAFT SINGLES BOUGHT THIS YEAR, WE WILL SEND A DOLLAR TO THE STARVING PYGMIES SO THEY CAN ENJOY THE CHEESE. JUST THINK OF THE SMILE A BLOATED STARVING PYGMIE WILL HAVE WHEN

HE POURS SOME MELTED CHEESE OVER THAT DEAD WILDEBEEST. MMMMM, GOOD!

KRAFT: NOT ONLY PROVIDING GOODNESS TO THIS COUNTRY, BUT ALSO GROWING SMILES ON THE FLY-INFESTED THIRD WORLD. THERE'S NOTHING LIKE KRAFT.

AND NOW, BACK TO OUR PROGRAM:

DEAR DIARY:

Last night my brother Larry peed the bed and soaked his Richard Petty bedsheets and Marlboro comforter. Mom was so mad because she had to smoke almost 300 packs of cigarettes to get that comforter. Mom said if he pees the bed again she's gonna stop chewin' Red Man and then he'll be five packs short a free BB gun.

Today at school, my boyfriend bookworm Earl dissected a frog and made me a bracelet out of his guts. It was so romantic. I really can't wear it, though, because its startin' to stink and is covered in ants.

We went to watch Larry's pee wee basketball game. His team is called the Skoal Bandits and they lost 62-5 to a team of black kids. They were pretty good. They were only 11 years old but the smallest kid was 6-foot-2. Larry's team did pretty good even though they all play wearing jeans and boots and have to use time-outs to spit. Larry had a great chance to score toward the end, but they threw him the ball and he missed it as he was standing still squishing his butt cheeks together.

ED NOTE: Every present we kids ever got until the age of 15 came from Marlboro miles.

DEAR DIARY:

Last night we had some problems at Grandma's house. My brother and his two buddies were lightin' farts in the living room and caught the curtains on fire and burnt down Grandpa's add-on porch. He crawled off his deathbed and chased after Larry for four blocks. Grandma tried to calm him down and broke her hip.

ED NOTE: I wonder who first discovered how to light farts. I didn't know this, but this frat party trick was traced way back to the caveman days. I guess they used to rub two sticks together in front of their asses when the enemy approached so they could shoot out flames, scaring off their aggressors. Strange but true. I heard that on that show with Leonard Nimoy though I do believe Paul Harvey also did something on it.

See, this book is very informative.

DEAR DIARY.

Larry got fired today as a mall Santa. He told a Haitian kid that Santa Claus won't go to Haiti anymore because there's too much disease. As part of our family tradition, we went to eat Christmas Eve dinner and Mom was mad because after we pulled away from the drive-thru they forgot her cole slaw. Second year in a row. I always tell 'em to check the bag.

I think she'll feel happier tomorrow when she gets her Christmas gift from all of us. We all chipped in and got her a Mark Martin bra and panty ensemble. There's a fancy #6 on each cup and a big V for Valvoline on the ass. She's just gonna go to squallerin'.

ED NOTE: Momma did love that. She still wears it but her ass has gotten bigger and now the V on her ass looks like a big upside-down road caution triangle.

And for the record, Haiti really is a big piece of crap!

Now, another word from Kraft:

MMMM. ROSES ARE RED, VIOLETS MAKE ME TINGLE, IT DON'T GET BETTER, THAN GOOD OLE KRAFT SINGLES!

Well, that's it for my sister's diary. The more I read through these entries, the more I wonder why we kids didn't grow up to run the fry machine. But this is just the tip of the iceberg. The next chapter deals with when I was a lot older and kept my own diary.

Before leavin', I would like to thank Kraft for sponsorin' this chapter. I enjoyed most of the commercials other than the poem at the end. Even though I wrote it, I thought it was a little lame.

Chapter 10

MY DIARY

YOU'VE JUST READ my sister's diary, but I also, later in life, kept a diary just to cover my ass in case of any sort of whatever. Unlike Doreen, I never wrote "dear diary" in my notebooks because I thought that was kinda gay, a grown man writing "dear diary."

Instead, I would start my stuff with "What up dawg?" I got that from rich suburban white kids trying to be rappers. To me it sounds more natural coming from Snoop Dog than it does Andy managing down at Radio Shack, but hey whatever. I just figured if they could use the phrase then I, too, wanted to fit in and roll with my rural redneck homies in a hipper fashion. Plus in this day and age of multiculturalism it seems to fit right in.

Check out the first one.

WHAT UP DAWG?

Last night I brought a girl home that was wearing edible mint chocolate underwear. We were so hammered that we both fell asleep and when I woke up the whole bed was covered in sugar ants! I had to spray her whole crotch with ant killer.

It's now Octoberfest, so everybody pretty much is gettin' hammered. I saw a drunk guy on the parade route syphonin' some gas out of a car and thought "damn! I hope I never get that thirsty!" Last year they wanted me to drive the wiener mobile in the parade and I hit a tree and rolled in the ditch and that was just from WALKIN' to the wiener mobile!

St. Patrick's Day is great. I can't believe Ted Kennedy got a whole holiday named after him. I didn't know he was that popular. Grandma won the farting contest down at the tavern. She pounded down a lager, laid on her back, and tore the roof off the place fartin' "The Devil Went Down to Georgia." She got her trophy then broke her hip.

She did better this year than she did last year, though, when she farted the Oak Ridge Boys' song "Elvira" and started to show off in the middle of the "oom papa mow mow" part. She got too low on the "mow mow," pooped, and got disqualified.

ED NOTE: Kraft isn't sponsoring my "What Up Dawg Diary." I had an offer from Nike, but they made too many demands.

WHAT UP DAWG?

Wow what an event-filled week. Ya know how they induct people into the Country Music Hall of Fame? I was just inducted into Cracker Barrel's wall of bad checks. I'm so damn proud. Tuesday was my girl-friend's birthday. I got her a gift where ya open up a big box and inside is a smaller box and then a smaller one. It was a great idea at the time, but I felt bad after I gave it to her because by the time she got to the last box, the kitten had suffocated.

Wednesday was fun, we were in the middle of cheese

week and I made a suit out of cheeseballs. It was pretty good but still not as clever as the sausage belt I made for wiener week. We used to have a big parade through town but the limburger float really keeps the crowds down.

I saw some girl at the Wal-Mart today wearing shoes. I couldn't believe it! It looks like the riffraff is startin' to move in. I found out this week that Willie Nelson and I have a lot in common . . . back taxes! The accountant told me I was gonna have to get an extension to pay 'em this year. I told him I was gonna need a ski mask and a gun to pay them! Good Lord Jesus and Kyle Bush, the government is rippin' us off!

I got so pissed I took a little poll to see if anyone was as sick of gettin' taxed as much as I am. I called 100 people one night and here's the results: everyone I polled said, "You dumb ass, it's three o'clock in the morning!"

ED NOTE: Ya ever smell limburger cheese? Put your head up Rosie O'Donnell's butt crack after some wind sprints and you'll get the basic idea. My grandpa loved that stuff, which explains why he's buried over the hill away from the other dead people. The grass is always greener, though.

WHAT UP DAWG?

I saw Sandra Bernhard on TV today. Good Lord Jesus and Molly Ringwald! That woman is so ugly, if she saw Jesus during a healing in the Bible days he would just look at her and say, "I'm stumped."

I laughed my ass off today. My aunt weighs about 400 lbs. and she went into Victoria's Secret and tried on a sexy white robe. She looked like the Michelin man runnin' around in there. When she asked me how she looked and I was like, "Damn! Ya look like about 200 bucks balanced and rotated!"

Was that wrong? Wrong or not, I ain't laughed that hard since I saw a one-armed bag boy trying to carry two jugs of milk.

I just saw on the country music channel tonight that Dolly Parton might tour with the group Emerson Drive. I wonder if she'll change her name to Emersome Bigguns? Well I have to go, I'm goin' over to eat at my girlfriend's house and she's a horrible cook. Last Thanksgiving she stuffed her turkey with Tums! One time we had a picnic and flies started divin' into the Mylanta!

I hope I'm alive to write more tomorrow.

ED NOTE: For the record a one-armed bag boy carrying two jugs of milk is a riot. However, there is one thing that trumps it . . . kickin' a midget in the nuts. Nothing is funnier. Period!

WHAT UP DAWG?

I ate some fat-free Pringles today and got the runs. I hate that fat-free crap. Now I know why Pringles come in a tube, 'cause if ya eat 'em you'll be huntin' for somethin' to poop in!

My nephew had a hot date tonight and I told him to take the Domino's sign off his car. I know he loves his job, but on the first date ya for sure don't wanna be too uppity and brag about all the money you're making. Ya got to just ease into that sort of thing.

My buddy just got engaged. I think she's a little too young for him though. She's registered at the Wet Seal and he's registered as a sex offender.

What's this world coming to?

My grandma was late for church the other day and she went up to an usher and asked, "Is mass out?" He said, "No but your hat's on crooked!"

I do have some good news. My sister'n-law Lester (named after her mother) just got named Luber of the Year down at the Jiffy Lube. We're all so proud of her. Just to think, last year she was just a no-name working the foot jack.

We hung her plaque right up next to that picture of the Last Supper with the Atlanta Braves replacing the disciples. The Lord sure has blessed us this year. Just when ya think somebody in your family's never gonna amount to nothing, they hit life's lottery. OK that's all for today. I went to Denny's and had a Grand Slam breakfast and now I think I'm need to go poop a two-run double.

More later.

ED NOTE: It was actually a base-clearing triple. Also the "Is mass out" joke is one that my grandpa told me and I promised to add it somewhere. He's the same grandpa that called Wayne Newton a pussy when we were kids on that trip to Vegas.

WHAT UP DAWG?

My fat Aunt Doris got remarried today. She's unbelievable! She ate those little Entenmann's donuts in the limo all the way over to the big fancy wedding. It was hilarious! Instead of kissin' the bride, the groom licked powdered sugar off her face.

The bridesmaids weren't much thinner than her. Instead of the Wedding March they played "Convoy" as they rolled up the aisle, and at the end of the service, instead of rice everybody threw Crunch 'n Munch at 'em.

There wasn't a dry eye in the bowling alley!

I hear tell from sources at the bowling alley that the groom hired a spotter to carry Aunt Dora over the threshold.

Here's something I didn't know. They did a poll of wedding songs and the song most played at weddings was Kris Kristofferson's "Why Me, Lord?"

I went waterskiin' this weekend and I was tryin' to do an Alan Jackson deal with my boots on when I fell on my back spread eagled. Half the lake shot up my hind end! I swear my large intestine came loose and it was trollin' bass for 200 yards. My hat went flyin' off and my Dick Trickle swim trunks went so far up my ass that I had dick comin' out one ear and trickle comin' out the other.

I took a poop twenty minutes later and out shot a bass and fourteen deep-water minnows. That's the last time I ski behind an airboat! I was layin' there in pain with alligators everywhere and then this cop shows up and says to me, "You been drinking?" I was like "Of course I been drinkin', Baretta! Ya think anybody sober is dumb enough to ski behind a fricken airboat in a lake full of gators?"

The next time my buddy says, "Hang on, I wanna try something," I'm heading for the house.

I'll write more later as soon as I poop out some shiners.

ED NOTE: True story. My ass looked like I'd just been spanked by Michael Jackson with a piece of orange Hot Wheels track after I didn't share at cookie time.

WHAT UP DAWG?

Grandma started an all-kazoo band at the old folks' home. We went to watch her do a little concert at the bingo hall. They started to do the macarena and she broke her hip. Another time they played at a Grand Ole Opry open-mike night for seniors and she had an asthma attack in the middle of "Foggy Mountain Breakdown" and got a standing ovation.

I went to see Charlie Daniels last night. I love the CDB. I found this out too, ya know what Ted Nugent, Charlie Daniels, Tom Petty, and Loretta Lynn all have in common? They've all called security on me!

I have to go. Springer's on.

ED NOTE: I had to watch Springer that day. I remember it vividly, it was the show I talked about earlier, entitled "Little People Klan." Midget Klan members.

Who says there's no more good TV?

WHAT UP DAWG?

I had some time off today so I was just watching a little news and got pissed. I found out their spending tons of money to build a Clinton library in Arkansas. Ain't that some crap. Spendin' all that money for a new Clinton library when all they had to do was remodel a Hooters?

Yesterday we went to the bass pro shops with the family and my grandma got the beenie weenie farts. Security stopped her at the exit and accused her of stealing a duck call and some stink bait. It was ridiculous! I don't know how the hell she's gonna steal them things. She didn't have any pockets on that nightgown she was wearing.

It was my parents' anniversary on Monday of this week. I'll never forget the story my mom told us when we were kids about their tenth anniversary. Mom tried to turn Dad on. At the time he was working two jobs, and there was never much time for romance.

So one afternoon she went to her stripper friend for advice and she told my mom to meet Dad at the door in sexy lingerie or something similar that was low cut in the front. Mom couldn't afford new sexy duds and the only thing she had at the time that was halfway sexy was an old nightgown that was low cut in the back.

Her friends advised her to put the older nightgown on backwards and then meet Dad at the door when he came home. Everything seemed to go as planned. She put some beer out on ice and had Merle Haggard singin' "Big City" softly in the background.

When Dad came walking in, she was waiting for him all sexy. He just walked past her and said, "Get me a beer." Devastated, my mom asked, "Didn't you notice anything different about me?"

"Ya got that old nightgown on backwards."

"How could ya tell?"

He said, "Because the shit stains are in the front!"
It's a lot funnier when Mom tells it.

OK, I gotta roll. I got tickets to Speedwagon. I'll
write more later.

WHAT UP DAWG?

Well this was a crappy week for my brother. He has
a real hard time holding a job.

I just found out he got fired from his job at the
police department. I thought he was pretty clever
when he got hired because he b.s.'d 'em and got a job
as a sketch artist in the investigation department.
But apparently he sent the police on a wild goose
chase last night trying to find a stick-up man with a
big round head.

He's as worthless as a box of rubbers on Michael
Moore's bed stand.

He quit his job before that because he said it was
too boring; he was workin' nights at the day care
center.

I remember last year he got a job holding the
stop/slow sign down at a construction site. He ended
up quitting that because it was too stressful! How
can that be too stressful?

I give up. I'll write more later. I'm too pissed off
at my loser brother to write any more.

**ED NOTE: How the hell do you apply for the stop/slow sign
holder's position? That has to be the dumbest interview around:**

Boss: "Now this job involves a lot of standing around and doing
nothing. Do you have any experience?"

Brother: "Hell ya, I used to work at a post office!"

Boss: "Well damn! Why didn't ya say so? Grab a sign and head out to mile marker 45!"

The only bad thing about this job would be having to explain your reasons for leavin' it to the unemployment office. I mean, how much easier can it get than holding the stop/slow sign job?

Unemployment dude: "Why did ya quit your last job?"

Brother: "It was too stressful, all that standing around and doing nothing. I'm actually more interested in a job that involves more sitting around and doing nothing instead. Better yet, is there anyone hiring that needs someone to sleep most of the day in between periods of television viewing? I feel this would be something more in my field of expertise."

WHAT UP DAWG?

Well I had a date last night with one of those high-maintenance girls. She was so high-maintenance she needed a crew chief. Talk about high-dollar girls, we went to eat and she actually wanted CHEESE on her nachos! Damn I ain't made outta money for God's sake. That's why from now on I have agreed to only date girls that are IN maintenance. I have my eye on a hot little number right now up at the Grease Monkey.

My friend Brad came over today all excited because he finally got one up on this girl he used to like. He was so in love with this high-society girl from the next town over. She came from money as her dad made a killing in the flea market selling titty lampshades. So they had a big log trailer up on a hill.

Anyway, every time Brad would ask her out, she'd

shoot him down because he wasn't in a job that paid the big bucks. I mean Brad ain't poor. At the time he was bringin' home two figures a year and had a good roof over his head. At least he did until the city tore it down as part of the downtown beautification process.

She shot him down left and right and always acted like she thought she was better than him. Well to make a long story short, he just got promoted to midway manager at that parking lot carnival down near the Kmart.

Tell me that girl ain't kicking herself in the ass about right now.

It always makes ya feel good when ya get dissed by a girl and then ya turn out successful so ya can rub it in her face.

Well anyway, I'm gonna go meet Brad for some BBQ to celebrate his big "kiss my ass" girl-dissin' moment, and he's even buying!

It's a good day.

ED NOTE: Brad ended up getting fired from that midway carnival manager's job for humping the mayor's daughter in one of the teacups after hours.

Well that's it for my dia— Hold on . . . I found some more.
Nevermind!

WHAT UP DAWG?

Man, I did a stupid thing today. I was leaving the country bar after getting hammered with the preacher. We was celebrating my nephew's confirmation and I was driving away from the bar when this cop goes flying by me like a bat outta hell with no flashing lights on.

Now I support the law enforcement of this country but when they ain't on a chase or going after illegal immigrants they need to slow down a little bit. I started flashing my lights at him and honking my horn to get his attention so I could make a citizen's complaint or perhaps even a citizen's arrest. He turned around finally and comes to my truck. I yelled, "Why the hell was you driving by me so fast for"

He said, "I wasn't. You were going backward!"

That cost me my truck keys, a ride to meet some new friends that didn't speak English, and 72 hours of cleaning up highway trash!

ED NOTE: Here's another good driving tip if ya drink a lot: putting one of those Jesus fishes on the back of the truck doesn't keep the cops from pulling ya over! I know I wrote that somewhere earlier, but it's a hell of a good tip and bears repeatin'.

WHAT UP DAWG?

I just got back from the Martina McBride concert. She's finer than a set of 38 Mickey Thompson truck tires.

Well, it's pretty close anyway.

I read this week in the paper that she got her start working with Garth Brooks selling T-shirts. That's awesome I think. One minute she's selling T-shirts and blam! She's a Big Star. Some folks have all the luck.

That reminds me a little of my dad's third wife, Doyle. She sold coolies for David Allan Coe for years and next thing ya know BAM! She still selling coolies for David Allan Coe!

Doyle actually tried to have a career in singin'. She went to a talent contest and took seventh place. The bad part was there were only five contestants. But everybody has a God-given talent and hers is selling coolies! At least she's still involved in show business, even if it is just bein' a coolie salesman.

Her sister was in show business as well. She was a roadie for the Statler Brothers for several years. Then she left for the Oak Ridge Boys where she got a job as a body double for William Lee Golden. She would wave to people from a distance backstage at fairs to keep the fans happy while he went out to get something to eat. Now she's in charge of taking care of the double-headed steer at the fairground and she's so damn uppity ya can't even talk to her. I don't know what is about showbiz that gives folks that "I'm better than you attitude," but it really drives me crazy.

I'll write more later. I got tickets to Molly Hatchet tonight at the bowling alley.

ED NOTE: I once flew through a major thunderstorm on a prop plane with Molly Hatchet. We were on our way to a music festival in Joplin, Missouri. As the turbulence shook us, I thought, *This is it. We're going down quicker than Michael Jackson at Webelos.* Thunderstorm plus a prop plane plus a southern rock band, these ain't good odds. I haven't been that scared and short of breath since I got in a 69 with a plus-sized model after a Lane Bryant fashion show.

WHAT UP DAWG?

I went drinkin' with some friends tonight. I can't believe Corona beer was 5 bucks. I've been to Mexico.

You can go to med school in Mexico for 5 bucks. That's way too much money for Corona.

The doctor told my dad yesterday during a physical that he needed to get his heart rate up. So instead of working out, which he hates to do, he went down to the horse track and bet his house.

I had to drive to my cousin's house Tuesday for a fishing trip. It was about a twelve-hour drive. Ya ever get so lonely and horny driving down the road that ya look out the window and see two dogs humping and actually say to yourself, "Ya know the line's really not that long."

How about this, have ya ever written something in a diary that later on ya wish ya wouldn't have written it in your diary, like say . . . watching two dogs humping and thinking "The lines aren't that long."

I wish I wouldn't have written that.

Here's something better to write down: Ya ever notice that celebrities die in threes. For example: Marlon Brando.

My grandma is about to celebrate her 96th birthday. I don't know if I wanna get that old. She's actually broken her hip every year since she was 73. Ya know you're getting a little too old when ya don't like bingo because you think it's too loud.

My great-grandpa was old when he died. I can't remember how old he was but Grandma said he was so old he actually remembered boxing matches between two white guys!

I'll write more later.

ED NOTE: Nothing at this time.

WHAT UP DAWG?

Today's Father's Day. If I had a dollar for every time my dad said he loved me I'd have . . . well, money's not that important. The point is it's Father's Day and if I ever find that bastard I'm gonna go off on him!

I know its hard for a dad to say those three words to his sons but one day he was in a loving mood and finally popped those three words out: "Get channel 7." My dad is tough though. He went horseback ridin' right after his vasectomy.

However, Dad did have a soft side. I remember he actually teared up at his father's funeral. Later I realized it was because he had told the deacon to pull his finger at the gravesite and he farted. He was crying so hard from laughing, it looked like he was in mourning.

Last I heard he was working with the Kerry campaign.

Talk to ya tomorrow.

ED NOTE: My dad was actually awesome and I loved him to death. I made this dad up. However my real dad did tell me to get channel 7 quite often.

WHAT UP DAWG?

My neighbor cracks me up. He's all into flying saucers and crap. He's one of them retards that camps out waiting to see Star Wars movies. He did that one year where he stayed in a tent in the mall parking lot before realizin' he was at the wrong theater. He ended up wastin' twenty-three days just to see "Turner and Hooch."

One time he called me freaking out that he'd been invaded by aliens because he had found three perfectly rounded little crop circles in his front yard. He wanted me to call the police. Turns out that I had just borrowed his trash cans to put some bait minnows in.

The guy really needs some help.

I just heard on the country music news today that Billy Ray Cyrus and Little Jimmy Dickens are putting out a duet called "Some Gave Half." I'm gonna have to get that one.

I'll write more later. I have to pick my drunk brother up. Evidently him and his buddies got thrown outta the Holiday Inn.

ED NOTE: What's the difference between a shower curtain and toilet paper? Ya don't know? Neither does my brother. That's why he got kicked out of the Holiday Inn. See ya.

WHAT UP DAWG?

Man it was hot today! How hot was it? It was so hot I saw Satan buying a Slurpie! Florida is horrible in the summer. Last night I was sweating so bad while playing horseshoes with toilet seats, I could have caught a bass in my pants. My girlfriend was sweating so bad I put my hand down her pants and felt a big red snapper!

Hahahahahahahahaaha Damn! I kill myself writing these diaries.

I went over to my grandma's house yesterday to help fix her air conditioner. I love my grandma and she looks exactly the same as she did 30 years ago: OLD!

Anyway her air conditioner fell out of her trailer window after a 20-mile-an-hour wind gust knocked her single wide off the front cinder blocks. I junked the air conditioner and just ended up putting in five ceiling fans. I told her not to use them all at the same time, but with her bad hearing she either didn't hear me or else she didn't care. She turned them all on at the same time and her roof took off!

I think I'm gonna do some charity work tonight and take my boss's ugly ass daughter to the baseball game because I got nobody else to go with. This girl looks a little like Cledus T. Judd only with smaller tits. They actually kept her at Glamour Shots for five days straight in intensive care! She's nice, though, and that's all that matters. I love baseball and this is the first game I've been able to go to all year since the city removed my ankle bracelet.

ED NOTE: I do love baseball. I love it so much that when I was a kid, before everyone had cable, I watched games on a black-and-white TV with rabbit ears. I was such a Braves fan that when the reception was poor, I watched an entire game naked while holding my left arm out the window with my privates wrapped in tin foil and a hanger on my head. I ended up getting thrown out of the Western Auto by the third inning. I think baseball is one of the last sports steeped in true American tradition. Nothing screams God bless America like a Rodriquez to Sanchez to Lopez double play! God bless baseball!

Some people would argue that football is better. Hey I love football as well but I was better at baseball. I played football once and actually lettered in concussions. I played for one year for the Devry Fightin' Vice Grips in college. We were so bad, our fight song was "The Beaches of Cheyenne" by Garth Brooks.

OK, this is getting ridiculous; let's hurry up and finish this chapter!

WHAT UP DAWG?

I took Mom and Dad out today for their 50th wedding anniversary and my mom accidentally, without thinkin', rolled the window up and the tray fell off! Root beer went all over the new Ricky Craven anniversary nightgown we got her. Ya know, ya try to do something special and somethin' stupid always happens to ruin it.

The good news, though, is when we got home Dad gave her the anniversary gift box he bought. Boy did she go to squallerin'. He had bought her one of those alligator back scratchers she always liked from the flea market and he also give her a some fat stretch britches from the Lane Bryant fat woman store. I knew she liked 'em cause after taking just one look at 'em, she threw 'em down and went off bawlin' like a stuck hog.

It's nice to see romance like that at their age.

My cousin had to go to the school Thursday because her son got thrown out of class for tryin' to kiss some girl in the playground. The teachers all said it was sexual harassment! This world really pisses me off. He's seven years old, for God's sake! If I had a dollar for every time I ran around droppin' my pants at school, I'd have been a rich man. Well maybe not rich, but I would have had 8 bucks and believe me in college 8 bucks comes in handy.

Oh well I'll write more later.

ED NOTE: Nothing at this time except I'm almost done with this chapter. But don't get too excited; there's a few more left. At least these are way more entertaining than the *Jim Lehrer Newshour*. Beside that you don't see Jim Lehrer ever begin his reports with "What up dawg?" It would be awesome but Jim won't do it. Maybe he should. He would begin to see a younger demographic watching the news.

Just thought I'd throw in a tip for the boys at PBS.

WHAT UP DAWG?

We had our family reunion today in the basement of the church. There were people there I didn't even know I was related to. When I seen some hot blonde eating a hot dog, I said to my grandma, "Who is that girl over there by the lemonade eating a hot dog?" Grandma said, "Shut the door I'm trying to poop!"

I guess I picked a bad time to talk to her, but I needed to know. My dad came over, so I asked him and it turned out to be my fourth cousin. I was like, well hold my beer 'cause I'm fittin' to make a retarded kid! I mean I couldn't be related to this girl. There was just something about her that made me think she wasn't a relative.

For instance, she was sober.

I ended up talking to her and the whole time people kept bummin' Skoal off her. That's what convinced me

we were family. Following dinner, we had the eighth
annual family reunion wet T-shirt contest. My aunt's
sister Doug Jr. took home the ball cap full of money
for the sixth year straight.

You should have seen Grandma. By God there she
was, still competing in a wheelchair after breaking
her hip doing a crossword puzzle four days before. It's
a wonder she didn't catch pneumonia. However, she
rolled one of her wheels over her dangling left tit
and it swelled up to the size of a balloon animal.
Later that night, after the festivities, I asked her if
she felt better and she said, "Shut the door I'm trying
to poop!"

DAMN! I did it again.

**ED NOTE: There were other family members there, but I guess I
left them out for some reason. I'll never forget my Aunt Doris. At
the time, she was the fattest woman in town. She was so big, she
stayed sitting in her truck throughout the whole reunion. We
would send her food and lemonade which she ate while she
watched the festivities from the passenger's seat.**

At one point, she came down with a sore throat and the doctor
had to run out to examine her in the truck. He got in bad trouble
because he told her to "open up and say moo." I thought it was
funny but the hospital said it was unprofessional.

OK, lets move on.

WHAT UP DAWG?

Today is National Abstinence Awareness week. That
pisses me off. Believe me, I'm fully AWARE that I ain't
gettin' laid. Do I really need the government cele-

bratin' my crappy sex life for seven whole days? They
already rip me off tax wise. Now they're gonna rub it
in for a week that I can't get laid.

Thanks a lot, Uncle Sam.

Well that's the end of 'em. There's actually more but I think I've
used up my "What up dawg" quota. I still haven't said it as much as
some suburban, wannabe rap star white kids but I got in as many
as I could considerin' as how it's not part of my everyday vernacu-
lar. I'm trying to be more cultured but it really sounds dumb when
I say it so I leave it to the pros.

However on paper, the reader can use his own inflections and
probably make it sound very hip. I hope you enjoyed reading this
as much as I enjoyed going through them and finding some I could
use. I didn't really sort 'em out by date; that's why they mighta
jumped around a little. So be it. All of the stories were kinda true
except for a lot of 'em.

It's now time for me to head to the next chapter, but first we're
bringin' you this important message from Verizon Wireless.

Guy on TV from Verizon: "Can you hear me now?"

Guy Walking by Him: "You piece of crap, I got the same phone
and my reception always sucks. I couldn't get good reception
if I was talking on a cell phone to a guy standing right next to
me. But you keep askin' 'Can you hear me now' as if you can
get perfect reception on a hill in the middle of nowhere! You
can take that cell phone and shove it up your lying commercial ass!"

(We HEAR the sound of a scuffle, yelling, and then gun shots.)
Blackout.

Chapter 11

I'LL DIET TOMORROW!

How many times have you said to yourself, "Look at the ass on Kylie Minogue!" Probably not very many times but I've said it a lot!

I know this has nothing to do with dieting, but I just wondered how many other people have said that when they saw her from the back on TV.

OK, how many times have you said this, "I'll diet tomorrow." I say it every day except on weekends because when I'm on a diet the weekends are my cheat days. The only problem with that is I always say "I'll diet tomorrow" on Monday night as well because I crave graham crackers and frosting. Then I'll say, "I'll diet tomorrow" on Tuesday night after I want some chocolate-covered graham crackers. And I always say "I'll diet tomorrow" on Wednesday after . . .

You get the drift.

Instead of having a cheat day, I have a cheat week. Which turns into a cheat month. Which turns into a cheat year. Which turns into me looking like a Macy's Thanksgiving Day parade float!

I was never a big kid. When I was born I weighed 8 lbs, 7 oz. That's just 2 lbs less than Calista Flockhart weighs now. My weight problems didn't start until I got older. It's gotten so bad that every time I go out to eat they have a guy waiting in front of the restaurant holding two flashlights. He guides me into the dining room like a Delta flight just arriving from Denver. It's embarassin'.

I hate them people that can eat anything they want and never gain a pound. I got a buddy that eats cheesecake and pasta 24 hours a day. He's so skinny he could fall through his own butthole and strangle himself (I know, I used that line earlier too, but it's so damned funny). Meanwhile I eat one cookie and I blow up like a tick on the vein of a boner! It's horrible!

So here's the deal. I wanted to write a chapter that maybe could help someone that struggles with their weight. Since I've started writin' this book I have lost 30 pounds. How did I do it? Have you heard of the Atkins diet? Well, I was on the Clay Aiken diet. Just before I ate something I would pop in a Clay Aiken CD and try to keep the food down.

ED NOTE: Ya know I did that stupid joke on the *The View* and got tons of hate mail and death threats from Clay Aiken fans! You believe that? I got nothin' against Clay Aiken, God bless him. I think his hair looks kinda like his butt's been humped by Rascal Flatts, but, other than that, more power to him. It was just that Aiken kinda sounds like Atkins, so hence the joke. People are so fricken uptight!

The Atkins diet has worked for some people but I tried it and wound up in the maternity ward givin' birth to an 8 lb. cheese turd. It was actually cuter than my brother's baby.

My dad went on that diet and it worked for him. Sorta. He lost 43 pounds. But then he died four months later after he swallowed 5 pounds of cheese up at the VFW club and farted next to an open flame.

Dr. Atkins definitely proved his critics wrong with that meat and cheese diet. When they said, "Watch the meat intake" he didn't listen. When they said, "Watch the cheese intake" he didn't listen. When they yelled, "Watch your step" he didn't listen and he tripped and hit his head on concrete! He ended up dying from falling down some steps after eatin' a big steak.

I still can't believe the pastor of protein, the Jehovah of finger wieners, the Savior of sausage links has passed away. Right now he's in heaven with Jesus and the shepherds takin' the bread off the holy hamburgers and dippin' the meat in mustard. He may be dead but he did prove 'em wrong.

The reason I liked him was that he proved that meat is good for ya. Hell even Duke University did a study on his diet and found out it was basically fine and safe. They also did a study on why Aaron Neville never gets that big-assed mole taken off his face, but the findings there were inconclusive.

Ya know P.E.T.A. and all them vegetarian, commie jackasses hated ole Dr. Atkins. I can't stand those vegetarian, tofu-fartin', health food fairies! My dad drank, smoked, chewed tobacco, and ate gravy on everything but titties and ya know what? He lived a happy 43 years!!!

I remember one time when I was home watching TV and picking food out of my teeth with a clipped toenail I saw a news story where these P.E.T.A. morons were tryin' to say that Jesus was a vegetarian. Jesus a vegetarian, pleeaassee!!!! The Lord ate loaves of bread and tons of fish and everybody knows it. It's right there among the red words in one of them verses.

These P.E.T.A. peckerheads need to live their lives whichever way they want and let us live ours the way we want and shut their skinny emaciated celery holes! And they need to quit dragging our Lord and Savior into their sick commie vegetable fantasies! What the hell do these P.E.T.A. a-holes think they had at the Last Supper, fried okra?

If the Lord came back today I bet ya tickets to Judy Juggs he'd be at the Longhorn steak house with his disciples downin' a fat prime rib! Before writin' this chapter, I always wondered why people said Jesus H. Christ and now I know.

The H stands for Hereford beef cows!

I've watched diet ads on TV since I was a kid! People are always trying to shed the pounds, but they want some quick and easy diet. It'll never happen like that. Let's face facts here. The only way to lose weight and keep it off is to put Hillary Clinton in hot pants on your refrigerator!

Seriously though, put her on your refrigerator and you'll never be able to eat again, thinking how that scumbag who once walked down a street in front of TV cameras, hand-in-hand with that commie terrorist Yasser Arafat might be our next president!

Sorry I lost it for a minute there.

OK, if ya really want to lose weight then ya need to cut out sugar and breads, exercise at least 30 to 45 minutes a day and don't eat late. That's basically it. My uncle Pat was always tryin' to find easy ways to lose weight and his wife ended up shooting him at age 43 for nailing a waitress at the Cracker Barrel.

And the moral of that story is . . . don't f*** with my aunt Cathy!

Whatever ya do, stay away from the Lean Cuisines. Ya ever eat a package of those? I've seen more food in Charlie Daniels's beard! All these get-small-quick diets are for the birds. Some people think they can just take a pill and—voilà!—they'll become Pam Anderson or Brad Pitt overnight. Believe me there ain't a pill like that.

Okay, there is heroin but I don't think you should go that route. I once went on the "liquid diet." I was supposed to drink nothin' but liquids for a week. But I got so damn drunk and sick of that Jim Beam and Coke, I'll never drink it again.

At least I admit when I'm fat. I don't cop out like my aunt Doris and say it's a "thyroid condition." My aunt is so damned heavy she doesn't get makeovers, she gets detailed! BADABING!

I know. I should have done comedy in the '40s!

I always laugh when she blames her thyroid. Then ya go over to her house and it looks like a burial ground for Little Debbie Oatmeal Creme Pie wrappers. She ain't got a thyroid problem, she has a 7–Eleven problem.

But I really shouldn't bitch that much because I still have to get in shape. I almost had a heart attack the other day throwin' eggs at whores. (Remember, I'm in a league.) I bought a Soloflex after seein' one of their commercials. Damn, those machines are hard to dust! I ended up hanging clothes off the dad gum thing.

That brings us to the one thing I hate other than illegal immigrants: the gym. I get so sweaty at the gym, my pork rinds get all soggy. I understand, though, that if ya wanna lose weight, ya have to get some sort of cardio activity. But the gym sucks for me because for some reason I always get the farts in there. I don't know what it is about the gym and good-lookin' woman, but the combination gives me the farts.

Farts attract woman like some sort of cologne and that's a known fact. Every time ya bust out a brown growler there's always a woman that'll show up to talk to ya. I could be in the middle of the Gobi desert, half dead from a plane crash, and not see any other living thing for four days. But just let one rip, and outta nowhere the Titty Sisters would come walkin' around the corner.

That gives me a great idea for anyone who wants to meet woman: eat a bowl of broccoli and cheese, then go stand in the mall somewhere. I bet 50 woman walk up and talk to ya!

But the gym is the worst. The other day, I was on the rowing machine and got popcorn farts. After 20 minutes, I sounded like a tug boat! I went to wipe the machine off with a towel. One of the trainers said, "Go ahead and take that one home. Ya can just keep it."

I started to leave but he stopped me and asked, "Why do you work out with a Skoal can in your gym shorts?" I was like, "Oh no that's not a Skoal can. It's a Stick-Up. It's part of my workout gear."

Here's another thing about health clubs that makes me madder than Star Jones jumping in the air and gettin' stuck. I'm sure you've seen those TV commercials for the big gyms. Everybody featured in 'em looks like a supermodel or a Chippendale dancer, right? But when ya actually go down there, the women resemble something out of a casting call for *Sweatin' to the Oldies V* and the dudes looked like Chips Ahoy dancers.

Now I understand that it's good for older folks to belong to health clubs. And I know the gym is a place to get into shape, not meet women. But these commercials make the whole thing look like a big pickup joint.

I saw this one Bally's commercial and it seemed like the Dallas Cowboy cheerleaders were in there working out, half naked and winkin' at guys while doing their splits. Where the hell is that gym at? I just went to the Bally's by my house and some 300-pound girl in red leotards came up and said, "Can ya spot me?" I was like "Hell yeah, I can spot ya, I spotted ya in the parking lot on the way in here from two blocks away!" And I didn't see a cheerleader or supermodel type in the whole place.

That's false advertising. Look, I know I need to get into shape but these folks got me all horny with their damn commercials. To be honest, I didn't join that gym to lift weights; I joined so I could hook up with good-lookin' girls.

I mean, if I wanted to lift heavy stuff, I'da got a job at Costco!

ED NOTE: Ya ever shop at Costco? That's where ya buy everything in bulk. I saw a guy leave with a crate of toilet paper. As he lugged it to his truck, I'm thinkin', *If you're buying a* **crate** *of toilet paper from Costco, you really do need to change your diet!*

They have that new diet now. You've seen it, right? Called the Subway Diet. That's where ya get on a New York subway, put on a Red Sox shirt, get off at your stop, and try to run your ass back to the hotel without being caught by a crazed mob of Yankees fans! That workout alone is good for a quick 7-pound loss!

OK, you caught me. I made that up. You know the real diet I'm talking about: Jared's Subway Diet. This guy's commercials come on TV every six minutes! Jared's like a turd that won't flush. He was supposedly fat until he ate nothin' but Subway sandwiches and lost 80 or 100 pounds or whatever the hell it was.

I say that's hogwash! Where was the Subway store, 200 miles away? I tried his diet once. I walked all the way to a Subway and ate my meal. By the time I made it back home, all that walkin' had worked up another appetite. So I ordered a damned pizza. That dude Jared must not have a job, because the last thing I wanna do after workin' all day is walk 3 miles for a turkey sub!

I got nothin' against Subway, God bless 'em. I took my mom there one Mother's Day and even though we walked, no one lost any weight. Let's see Subway work some magic with Rosie O'Donnell. Ain't no amount of walkin' gonna thin her out. She's about two subs away from Holy Shit! Rosie can walk to a subway four states away and jump rope while she eats, but this bacon bit ain't sheddin' no pounds!

Richard Simmons's Deal A Meal was another popular diet. Me and my buddy Brad used to watch his infomercials. We'd get great ab workouts laughin' our asses off, watchin' Ole Ritchie in them shorty-shorts, dancing around with a parade of fat woman to KC & the Sunshine Band.

That was the funniest thing on TV since Larry King. Ritchie called the show *Sweating to the Oldies*. They shoulda changed that name to *Laughin' at the Fatties!* I mean I ain't no Skinny Mini, but I know better than to let anybody videotape me in stretch pants, dancin' around like a wounded hog to old disco songs with some gay guy in candy-striped shorts. If ya looked close, you could actually see Ritchie's nuts poppin' out. It was disgusting!

That was the funniest video I've seen since that movie *Retard and the Kitty*. But I'll tell you what was even funnier. Richard's actual Deal A Meal Diet. That's the one in which you deal yourself food cards for every meal. My mom did that. She got a full house and gained 47 pounds!

Dealin' yourself food cards, of all the stupid ideas. Can you just see how that works: "Hey I'm starvin', let's get a game goin'." And by the way have you seen ole Richard lately? Good Lord, Jesus, and Betty Crocker! He looks like he's been humpin' Big Boy! I seen him on Hollywood Squares a while back and I thought the top row was gonna come falling down. The Lord and Savior of cellulite victims looks like he'd been hittin' a few too many buffets. His hind end must have been starvin' too; it was suckin' them candy-striped shorty-shorts up his ass crack like a vacuum.

I'd be in pretty good shape if it weren't for cereal. I love cereal. That's my dad gum downfall. Cap'n Crunch, Frosted Flakes, Fruity Pebbles, Super Model Vagina Crunch, boy, are those good in the morning.

I was all set to diet today. Then I saw a box of Super Sugar Crisps sittin' up in the cupboard and thought, *What the hell, I'll diet tomorrow*. I tore into them Sugar Crisps while watchin' the

Flintstones on the Cartoon Network. I had me a smile bigger than a male cheerleader holdin' up a pom-pom girl by the squishy parts. Cereal sure does take me back to the good ole days.

Just when ya start gettin' on track with your diet and lose a few pounds, here comes the holidays. Nothin' kills a diet worse than Thanksgiving, Christmas, and the five-dollar lunch special at a strip club. Holiday eating is the worst thing to happen to dieters since they invented microwaveable s'mores.

I was doing awesome goin' into last Thanksgiving. I had lost 12 pounds and was getting into my pants, as well as the neighbor girl's pants, fairly easily. Then came Pumpkin Pie Day. I pooped a wicker chair Thanksgiving night. Ain't that a shame? The Pilgrims discover America and all I get for it is gas and Pepto breath!

Damn Pilgrims. I wish when they came here they woulda celebrated at some titty bar instead. I know I'd rather celebrate Thanksgiving with a redhead on my knee, wigglin' to Mötley Crüe than layin' on the floor with my pants unsnapped and my feet up on the coffee table, shootin' out pumpkin farts!

Last time I had that much gas they gave me a set of Bobby Labonte coffee mugs! And the worst part is just when ya get your plumbin' back to working, here comes Christmas. The main phrase at our house during the holiday season isn't "Merry Christmas" or "Happy Thanksgiving." It's "Where's the plunger?"

I saw somethin' disturbing the other day. No, it wasn't the TV show *Fat Actress*. As disturbing as that is, it's no match for this news story about the 150-pound three-year-old. I ain't kidding ya. Now it's one thing when adults get a little large, but they have the brains to do something about it provided they have the willpower.

This poor kid, though, needed someone in charge to say no every time he reached for that extra helping or four of dessert. I mean, it's one thing to be a chubby kid. Many kids have some baby fat to lose. It's natural.

However, a 150-pound three-year-old is a bit over the top. I mean for God's sake, when you see your child eating your pets, it's time to say, "Enough's enough!"

I bet that two-ton tot goes through a crate of Gerbers like a Somalian attackin' a buffet. What the hell do they feed this mini–Rosie O'Donnell for breakfast, a whole hog? These parents are either brain dead Mongoloids or else they're doing it on purpose so they can start a circus.

It's just ridiculous. It wasn't a disease that put on those pounds either; he just got fat from eatin'! I'd have these parents arrested for child abuse. Whatever happened to the word "NO!" A kid that heavy starts to become a health and clean air problem after a while. Can you imagine changin' that boy's diaper after he downed down 47 jars of Gerber stewed prunes? He'd make elephants look like amateurs! They'd have to call in a loader, dump truck, and twelve city workers just to dispose of this damn two-ton tot's Ripley-sized diaper accumulations.

Can ya imagine what his neighbor's must be sayin'?:

Man: "Hey honey, look at all them trucks pullin' up next door. They must be doing road construction."

Wife: "No, I think the Willis kid just pooped again and they're fittin' to change his diaper."

Man: "Oh damn! That kid can poop! Hey, speakin' of crap, did you see that show *Fat Actress*?"

Wife: "Ya, that was the dumbest thing I've seen since I saw Richard Simmons on *Hollywood Squares*. Tell me he didn't look like he gained all his weight back?"

Man: "I know it's hilarious! Boy that Larry King's an old sumbitch, ain't he?"

Wife: "These pretzels are making me thirsty!"

Man: "Isn't that from *Seinfeld*?"

Wife: "Yeah, I only said it because Larry the Cable Guy thinks it's hilarious. He's a big *Seinfeld* fan."

Man: "Hey look it's Jerry Seinfeld. What are you doing in this bit?"

Jerry Seinfeld: "I was just walking by and heard y'all writing about me so I thought I'd say hey. Tell Larry I said hey. I got his book and I think it's funny."

Wife: "Hey, Jerry, it looks like you sat on something. Your pants have some food stains on the back."

Man: "Yeah, it looks like Drake's Coffee Cake."

Jerry Seinfeld: "NEWMAN!!!!"

ED NOTE: Bill and Sheri Alderman played the roles of the man and his wife. I would like to thank them for participatin' in this book. Also thanks to Henry Skokel for his role of Jerry. I wish I could have gotten the actual Jerry Seinfeld, but at the time I was writing this book, he had a corporate event.

And now, back to "I'll Diet Tomorrow."

Diets are fine if you can find one that's comfortable and fits your daily routine. However, as much as people need to watch what they eat, they must remember that some of these diet foods can have horrible aftereffects. The manufactuers never tell ya that. In their commercials or ads, they always have somone drinkin' this low-fat drink and they act like it tastes better than peanut brittle–flavored panties.

Have you ever had one of those drinks? Most diet drinks taste like ya just licked Cher's ass crack while she had the flu! Now that can't be good for anybody!

Here's somethin' else them commercials don't tell ya: 98 percent of them drinks make ya feel like ya just ate the butthole out of a skunk. They leave your ass soundin' like Uncle Jim fell asleep with a lit cigarette in the firecracker tent!

They don't show that side of it, do they?

I've only seen one diet drink commercial that was honest enough to admit what it might do to ya. I can't remember which one it was because I'm still laughing over the line ". . . lick Cher's ass crack while she had the flu." Brilliantly funny. I remember, though, that the commercial said that the drink could make ya gassy and give you an oily discharge.

Finally, here was a company on the up and up. They said, "Look, this thing'll help ya lose weight. But we're warning ya right now: cancel all dinner reservations and appointments for the next few days because shitting will be your top priority!"

At least they spelled it out for us. And the thing is people still bought the stuff faster than the Princess Di Beanie Baby (well, it was close). Even though they knew this drink would have 'em bent over, haulin' ass to the stool to shoot out colors Crayola never thought of, they still purchased the product.

That's why diets are such big business. People will buy a pill or drink that will make 'em crap out their livers just to look like Brad Pitt or Donna Fargo (I could have used Pam Anderson there, but I've always had this thing for Donna).

I don't know about you, but I'd rather be fat than run around fartin' all day with oily discharges! If I was on that drink and had a 9:30 p.m. movie date with a girl, I'd have to map out a route that took us past gas stations with toilets in 'em every 10 minutes. I'd be stopping at every one of them damn things. Why, I'd have to pick the girl up at 4 p.m. just to reach the movie theater on time. And can you imagine the poor sumbitches that had to research and test this product?:

Merle the Dietitian: "Jim, does this feel like an oily discharge to you or just a regular watery discharge?"

Jim the Dietitian: "No, that's definitely oily, we better write it down in the log book."

Andy the Supervisor: "These pretzels are making me thirsty!"

Who in their right mind would drink this stuff? A person would have to be crazy:

DeWayne: "Hey Bill, How's the diet comin'?"
Bill: "Well good and bad. So far I've lost seven friends, cleared out two whole sections down there at the Bonanza Buffet, and ruined 16 pairs of Wal-Mart underbritches! But on the good side I'm 27 pounds lighter. I lost 3 pounds off my waist and pooped out 24 pounds of spleen that was causin' me problems.

ED NOTE: For those of you not into country, Donna Fargo was a fine, country-western singer during the '70s. Ya might remember some of the words to one of her hits:

It's a skippity do da day,
I'm the happiest girl, in the whole U.S.A.

You don't find clever, thought-provoking lyrics like that any-more in music. Donna sang that song with a little lisp so it sounded like she was singin', "I'm the happiest girl, in the whole U.ESH.A." It was very sexy.

When I was growing up, there was a diet candy called AIDS. They were little caramel fat busters and when ya ate 'em, you were supposed to lose weight (yank, yank). These candies were real popular until the horrible epidemic hit.

Talk about bad timing. Those poor AIDS candy folks shoulda sued somebody's ass off. Out of all the things doctors could have named one of the worst diseases in the world, they named it after a diet candy. I'da been pissed if I was the manufacturer. However, my mom tried those candies and never dropped a pound, so the new improved AIDS probably works much better as a weight-loss program.

Boy, that disease makes ya long for the good ole days of clap and herpes, don't it? I still remember that time when my brother called from the hospital to say they'd found a problem with his blood tests. We all thought the worst and he was on pins and needles until the final results came in. You shoulda seen the look of relief on my brother when he learned that it was just syphilis. Thank God up above. We had a big celebration that night at the church in his honor and the choir sang "Lookin' for Love in All the Wrong Places."

Compared to that AIDS thing, all other diseases are a piece of cake. I remember one time a girl phoned me (OK, a fourth cousin I'd met at a family reunion) and said "You better go to the doctor! I just got back and he said I had the clap!" I was like "Big deal, I sprinkle that stuff on my ice cream!"

ED NOTE: I kinda got off topic a bit here but it tied in well with the AIDS candy thing. I used to eat those candies when I was a kid because they kinda tasted good. I still think that candy company oughta sue because they took it right up the ass in that deal!

Tell me I didn't just write that.

In case that last joke offended somebody send your comments to

> **Kiss My Ass**
> c/o Larry the Cable Guy
> That Was Funny As Hell Blvd.
> Lighten Up, Florida OU812

OK, there's tons more diets and weight-loss things out there that we could cover, but I wrote only about the ones I've tried. The main point here goes back to somethin' my trainer always tells me.

That's right, I have a trainer, so when your done laughing I'll continue.

Ready now? Here's what she constantly says, "Quit staring at my tits."

OK, so maybe that's not helpful, but here is what experience has taught me about losing weight. It's like I said before, lay off the carbs, cut out the sugars, work out at least 45 minutes to an hour a day, and don't eat late.

That's it.

Professional trainers will tell you the same thing. Save your money on all these stupid diets and do it yourself. Believe me, if I can lose weight, so can you. It's like my trainer's mom often says to me, "Quit staring at my tits!"

OK, still not a good example.

In closing, let me remind you, I don't claim to be a dietitian. However, I did stay at a Holiday Inn Express last night. Now I gotta run and get something to drink. These pretzels are making me thirsty!

Chapter 12

EVERYDAY OBSERVATIONS

WARNING: You're about to read one of the longest chapters in the book, unless I add a chapter where I explain what I'd like to do to Jenny McCarthy. This is where I'm gonna ask my readers, all eight of them, whether they notice the same things I do, be it news stories or events that occur in everyday life.

For example: Is it just me or are gas stations starting to turn into little mini-malls for the less fortunate? Is there really anybody driving around in a car saying, "Boy I could really go for that T-shirt with the picture of a coyote on it," or "Damn, I could really use a combination bottle opener, fingernail clipper, and pocket knife with a picture of Jesus on the side of it." These are the kinda items people buy at gas stations and it really frosts my ass.

Which, by the way, is one of the things I'd like to do to Jenny McCarthy.

I have tons (OK, a few pages) of examples like these that I've gathered throughout the years. I've written 'em all down with my combination tire gauge, compass, and ballpoint pen with the picture of Elvis on it.

Prostate Exams

Let me start off by telling you about my prostate exam. Now I know only guys and a couple of WNBA players can relate to this but here goes. Why is it that the doctor who gives that exam is always female and attractive? At least that's how it always is in my case. Not that I mind, but what if she hits on me and then makes me drop my pants and my tighty whities look like turn 4 at Bristol.

I'm not sayin' she'd hit on me but it does happen in porno movies, from what I hear.

Let me tell you about my first prostate exam. I went into this little room and here comes my doctor. Holy greased ass crack! She was a major MILF! I got Stifler's mom fixin' to lube me up like I'm headed to an Elton John backstage party.

Remember now, I've never had an exam like this, anyway not without dim lighting and Richard Marx playing in the background. So I was a little apprehensive. She asked if I was ready and pulled on a rubber glove.

I bit down on a small block of cedar while Stifler's mom began searchin' for polyps. The weird thing was she ran out of lube and had to use mustard. Fortunately, she didn't find any cancerous growths. However she did find a Professional Bull Riders pocket knife that I had shoved up my ass to keep security from takin' it during a flight to Baltimore.

My bill for this hot-lookin' nurse sticking her finger in my hind end for 30 seconds was 82 bucks. WAAAY cheaper than what I'd pay downtown! I walked out of that office looking like Joe Paterno after a Bikeathon.

Don't ask me. I have no idea what that means.

Dial 10-10-220

Anyone with a TV has seen the commercials for Dial 10-10-220. If you haven't, you've either been dead since 1988 or you're an Amish. The commercials claim that you can save some money if you dial these numbers before calling someone.

Fine except that by the time I get done punchin' in all those numbers, I forgot who the hell I was phoning in the first place!

Then to piss ya off even more, all the competing companies try to outdo each other. One ad goes, "Save an extra penny and dial 10-1-220-32-546 and you'll be instantly connected."

OK, that's not too bad, but how about the other ad that says, "You can save an extra 4 cents with our service just by dialing 10-10-220-4354-777-888-90605-4354-22-556-2. Then after the beep punch in your date of birth followed by the # sign. After ya hear another beep, stick a carrot up your ass, do a backflip, and you'll be instantly connected. It's that easy!"

I got a better idea. Just make every call a cheap call and knock off the Abbott and Costello routine.

The West Nile Virus

This should make ya feel safe. I was recently listening to the news while watching the stars with my telescope after my neighbor had just put her top back on. I heard some anchorwoman say that foreigners were bringing in the West Nile virus by crossing our borders with mosquito eggs hiding in their clothing and shoes.

Great, out of all the crap we've already got to worry about in this country, we really need foreign Ebola mosquitoes sneaking past

Customs. What are we getting next, piranha swimmin' through the sewers and shooting up my toilet pipe to nibble at my nuts during an after-dinner poop?

We need these mosquitoes like we need another *C.S.I.* show. They should start sprayin' foreigners at the airports for ticks and stuff before we all wind up dead. Call me insensitive or whatever ya want, but when your blood's full of Ebola because some foreigner carried a mosquito into this country in sandals made outta cow pies, don't come running to me. I'll be at the airport covered in cellophane welcoming foreigners with cans of Raid.

Toaster Troubles

Ya ever notice that everybody is out to make a buck because they did something stupid and it's always somebody else's fault but theirs. Case in point: I just read about this couple whose house burnt down after the wife left some Pop-Tarts in the toaster too long. Now these two breakfast bozos are suing the toaster manufacturer.

Excuse me, but how is that the manufacturer's fault? Either this braindead Mama Cass needs to lay off the carbs (see the previous chapter) or try waiting at least 45 seconds for that piece of pastry to toast. After all, it ain't a turkey, it's a Pop-Tart. Too bad she didn't stick a knife in there to see if it was done. We'da had a fully toasted tart and one less dumb ass tyin' up the already overworked court system.

Here the deal: just because you're an idiot doesn't mean you can sue companies for every bad decision you make in your life. No wonder insurance rates are so high, when ya got people in this country too stupid to operate a two-slice toaster!

Save the Planet

OK, here's a good one. I was leaving the mall the other day after hittin' on the chick workin' in the candle shop and saw a guy drivin' down the road with a bumper sticker that read "Save the planet don't use aerosol." Meanwhile, the guy had white smoke flyin' outta his mufflers. Ya woulda thought the car had just elected its own pope.

These environmentalists crack me up. Save the planet. I can barely save the oak tree out by the creek from beavers, how the hell am I supposed to save the planet? Don't use aerosol? The earth has survived earthquakes, volcanic eruptions, tidal waves, forest fires, and the New Kids on the Block. You think Edith sprayin' hairspray on her hairway to heaven before goin' to the Dolly Parton look-alike contest is gonna screw it up!

Why don't you enviroqueers buy three or four acres, see what you can do with that, and then work your way up to the whole planet. Is everyone insane?

Unfunny Cartoons

Ya ever read the Sunday comics and realize that the miniseries *Roots* provided more laughs? That damn Beetle Bailey ain't been funny since I was two. And that whore Mary Worth never belonged in the funny papers. I've read obituaries funnier than her. All them other cartoons used to be funny until they got so politically correct. Now they're so careful not to offend anybody, I wouldn't wipe my ass with one.

Well actually I was campin' once and had to wipe myself with Dagwood and Blondie plus a couple of panels from Marmaduke after some bad potato salad. I must admit they did the job, but that's about all they're good for.

Cartoons are supposed to provide laughs, not lessons in sensitivity and political correctness. I haven't laughed at a cartoon since Snoopy sniffed Lucy while she was doing a headstand.

Come to think of it, that was in *Penthouse*!

Root Canals

Is it just me or are root canals as painful as watching an episode of A&E's *True Hollywood* featurin' Paulie Shore? I'd rather dip my nuts in sweet cream and lay naked among a barnyard full of tomcats than get a root canal (I actually did the tomcat thing as part of my F.F.A initiation, so I know).

I remember when my cousin had a root canal. He was in so much pain he got dizzy and fell off the water tower while tryin' to write *God Hates Fags* (I don't condone that, by the way). But when it's all said and done, havin' a root canal is like getting herpes from Shania Twain. It's worth the pain.

Wilt Chamberlain's Ball

An autographed ball from Wilt Chamberlain recently sold for $551,884. You believe that?

I wonder what his other ball went for? (I could do this all day.)

I can't believe people spend money for crap like that. People are starving in other countries and some rich dude just spent the entire income of Jamaica on Wilt the Stilt's ball. I learned my lesson about that crap. I once paid 125 bucks at the flea market for a little white cotton patch out of Faith Hill's panties and it only lasted seven sniffs.

Is it just me or is half a million for a dumb old ball a little steep?

The Price is Right

I love that TV game show, *The Price Is Right*. I try to use the word "plinko" everyday during conversations. In my family, *The Price Is Right* has survived two sets of grandparents and five pets. But the one thing I hate about the game is those number blockers, the idiots that bid a dollar over another person's bid. They're like that cock blocker guy at the beer party. He comes in at the last minute to hit on some girl you've been workin' on for two hours and then blows it for both of ya. I can't stand those people.

If I bid 1,200 bucks for somethin' on *The Price Is Right* and the idiot next to me bid $1,201, I'd stab him in the neck with a pair of scissors (in a good Christian way of course).

I always feel sorry for the poor soul that never makes it off the front row of bidders. Just kinda stuck there in Bidders' Limbo, where everyone can see what a big loser you are. The only one outta the bunch that never advanced.

Kinda like me in 8th and 11th grade.

It's embarassin'. Just think, family and friends watching back home. The camera pans on you. Your nephew at home yells, "Hey, Dad, there's Uncle George!"

"Yeah, I know. The big loser, he's been standing there since last Thursday! They said if he loses a couple more times they might make him a regular."

I like *The Price Is Right* but they really need to stop the number blockers.

Deaf Guy Suing Millionaire

Remember back when *Who Wants to Be a Millionaire* was at the peak of its popularity? All right, it was never quite as popular as that *Happy Days* episode when Fonzie jumped over the shark tank, but *Millionaire* attracted a lot of fans. Well some deaf guy out for a quick buck recently tried suing them. He claimed he couldn't be a contestant on the show because his hearing handicap made it impossible for him to answer questions on that 800 number the producers had set up. He hired a lawyer and cried discrimination.

He sure as hell could hear on the phone well enough to call up and get a lawyer to file suit, though, couldn't he?

I oughta sue *Playboy* because I can't hump the centerfold! I mean, come on! Enough already. Everybody's gotta bitch about something. What's next, somebody gonna sue Regis Philbin because his questions are too hard! Life ain't fair, deal with it. The public ain't gonna watch an all sign language quiz show and that's for damn sure.

Shaving the Privates

I read an article in the paper that said women shaving their private parts was like a 200-million-dollar-a-year business.

Damn, that's a great way to make a living. Waxing and shaving women's private parts. I think I'm going to do that when I quit doing stand-up. I already got my business registered with the government. It's called Bushwackers.

I think it's sexy when woman do all that waxin' and shavin'. It ain't like the old days when a girl would take off her overalls and a bunch of quail would come flying out of the underbrush. You didn't need a rubber; you needed a hunting permit back then. I coulda gotten laid and bagged my limit in 15 minutes flat back in '85.

Nowadays women are all groomed up and it looks good. However there are women that think its sexy if guys shave their privates, too. I draw the line there. I once tried to turn on a girlfriend by trimmin' down there. I came outta the bathroom with little red bumps and toilet paper squares all over my testicles. I looked like a grub worm with a turtleneck on. It was embarrassing.

I do think men need to groom and trim, though. This friend of mine sent me a photo of some naked couple over the Internet once and the dude had so much pubic hair it looked like an aerial photo of a rainforest with a small missile installation in the middle of it. That's a little much.

Gays and Lesbians

OK look, I couldn't care less who's gay or who's not gay, I couldn't care less if people wanna stick carrots up their asses and run around the park singin' "Looks like chicken tonight." But for God's sake, do I have to hear about gay rights 24 hours a day? Seems like every day it's gay this and gay that. Who gives a damn! You're gay, congratulations! Ya want me to do backflips and start pulling rabbits outta my ass? Enough already. I got friends that like sheep but they don't throw a parade every weekend!

It's ridiculous. These folks act like they're the dad gum holy grail and better than everybody else. You're not. You're just like me and everybody else except ya own more flannel and have a slight limp. Just last week, I went to the music store in the mall to find the new Jerry Reed live CD for my dad to put on as background music so he could get mom all turned on for their anniversary.

This store had a Gay and Lesbian music section!

Good Lord, Jesus, and Elton John! Ya know for a group of folks that say all they want to do is blend in, they sure go outta their way to stand out. We already have gay and lesbian music. It's called Adult Contemporary and they have a section for that.

Look, if you're gay, fine. God bless ya, who cares. I don't think it's right but I'm not the Lord and I'll let him deal with it at the end. Gay people are still individuals. Even though I disagree with their lifestyle that doesn't mean I can't love them as fellow citizens and be friends with them. Long as you're not an asshole, more power to ya. Believe me, I'd much rather hang out with gay guys than any member of the Kennedys. But do me a favor. Try shutting up about it for at least 10 minutes. I heard ya the first time.

Playing with Yourself

First off I bet I'm the only person to ever write a book with a section entitled "Playing with Yourself." This was inevitable. I have noticed that there are two things in life I really enjoy doing: watching *All in the Family* and playing with myself.

In fact, sometimes I'll play with myself while I'm watching *All in the Family.* I believe everyone has done this sometime in their lives. I'm talkin' about playing with yourself, AND DON'T LIE!

I may have a problem, though. I remember the time when I sat naked in my doctor's examination room and asked him, "What's wrong with me, I can't stop playing with myself?"

He said "How the hell do I know, I'm a dentist."

But in all seriousness, there's so much temptation out there, it kinda gets irritating. I had to run to the bass pro shops bathroom the other day after I saw a mannequin wearing a camo miniskirt and a "NAPA" tube top! I wish I didn't do that so often, but that's the society we live in. Ya can't turn on the TV anymore without see-ing some girl that gets ya going.

The other day, I was watching, of all things, the Learning Chan-nel. They had on some emergency room show and there was this attractive, fortyish woman laying on an operating table, out like a light. When the camera panned down, her nipple popped out. I was in and outta the shower before they took out her kidney.

It really gets frustrating. I know I'm not the only one that has this problem so I figured I'd write about to let ya know you're not alone.

Okay, I gotta go get a towel. *All in the Family*'s coming on.

Weddings

Wedding invitations are a major pain in the ass. Anybody that's been to a wedding knows what I'm talking about. In most cases you have a couple that has lived together for years and are basi-cally married without the paper from the state.

They invite ya to their wedding, which is really a nice way of say-ing, "We want money and free stuff from our friends." Ya get all dressed up and drive 1,200 miles to attend the ceremony and reception. Then you barely talk to either one of 'em.

After they haul ass down the road for their honeymoon, you're stuck twiddlin' your thumbs, hangin' out with people you don't know. Ya end up talkin' to the bride's drunken brother for 45 min-utes. The rest of the time is spent dancin' with her 300-lb. loud-mouthed aunt.

It's ridiculous and I'm never going to another one. I'll be damned if I waste a whole day in a church basement watchin' Dar-win and Doris exchange wedding vows of eternal love after I just seen 'em two nights earlier cussin' and smackin' at each other because someone didn't put his beer on a coaster in the add-on porch! I'd respect folks more if they were honest about their motives. Screw the ceremony. Just call up and say, "Hey, we're now having sex legally. Can ya send us 20 bucks and some house-wares?"

I'm all for the institution of marriage but weddings are nothing but headaches! And I don't see any couples all gung ho on invitin' everybody back for the divorce ceremony, so we can divvy up the cash and get our shit back. That would be only fair, wouldn't ya think?

Homeland Security

Can I ask who's in charge of Homeland Security? It has to be the special ed department of this country, because they've got nothing but retards working airport security! Half these people look like they just got fired from McDonalds for ringin' up fries on the salad key and they're the ones checking for bombs in bags!

God help us!

I had a guy remove my fish hook from my hat. He claimed that decorative hat clip could be used as a weapon. In the words of Billy Graham "You gotta be shittin' me"(once again, I don't know if this is an actual quote). My fish hook a weapon. Who'da thunk it? What, are the pilots biting on worms this time of year? Good thing I cooperated. I'd be the only guy ever placed in a maximum secu-rity prison for carrying fishing supplies onto a Delta jet!

It's really frustrating how the government lacks common sense. I actually saw airport security confiscate a big rubber band from someone. They considered that a weapon too. I have never in my life seen a rubber band hurt anyone really bad. However I did see a wedding band beat the hell out of my brother in 2003!

Okay, I know I used that joke before too. But he's been married more than once.

I wished these security people would quit trying to be so damn politically correct and start profiling. I really don't look like a Middle Easterner between the ages of 18 and 28, do I? Can you see anyone mistaking me for Larry Allah Bin Cable Wada Wada Guy Laden or whatever the hell these terrorists call themselves?

It cracked me up when the Homeland Security folks recommended that everybody get duct tape and bottled water in case we had another attack. How the hell can those items help us? Unless you tie a long string of tape to a gallon water bottle, then swing it around and whack an extreme Muslim in the head while he's boarding a plane, that stuff is pretty much useless. I think companies make this crap up when business is down just to sell products in a time of panic. Can't you see how it works:

Panicked Man (after dialin' 911): "I just seen two Middle East sumbitches sneaking around the back of my house with a bag of Ebola viruses. What do I do?"

Operator: "OK, don't panic, go to the store and get three bottles of Prell, a box of Pecan Logs, and sit tight."

Panicked Man: "How will that help?"

Operator: "It won't, but the manufacturers' stocks'll go up, your hair will smell better, and your belly'll be full!"

ED NOTE: Here's a bit of cool info; the Panicked Man and the Operator in this sketch were played by the same guys that did the announcers in the NASCAR bit earlier in the book.

I wouldn't be surprised if one day ya turned on your TV and found a message like this from the Homeland Security Department scrolling across the bottom of your screen:

> *WE HAVE INFORMATION [pretend this is scrolling . . .]*
> *WE HAVE INFORMATION THAT LEADS US TO BELIEVE*
> *THAT THERE ARE SOME TERRORISTS FLYING DOWN*
> *THE TURNPIKE ON A MAGIC CARPET THROWING RAT*
> *POISON ON MOTORISTS. PLEASE STAY IN YOUR HOMES*
> *WITH 4 BOTTLES OF WATER, LIQUID CRISCO, AND A*
> *BAG OF NUTTERBUTTERS. PLEASE MAKE SURE YOU*
> *HAVE PLENTY OF BATTERIES AND STINKBAIT. WE'LL*
> *ISSUE FURTHER INSRUCTIONS IF THE SITUATION*
> *HEIGHTENS. MEANWHILE BLOW UP 8 BALLOONS AND*
> *TWIST THEM INTO POODLES AND THEN DUCT TAPE*
> *YOUR KIDS TO THE BED. THEN DOUSE THEM AND YOUR-*
> *SELF IN PICANTE SAUCE . . . MLB . . . ATL 5 MIL 3 . . . CHI*
> *3 CIN 1 . . . OAK 6 CLE 4 . . . DON'T MISS ARLEN SPEC-*
> *TOR TONIGHT ON HANNITY & COLMES . . .*

I could scroll on and on, but you get the idea.

Miss America

It's a shame they don't stage this competition on TV anymore because it always felt good to root for the girl from your home state. The Miss America Pageant was fun even though I hated how some contestants preached to ya about some goofy cause they supported. "My name's Tina and one of my goals is to work with the starving kids in Africa and help educate them on democracy. Either that or be a Bud girl!"

That crap kept the PC morons happy but the majority of the viewers thought it was stupid. People never bought into it. Who in their right mind is really gonna believe that this girl, who's biggest decision in life was what pair of shoes to wear during the evening gown competition, really gives a rat's ass about the Zulu and their struggles against oppression.

Just put a T-back on Tina and shut up! If I wanted to learn about Zulu oppression I'd watch PBS.

Now maybe she does know about that stuff. More power to her. Even so, who are we kiddin' here? The Miss America Pageant was basically a classy bikini contest. God bless Tina's intelligence but that doesn't win ratings.

Case in point: Showtime once carried a show that featured nothing but women in sexy tights working out to music in front of a camera. Every episode was nothin' but close-up crotch shots. There was no dialogue and you know what? PBS still has never produed a show that could match the ratings of that Showtime series.

Here's another thing that pissed me off about the Miss America pageant. The politically correct morons that ran it made sure every race was represented so as not to offend anyone. Whatever happened to just pickin' the best-lookin' women? One year, they had some Asian girl in the finals that looked like Yoko Ono BEFORE the glamour shots. Good Lord, Jesus, and Long Duck Dong! I could have thrown a rock at the flea market and hit 15 girls better lookin' than her.

So thanks political correctness for ruining another good TV program.

Rosie O'Donnell

Settle in for this.

When I heard Rosie got married a while back, I thought, *Wow, just what she needs, more cake!* I've been pissed at Rosie ever since she badgered Tom Selleck for being a member of the NRA. Everybody used to say, "Leave Rosie alone!" (OK, not everybody, just my mom and the gay guy from Super Cuts). They'd say, "She's so nice and sincere and she helps people."

But after she left her show, the real Rosie started to show through. She behaved like an asshole to everybody but Little Debbie. Rosie sure got big, though, didn't she? I have never seen size 68 Levis before. I actually read in *Variety* that she's been cast as Hoss in the new *Bonanza* movie!

Remember when she got that Mother of the Year award? What a joke that was! It was like the P.E.T.A. honoring Ted Nugent. Mother of the Year, my ass! Rosie adopts a couple kids, hires round-the-clock nannies to raise 'em, then shows up every now and again to buy 'em cool stuff.

She ain't a mom, she's Santa Claus. Only less shapely.

I'm sure Rosie may be nice to those kids but she ain't qualified for that award. Mother of the Year should go to that gal with four kids, a scumbag ex-husband who cheated on her and still owes back child support. She has to work two jobs, plus help the kids with homework and take 'em to their daily activities. That's a Mother of the Year! I'll give Rosie an award, how 'bout "The pull the wool over everyone's eyes award!"

ED NOTE: I gotta tell ya. I'm not in the least apologizing for ragging on Rosie. What she did to Tom Selleck was uncalled-for. He's Fricken Quigley, for God's sake! Ya don't screw with Quigley!

X-bay

I feel I should offer some observations about one of the most popular features on the Internet, orientalwhore.com.

Oh sorry, that's only popular in my circles.

Of course I'm talking about eBay. The cool thing about eBay is
you can buy and sell almost anything ya want on there. If ya can't
find it, go to eBay. It's just like going to the flea market minus the
Mexicans and corn dogs.

The wild thing is people make pretty good money thinking up
crazy things to put on eBay. Now they also have X-bay. That's the
dirty alternative to eBay and you never know what might turn up
on it. A few years back, a girl sold her virginity on X-bay. I'm not
lying. She got 20 THOUSAND bucks.

Boy, somebody was hard up. I had a virgin once; she only cost
me a pack of cigarettes and two tickets to Mötley Crüe! Ya got to
hand it to this X-bay girl for having a keen business sense. I
pimped out my sister last year in the Auto Trader and all I got was
some retreads and a brush guard. And that was from my uncle!! I
mean 20 grand is ridiculous. For 20 grand that girl had better be
able to tongue-tie your wiener in a knot like a cherry stem!

**ED NOTE: I have no idea what to say here other than Mexicans
love flea markets.**

Crippled Golfer!

OK, I really have to make an observation about this even though it's
an old story. A while back there was a case involving the PGA and a
crippled guy named Casey. Because of his handicap, he needed a

golf cart to get around the course. The PGA said he couldn't play in its tournaments because the rules required all the participants to walk the course.

Now I know with all the world's troubles this is insignificant. However it was all over the news back then. I sure didn't lose any sleep over the dispute. I couldn't have cared less if Hopalong Cassidy took a bus from hole to hole. I hate golf.

But I just couldn't believe golfers were getting pissed off at the guy. Damn, excuse him for being crippled! If it was up to the PGA, we'd be arrestin' crippled folks and tar-and-featherin' retards. It don't matter if the guy walks, rides, or takes a cab, he still has to knock the ball in the hole don't he?

I hadn't seen this much narrow-mindedness since my hometown fair when the mayor tried to keep a Haitian crack whore outta the pie eating contest. He eventually got to play and everybody has since forgotten about it. However in another recent case, a guy with no legs sued to play shortstop for some baseball team. He won the suit, but now he's pissed because every time someone for the other team smacks the ball into the outfield everyone yells, "Hit the cutoff man!"

Nude Beaches

When I was a kid I heard about nude beaches and thought it would be cool to visit one and check out the good-lookin' naked chicks. That's how little boys think. Their main goal in life is to see a girl naked and perhaps (cross your fingers) feel her up! Wow! That would be like winning the lottery.

Well guess what? Nude beaches are a major letdown. Nude beaches are full of nothing but old people, fat hippies, and gay guys! Me and my buddies were eating at the fish camp one day and decided we'd go to the nude beach down the way to check out some sexy ladies. All we found was a beach full of big naked red asses, old women hunched over with danglin' boobs that looked like a 7–10 split and the Village People.

I asked myself that afternoon, why do old people have this strong yearnin' to get naked? I'm sure my grandma was quite a looker in her day but I really don't think anyone wants to see her at 87 bare-ass naked on the beach, leaving snail-size marks in the sand with her nipples. When we went, I saw three naked lesbians that could have passed for a ZZ Top tribute band. All I'm saying in my observation of nude beaches is don't waste your time if you're going for the sights 'cause there aren't any.

ED NOTE: When I use the term "feel her up" that's actually something really important to a kid whose hormones are raging. Look, I don't make the rules, I'm just the messenger. Here's a list of turn-ons based on the different age groups:

> 5–10: Ya don't care about the opposite sex as long as ya have the Cartoon Network and plenty of sugar to eat.
> 11–12: It's always "Did ya hold their hand?"
> 13–14: It's always "Did ya kiss her?"
> 15–17: It's always "Did ya feel her up?"
> 18 and up: It's always "Did ya nail her?"

Now this chart is based only on my experiences while growing up durin' the '60s, '70s, and '80s and I had strict parents. So depending on the decade in which you grew up or how a person was raised or whether you visited Michael Jackson anytime in the last 15 years as a kid, this chart is probably way off.

Chopsticks

Not the song, the eating utensils.

I can't stand chopsticks. No wonder Chinese people are so skinny; they drop more food than they eat. People think they look really cool and cultured when they eat with chopsticks. They kinda portray that "I'm better than you" attitude, all because they know how to eat like they're living back in the Ming Dynasty.

I'd say only a small percentage of people eat with chopsticks at Chinese joints. The rest of the people are usually like me. Until our food comes, we use them as drumsticks while playing "Wipe Out" on the glasses and plates like we had a miniature drum set.

Honestly, I don't know why chopsticks bother me, they just do. Its like Jared from the Subway Diet. I never met the guy and I'm sure he's probably a sweetheart. But for some reason I wanna whack the shit out of him with a shovel.

I dunno, is that wrong?

It's like the TV show *Becker*. I've never seen it but I hate the damn thing! It's the same with people that eat with chopsticks. I guess in a nice upscale Chinese restaurant, it's no big deal when people use them.

However, I once saw somebody in a food court at the mall using them and that's where I draw the chopstick line. I mean, excuse me there, golden child sitting in front of the China Wok. You're not impressing anyone in the strip mall with your mastery of Chinese tableware. Just for the record, after everyone that could see him left, the guy acted like a true American and picked up his fork.

Nice move, grasshopper, your master would be proud!

ED NOTE: OK, I'll admit I got too worked up over something so stupid. But I know that you've used chopsticks to play "Wipe Out" at a Benihana at least once in your life.

Tracing Your Family Tree

One day after turning off the TV when *Becker* came on, I decided to trace my family tree. I got the idea after talking to my preacher about his great-grandpa. At the time, we were both peeing in a toilet together, trying to sink a cigarette butt. He said his great-grandpa was a general who had won the Purple Heart during WWI. After I started tracing my own family history, other people told me stories about their famous relatives.

One dude said he had traced back to a family member who had crossed over on the *Mayflower*. Another lady told me she had a relative that helped start the Pony Express. I was getting excited thinking, *I wonder what great things my ancestors did?*

What I discovered discouraged me. After all my in-depth research, the only semi-famous person I could find was a great-great grandpa who accidentally shot himself in the head with a potato gun. We had another distant relative that laughed all the time and made fun of Noah. He ended up drowning at age 43. And now I just found out from a telephone call only 10 minutes ago that my dad's in the hospital for zippin' his nuts up in his pants. I think I'll just cut down our family tree to save everyone any more embarrassment!

ED NOTE: I did have one grandpa who was famous only on New Year's Eve. Everyone would go over to his house at midnight to watch his balls drop!

Cher

I know a lot of people enjoy Cher. I had no problem with her either until she sued the estate of Sonny Bono for some ungodly amount of cash in back child support. BACK CHILD SUPPORT! I've seen her kid and believe me she sure wasn't starving. What's she weighin' in at now, about 310?

I can't believe Cher sued Sonny. That plastic, big-nosed, Chief Crazy Horse-lookin', gypsy goofball oughta be ashamed of herself. If it wasn't for Sonny Bono this AARP card-carryin', black-haired beanpole would be sellin' sharktooth necklaces and cold syrup for gambling money. This has nothing to do with her singing. I'm sure she sings well and I loved the song "I Got You Babe," but she shouldn't have sued Sonny Bono when he was already dead.

ED NOTE: *The Sonny and Cher Show* **was magic. I think it's also cool that Cher is still performing. However, my grandma's about the same age and I don't want to see her in black fishnet with a t-back on either.**

The Bathroom

Why is it when you're still living with your relatives and you're on the toilet, they think it's OK to just walk right in and grab something they need. I mean pooping is the one small moment of private time many people get in this world. If it wasn't for the toilet, I would have never finished readin' that book about Walt Garrison. I mean a private poop is something that ya don't take for granted; it only comes around twice a day on average (unless you attend a chili cookoff, then the numbers shoot way up) and by God a person wants to enjoy it!

I was in there one time trying to get rid of a rancid corn dog and lookin' at the latest Victoria's Secret catalog when in walks my sister without even knockin'!

"Damn, it stinks in here!" she said.

I was like, "No shit, Sherlock, I ain't poopin' out cinnamon sticks!" She heard me gruntin' and groanin', what did she think I was doin' in there, lifting weights!! All I'm saying is people should be respectful of a person's toilet time. They should remember that Einstein thought up a lot of his greatest theories while pooping.

ED NOTE: I'm not really sure about the Einstein thing, but he was smart and I know for sure that he pooped.

Fast Food Restaurants

I love fast food. It's not good for ya, but then again neither is twisting your penis into balloon animals (it was a party and I was drinking AND they double dared me). In any case, I'm going to quit going until they start hirin' some employees that speak English. I mean it's a fast food restaurant in America, for God's sake! You walk behind a McDonald's nowadays expectin' to see a boat and paddles sittin' out back! That's how fresh the employees are. It's frustrating!

And I'm telling ya right now, I got nothing against Cuba or Mexico, God bless 'em! But is it too much to ask that if you come to our country and work at a job where ya have to communicate with people, you at least learn the language? I mean, good God, if I had a dollar for every time I asked for a cheeseburger and large fries and received a chicken sandwich and onion rings, I'd be a rich man.

ED NOTE: How do ya say, you're a fricken idiot in Spanish?

UFOs!

How come UFOs always land in the middle of a trailer park and pick up DeWayne the toothless drunk and diddle his ass, then drop him off at a convenience store? It happens every time. Then when you hear the guy getting interviewed later, it's always the same damned story:

Reporter: "What happened, DeWayne? Tell us about the aliens."
DeWayne: "Well, I was coming home from the pig race with a sack of Schlitz and all of a sudden these green dudes come out from the bean field. Next thing I know I was bent over a sparkly lookin' sawhorse with my pants down getting' butt-diddled by a green guy that looked like Alf with the mange. Then I blacked out and woke at the Stop 'n Shop right next to this here Dumpster."

These abductees always say that the Martians that took 'em are of a high intelligence. I say that's a bunch of crap. It seems like to me, these aliens are all a bunch of perverts with ass fetishes.

Hey, come to think of it, maybe my Uncle Bob's a Martian!

These aliens never come here lookin' for water, or petroleum, or to find out how we grow crops. They never do anything but look for people to ass knuckle. It's obviously nothin' but a plea-sure trip so they can get their Martian rocks off.

Tell ya what. If I'm ever walkin' down a dirt road and see bright lights flashin' in the sky, I'm grabbin' a shotgun and duct tapin' my ass crack shut! If these intergalactic sodomizers are so smart, you think they'd wanna land by the Dallas Cowboy cheerleaders and snag their little nice butts, rather than the Miller boys from the Ozarks.

That's why I'm not scared of extraterrestrials. You wanna get rid of sightings in the sky? Send a bunch of blowup dolls into space and let 'em go to town on them for a few years.

I read a while back that the Mexican government has pictures of some UFOs that their Air Force took. Tell me that ain't scary. Not the UFO thing, the fact that Mexico has an Air Force.

What is it? A hot air balloon tied to a '74 Impala with no tires?

They had pictures of 11 UFOs. And you could tell they were Mexican UFO's because they were all lined up in front of a Taco Bell. Amazing pictures! They actually have videos of each space ship bouncing up and down with their speakers blaring the song "La Bamba" as they flew into space.

In the article, many government officials said they believed that the rims of the spaceship were actually nicer than the craft itself. They were rather small space vehicles although one official thought that there might be as many as 40 aliens packed into each vessel.

There were no reports of crop circles, but several witnesses claimed that the spacecraft left fuzzy dice hanging in a number of specified cars. Sources indicated that the aliens appeared rather peaceful. Before they left, two ships landed and its inhabitants got out and sold oranges at a red light for about two hours.

From all accounts, members of the American government have expressed concerns that the Mexican aliens may be entering our country to take away jobs that some of our own aliens already fill.

ED NOTE: I don't care who ya are, that paragraph was funny as hell. By the way this is a fact: the only objects visible from outer space are the Great Wall of China and Charlie Daniels's belt buckle.

The Moon's Aligning

Not long ago, people were up in arms and attending church a lot more often after reading a story that claimed the planets "were aligning" with the moon. They all thought the world was about to end.

It's funny to me how people get real religious when they think they're gonna die or when there's a tragedy. It's like, after 9/11, all those senators and congressmen gathered on the steps of the capitol and sang gospel tunes and prayed to the Lord. This from the same assholes that have basically tried to eliminate God from every walk of American life, from religious pictures or statues in government buildings all the way down to getting rid of pre-prayers at football games. Now all of a sudden, when it looks like they might need the Lord, they sing religious songs in front of the cameras.

If I was God, I'da struck all them government hypocrites dead right there. The government treats God like a whore, they only call on him when they really, really need him. It's unbelievable!

Anyway, as I was saying before I got into that little sermon, was that everyone thought the world was gonna end on the day the moon and the planets aligned. Well they did align and guess what? The day it happened was no different than the day before, except it was cooler and my dog crapped on my rug.

I'll admit to being a little worried when Y2K was around the corner. That's why I was the first person in my neighborhood to lock himself in a homemade bunker. I spent the night up to my ass in bottled water and Spam while holding an AK47.

And, as you well know, absolutely nothin' happened.

So, when I heard about this alignin' thing, I said, I'll be damned if I'm gonna fall for this crap again! Forget the planets, there are so many more real worries in this world. For instance, a real disaster would be if Rosie O'Donnell, Ricki Lake, Star Jones, and that fat Dixie Chick all lined up in a row! Good Lord, Jesus, and Jenny

Craig! That would create enough magnetic pull to send boxes of cake mix flyin' all over the country. You'd see tin roofs ripping off buildings!

Compared to that catastrophe, this planet thing was ridiculous. It was just another ploy hatched by Eveready to sell more batteries. Nowhere in the Bible does it talk about planets aligning and ending the world. However, there is a little mention in Daniel about four fat woman ransacking a Krispy Kreme. I can't really remember the verse right now, but I know it's in there.

Waiting Tables

Every time you hear people talking about bad jobs, somebody always chimes in with "at least it's better than waiting tables!" I have a buddy who empties septic tanks. When I told him, "Dude, that has to be the worst job ever." He said, "Ya, but it's better than waiting tables!"

I thought, *Man, waiting tables must really suck if a guy that empties poop is dissin' it.*

But I bet there are many jobs worse than bein' a waiter. For instance, here's a job that would really suck: head doucher at Wimbledon.

If waiting tables is that bad, then maybe they oughta get rid of the death penalty and sentence criminals to being waiters and waitresses! I'd love to be in that courtroom:

Judge: "Mr. Anderson, you have been convicted of 32 counts of murder, 12 counts of mutilation, and 1 count of doing a bad Jack Nicholson impression during open mic night at a comedy club in St. Louis. I hearby sentence you to working the night shift at Denny's for the rest of your life!"

Killer: "NOOOOOO!!!!"

Lawyer: "Your honor, I object! This sentence is inhumane! Surely you could find enough compassion in your heart to give my client the electric chair. Even Ted Bundy wasn't subjected to this kind of barbarism!"

Judge: "Overruled!! Bailiff, get this piece of trash an apron and a time card and get him the hell outta this court room!"

Killer: "Pleeease, don't make me do this!"

The killer puts his hand to his forehead and pushes his hair back and pretends to be Jack Nicholson. The bailiff zaps him with a Taser.

The End.

ED NOTE: I have never waited on tables so I can't really comment, but I bet a pin setter at the Baghdad Lanes in Iraq would be right up there as far as crappy jobs are concerned.

Westerns

I've always loved westerns. When I was a kid I used to play cowboys and Indians 24 hours a day. When I was a kid there was nothing I wanted more than to be John Wayne or Morgan Fairchild's bicycle seat.

Gunsmoke was my favorite TV western. The cool thing about *Gunsmoke* was that everyone loved Miss Kitty. I did, too. But in reality, Miss Kitty was a whore. She never really was seen givin' it up. But let's face facts here, she was the *main saloon girl*. Whattya think that means? No disrespect meant to Miss Kitty, but back in those days, saloon girls were the ones givin' it up like Paris Hilton at an F.H.M. after-party.

So Miss Kitty was a whore, but she was a whore with morals. It didn't matter to me if she banged half of Dodge City, it was a great western. Matt Dillon, Festus, Newly, Doc, Chester . . . man, those were the good ole days.

Westerns were one of the few forms of entertainment the whole family could enjoy together. They had cowboys shooting Indians, lawmen hangin' outlaws, whores gettin' plowed on the top floor of the bar and everybody gettin' into fights over a bottle of whisky! Now you know why kids today grow up all screwed up. They're watchin' MTV instead of pickin' up all those wholesome family values from television westerns.

Showering With a Fat Girl

Ya ever take a shower with a fat girl? I think I did but let me tell ya why I'm not sure. First ask yourselves these critical questions:

If you put food in your mouth and don't chew it, are you eating?

If a midget falls out of a tree in the forest and there's no one around to see it, is it still funny?

If you put your wiener in anything, and don't move it, are you having sex?

The answer to all three is no (anyway that's what a judge told me on the weiner question). In my case, I was in the shower with a fat girl but I never got wet. Why was that? Because I was standin' in the back! My baseball cap didn't even get wet! So I don't know if ya can rightfully say I ever took a shower with a fat girl. I have, however, stood really close to a wet naked fat girl while I was naked too. Here's what happened:

I was in a bar sweet-talkin' the ladies when the next thing ya know, I'm strapped to the hood of a '72 Plymouth looking at Violet

Beauregarde from *Willy Wonka and the Chocolate Factory* only a little less purple and not as shapely. The next thing ya know we were naked in the shower. I was behind her and I was freezing. Not a drop touched me. The water didn't even bounce off her; it just disappeared like a hot coal in a snowbank.

It was so cold my little nipples around my regular nipples were hard. It was obvious I had to get around her somehow and get under some of that hot water. I decided to risk life and limb and tried crawlin' through her legs.

First, I had to make room so that I could get down on my knees without getting my head stuck in her hind end. That's when I noticed there was really no opening between her legs until somewhere around her ankles. Her thighs were like a roadblock and her calves were actually in a herd. It all looked like a giant igloo with a tiny entrance, but not as shapely.

Water began filling the shower from the drain being clogged so when I began to crawl, my whole face went underwater. I got stuck halfway and started drownin'.

She bent over to pull me up but that movement only doubled her width and the glass shower door shattered. It looked like that scene from *Lethal Weapon 2* when Mel Gibson shot out the glass in that huge aquarium and the fish and lobsters came flyin' all over the floor. When she bent over, I think I saw a starfish but I don't want to talk about that right now. Once that glass broke, the waves carried me clean out of the shower. I ended up on top of the dresser in the back bedroom.

And that's the story of the night I met Ann Wilson from *Heart*.

ED NOTE: I know for a fact that there are tons of lesbians showerin' with fat woman on a constant basis. But this particular observation was meant exclusively for straight men to read so they

could see if they've ever had a similar experience. If you lesbians out there would like, I will touch on this subject later in a chapter you might enjoy entitled, "Lumber Yards, Flannel and Other Turn-ons." Also, I apologize to Ann Wilson. She's a great singer and I'm a big fan, but that was damn funny.

Motorcycles

Ya know what makes no sense to me? Seein' some guy ridin' one of those giant motorcycles pullin' a TRAILER!!

Get a fricken car, jackass! At this point, your trailer is the same thing as a set of training wheels, in case you didn't know it!

ED NOTE: And if you really want to get your ass kicked, just try pullin' up to a biker bar on a motorcycle with training wheels.

Just Sox

I was at a mall awhile back and saw a store called "Just Sox." It's gotta suck working at "Just Sox" (but still not any worse than waiting tables). First off, the whole store is the size of Jay Leno's chin so you can't even stand up to help customers.

Second, and this is the ironic thing, the girl that worked there wasn't *even wearing socks*! I started thinkin', *Hot damn, she's working at Just Sox without wearing any sox. I oughta head down to Just Bikinis!*

Ya see, I think if you're working at a store called Just Sox, damnit you oughta wear some socks. If I owned a store called Just Bikinis and went in there and all my employees were naked I'd . . .

OK, that's a bad comparison, but you get the drift.

ED NOTE: Turned out the girl actually was wearing hose. It still wasn't socks. The store sign read JUST SOX not JUST HOSE.

That's H-O-S-E, by the way. Otherwise it would have been a whole different kinda store.

Handicapped Spaces

I ran for president back in the early '90s on a great platform. I proposed allowin' hot-lookin' illegal immigrant women to dance at local strip clubs while patrons touched and groped them to earn them free green cards.

I also said we needed to get rid of crippled parking spots at bowling alleys and skating rinks. If these folks are able to bowl and skate, I think they should park and walk like the rest of us. I have a buddy with one leg that bowled a 210 the other day while I bowled a 47.

You tell me, who should get the crippled spot?

I think bowlers oughta park based on their scores: shitty bowlers up front, good bowlers head to the back. That's the only fair way.

I also hate it when ya have to use the crippled stall to drop a major stinkpickle. People see ya come outta there and give ya a look like you just kicked Melissa Etheridge in the nuts or somethin'. They give ya that "I can't believe you just pooped in the handicapped stall" look. I can't stand those people who think, *I'm better than you.* Like they've never let loose of some Egg McMuffins in a crippled toilet stall after a long car trip.

Hell, not only have I done that, but I had the courtesy to put out road flares in front of the damn stall warnin' people that they were fittin' to run into some friendly fire. Everyone has pooped in a crippled stall at least once in their lives. If ya say ya ain't, than you're a dad gum liar, liar, pants on fire!

And who cares if I used the handicapped stall anyway. It was empty. It ain't like I went in there and ripped some constipated paralyzed guy off the shitter just for giggles. If it was occupied I wouldn't have used it!

Lighten up for God's sake.

I'll tell ya why I like the crippled stalls: because they give ya lots of room to stretch your legs. Plus, if you're constipated, they have them metal rails to grip for power squeezin'.

But the main reason I like them is because they're clean. Regular public toilets always look like a van of gay guys with Down syndrome just got done havin' cock fights in them, then left an aftermath of urine and ripped-out pubic hairs everywhere. Those things are disgusting!

That's why I hate those adopt-a-highway programs. Forget adopting highways, what people oughta adopt is a toilet stall in a truck stop restroom somewhere. Most highways actually look pretty good; it's the toilets that could use a little foster care!

PlayStations

Have you noticed lately how vidcogames are getting way more sexually explicit and violent?

I really gotta buy me one of them games!

I enjoy PlayStation but the thing is so dad gum hard to play. You either have to be a Harvard graduate or a 4th grader to figure out all the games you can run on it.

When I was a kid I kept wishin' some company would invent a realistic football simulation game. Ya know, something I could play on those days when I sat around the house while my parents were out trying to sell me on the black market for 3,500 bucks.

But I could never play one of these PlayStation games. I once asked a kid how I could make my simulated quarterback pass the ball to his receiver. He said, "It's easy, just hit the 'A' button and then hit the 'B' button twice, and hit the 'A' button once again while holding the trigger down. Then hit the 'C' button and he'll throw a pass."

Good Lord, Jesus, and Joe Namath, why do they gotta make it so hard? Why don't they just make a button that says, "PASS"? These games are a waste of time anyway. Kids oughta be out spray painting pictures of vaginas on train cars like we did when I was a kid and getting some exercise, rather than spendin' all those hours with this PlayStation garbage.

ED NOTE: I actually tried spray painting vaginas on train cars, but I wasn't very good at it. My vaginas always ended up looking like Venus Fly Traps wearing toupees.

Is that funny? I can't tell anymore.

Centerfolds

I've always wanted a forum to write about women that pose for centerfolds and now I got it. I think it's ridiculous when you hear some famous Hollywood retard announce that she only agreed to pose for the nude photo spread because the magazine guaranteed it was gonna be tastefully done.

Gimme a break. Like this girl's parents are gonna see it and say, "Hey there's a picture of our little girl spread-eagled on a floor mat with her tits squeezed together. And it's right next to an ad for a penis enlarger. We're so damn proud! At least she did it tastefully so the folks at church won't be too upset about it."

Enough of this artsy fartsy "I did it tastefully" crap. Show me a nudie magazine with tastefully done pictures, I'll show you a nudie magazine that's bankrupt.

ED NOTE: The *National Geographic* doesn't count. I understand that those women are topless but it's not a turn-on and here's the difference: whip cream rollin' down a boob is sexy; flies crawlin' 'round a boob is not.

By the way, I ordered one of those penis enlargers and it was a ripoff. They sent me a magnifying glass and some black paint.

OK, I've finally finished this part of the book. I could go on with tons more of these observations on all kinds of stuff. Unfortunately, my fingers are starting to carpel tunnel like they belonged to a 17-year-old looking at tastefully done spread-eagle pictures in *OUI Magazine*.

I hope ya enjoyed this chapter. If you're reading this as a school project, then ask your teacher if you and your classmates can have a discussion group on whether the line "My vaginas always ended up looking like Venus Fly Traps wearing toupees" is funny or not. I still can't decide.

Anyway, if you're politically correct and nothing in this book has offended you yet, God bless ya for having a sense of humor. However, if you were figurin' to be pissed at something and still aren't, I think the next chapter'll more than live up to your expectations.

Chapter 13

POLITICAL RAMBLINGS

POLITICS! Though I can't always spell it, I think it's an area where I'm pretty knowledgeable (not sure I can spell that word, either).

Here's the situation. When I started in stand-up, I developed my following while doing social commentaries that were heard on 27 radio stations across America. That probably doesn't sound like many, but when ya have to call each one of them almost every day from 6 to 11, it's a ton.

I approached major issues with no holds barred. I said what I felt without apology. I mean, if ya can't speak your mind in a free country then what good is livin' here? Ya don't find many people expressin' how they feel anymore, because America has developed this "Be careful about what you say" climate. We basically have rules against anyone holding an opinion—no matter what the subject—that doesn't conform to the political correctness that binds us like a cheese wheel at a Packers' game.

Because of that mentality, nothing ever gets done and problems never get solved. Our leaders are too scared to really address important issues for fear of—here we go—offending anyone. It really blows.

I believe I'm pretty much as regular a guy as anybody. Yes, I've finally achieved some success in my field but it doesn't change the way I was raised or the way I think. I grew up in a small town, raised pigs, went to church on Sundays, and tried to feel the girls' tits as they ran by the ice cream joint after the football games on Saturday nights. People who visit my website send me e-mails telling me they love my political rants. I thought it was hilarious when I saw them posted on political chat boards.

You didn't have to read this far to figure out I'm a George Bush fan. I don't think he's perfect and he's pissin' me off with not doing anything about our borders. He has all this homeland security crap in place to monitor illegal activity and then he leaves the borders unguarded. That's like wipin' before ya poop—doesn't make any sense. He's still way better than the alternative but for God's sake I hope he shakes the retard phase he's going through! For the most part, I think he inherited a shit pile of problems and has done pretty good. However every now and then lately when he gives a speech I keep thinkin' the *Hee Haw* fence is gonna slap him in the ass!

In this chapter, I want to list a few things that really piss me off politically. Hopefully you'll read them and find a little ammunition to fight off the tree huggers, the tofu-fartin' fairies, the commie environmentalists, and any other politically correct thought and speech control retards you may encounter. Then you'll fall asleep with visions of John Wayne, Ronald Reagan, and the cast of *Smokey and the Bandit* dancing in your heads.

I think I'm gonna cry.

OK, here we go. Now remember I'm a comedian and these are just my opinions. But the great thing about America is we're free to have them. That being said, it still doesn't mean I won't make some good points.

The good news is I'm not pretending to be a political master-mind and use my celebrity to act like I'm smarter than everybody

else like some other dumb asses in Hollywood that take themselves way too seriously. That's crazy, ain't it? Here ya have guys
like Sean Penn who has acted his whole life (and he's great by the
way), but because he has fame and power, all of a sudden he
becomes an expert on foreign policy! I don't get it.

Look, I don't mind him speaking his mind. More power to him.
But he's no foreign policy expert, so he needs to shut up and go sign
some head shots. Unfortunately, the world is full of sheep and they
feed Penn's "I'm smarter than you attitude" by actually thinkin'
this dude knows what he's talkin' about just because he's an actor.

Arnold Schwarzenegger may not be the best person for the job
in California but at least he had the balls to actually run for an
office. He was like Ronald Reagan, puttin' his money where his
mouth is instead of hiding behind the protection of the liberal
Hollywood blowhards.

Give the Terminator a break. When he took office, California
was in worse shape than Liza Minnelli. I know he's better than the
last governor they had. You coulda dressed a turd up in a hat and
tie and had a better governor than that guy. I can't say whether
Arnold's a good governor. I don't live in his state. However I do
know him as the Terminator, so deep down inside my gut I hope
he's gonna show up at some P.E.T.A. meeting and start beatin' the
hell out of everybody, like he does in his movies.

I must admit, though, that when he talks, I don't always hear his
point because I'm laughin' too fricken hard!

Global Warming Advocates

These folks really need help. They actually believe that we can kill
the ozone layer that's been around since the beginning of time
and that we're all gonna burn to death because of it.

Yeah right! And Lisa Marie Presley is gonna get naked and rub my back while I eat a pizza and get a nut rub from Barbara Mandrell!

For every scientist that says global warming is a fact, just as many say it's hogwash! Of course you never hear from the doubters because the politically correct, environmentalist friendly media write them off as loony tunes. Besides, the more things that scare people into environmental submission the better. Global warming is big business in this country. There's a lot of executives with environmental safety companies who are driving new cars and getting big houses because of this so-called global warming BS!

I remember when Mount St. Helens erupted and blew out more toxic gas than Michael Moore after two enchiritos. I mean it was bad. Scientists said that a volcano puts more toxins into the atmosphere in one day than we humans could produce in hundreds and thousands of years. Yet they think Lydia drivin' her kids to school in an S.U.V. is ruining the ozone.

Every year since I was born in 1963 the news media has covered some terrible blizzard. I mean every winter it snows so bad somewhere in this county that Santa Claus cries uncle!!

Then in the summer, there's always some place in the country that is hotter than hell. I mean, the kinda heat that makes your nuts stick to the side of your leg.

Every summer there's old people dying from the heat. I myself almost died last summer. The heat didn't get to me, but all the shitty shows on UPN's summer lineup had me gasping for air. Environmentalists call it global warming. Not UPN, they call that a crappy network. They call the excessive heat and cold the symptoms of global warming.

I call it summer and fricken winter and it happens every damn year!

I mean, are these people insane? It's cold because it's winter, it's hot because it's summer! My buddy called me last summer, really concerned because it was 127 degrees that day. He was jumping on the global warming bandwagon. I told him the temperature sounded pretty normal since he had just moved to Phoenix and it was JULY!!!!

One mornin', I was leaving church after asking the preacher whether the new blonde pianist put out. There was this lady, a member of some save the planet group, talking about global warming on the front steps. She said she was a Christian but, I got to tell ya, you can't be a Christian and believe in global warming. Sorry, you politically correct Church-going enviromentalqueers! I believe God put a rainbow in the sky as a promise that he would never flood the world again.

Now that ain't no fairy tale and it shoots down the global warming crap right there. If global warming is true, then the polar ice caps would melt, flooding everything and everybody. I'm looking out the window right now and I don't see no one buildin' an ark. So that just ain't gonna happen. That is if ya believe the bible and, by God, I do.

So kiss my big truck-driving ass!

ED NOTE: By the way, true story: the global warming conference two years ago was canceled because of a snowstorm!

Evolution

Oh boy here's a humdinger: evolution. The theory (and I repeat *theory*) that we all come from monkeys. If that's how humans got here, don't ya think we'd still see some sort of movement on that theory at the zoo somewhere. I mean, for God's sake, you'd think we'd see one or two chimps or orangatuns eventually assume some sort of human features. What happened? We evolved but these are just some special retarded monkeys that just can't handle progress! Gimme a break. It's been God knows how many years since we became humans. Did evolution just all of a sudden take a holiday?

ED NOTE: Anyone that has really studied the theory of evolution knows that Darwin never said we actually came from monkeys. That's BS. According to him, we went one direction and monkeys went another. Of course, it's more complicated than that. But since I'm more into fart jokes and titty stories, this is basically just the Cliff Notes version of evolution.

However, some people actually think evolution means we came from monkeys. These are probably the same folks that think Sean Penn is a foreign policy genius.

Now I'm not trying to show off my knowledge of crap like this. I actually avoid these conversations because evolution is not only BS, it's kinda boring. I did, however, write a college paper on this topic, so I do know a little about it. Also my wife is really smart and helped me out with the Darwin stuff.

By the way, in college I also learned how to make a beer bong out of an old trumpet, but that's really not applicable here.

Public Schools

I have no problem with public schools except that the people in charge are anti-God commies teaching a bunch of crap while molding young kids into politically correct robots that have no independent thought.

Other than that, party on!

I went to public school for the first 10 years of my life and I learned a lot. Mainly about multiculturalism and how all of my forefathers were criminals, womanizers, rapists, slave owners, and murderers. Some heritage, huh! It's a wonder I just didn't shoot myself in the head after the 9th grade.

The teacher said my great-great-great-great-grandpa was an asshole without even meetin' the guy. It wasn't until my parents put me in a private school that I realized that schools actually taught math, science, and history. Wow! Real learnin' stuff (notice how I left out spelling and grammar). The teachers there even said nice things about Thomas Jefferson. In public school, he was screwin' the help!

I notice that the older I get, I'm glad that I read books on my own. People often look amazed when they hear that. Their eyes pop out and they say, "You mean you actually *read* books?"

Yes I did, by God! I go in and out of the book-readin' phases. In between *Hustler* and *Letters to Penthouse,* I manage to squeeze in some real learnin'! But when you read things on your own and develop an independent thought process, you discover how actual historical events are being rewritten to appease the politically correct minority. It's unbelievable! You can't change history because you don't like it. History is history!

It's like when some women's rights groups wanted Disney to redesign the ride "The Pirates of the Caribbean." They thought it set a bad example for kids to have the pirates chasing after the women in the town.

Hey, they weren't called "The Altar Boys of the Caribbean." They were pirates, which meant they looted and tried to hump anything with a hole and a heartbeat. Leave it alone. I'm pretty sure none of those kids tried to steal a pig or screw their neighbor's mom when they came back home from vacation (I actually did that when I came home from a trip but I was 24 at the time).

People want to change history because they're afraid the truth might offend or hurt someone. So every few years they rewrite the history books. Depending on how PC this country gets, the next thing ya know we'll have teachers tellin' 4th graders that Abe Lincoln was bangin' transvestites and sodomizing crippled kids! You think I'm kidding? It's just too bad that our great forefathers aren't here to defend themselves from propaganda like this.

I remember when they started giving Columbus a hard time after some historian wrote that he was worse than Charles Manson. Despite all the good things that have been written about Columbus, the PC crowd automatically jumped on the anti-Columbus bandwagon. All because this one guy's research indicated he was an asshole, and then he wrote a bad book about him. Like I'm gonna buy this researcher's conclusions!

Most of all the early American History books written about Columbus praise the guy. Now all of a sudden, they are all wrong and only Jimmy from Grand Rapids knows the truth. If you stood 25 people in a line and whispered "Johnny kissed Sally" into the first person's ear, and he whispered into the next person's ear, and you repeated this same process all the way down, the last person in line would repeat the phrase as, "Donnie missed pissing on Sally on weekends."

The point is, who knows where this dumbass got his Columbus information from? Was it from the book the first guy in line wrote about Columbus, based on firsthand sources, or was it based on what the last guy in line wrote in his book off fuzzy information?

The point is this: my nuts itch!

No, really, here's my point: political correctness often changes history so that it doesn't offend anyone. And that distorts the truth, which can be hurtful at times. Just remember that the next time ya read commie propaganda about what a bunch of assholes our forefathers were.

ED NOTE: I have never peed on a girl. Not even on a weekend!

GOD

Oh boy here's a topic ya can't talk about in any sort of government forum anymore. That is, of course, until some tragedy occurs. Then ya got people prayin' to God on the capitol steps like they were the cast of *Queer Eye for the Straight Guy* after a blood test. For some reason, Washington, D.C., has a major bug up its ass about our creator. I say our creator because, as I said earlier, I have yet to see a monkey driving down the interstate with human features.

Our forefathers only mentioned God . . . oh gee . . . let's see . . . I guess . . . they only mentioned God in only ABOUT EVERY OTHER SENTENCE! If you actually read about George Washington or Abe Lincoln, you'da thought Billy Graham wrote their bios. These dudes made more references to "God" and "our Savior" than the Wu-Tang Clan after they won an MTV award.

Now you can't deny the majority of our constitutional framers were very Christian and very bad wig wearers. People can deny that until Alabama has another farewell tour, but facts are facts. I know the politically correct crowd doesn't approve of this, but who cares? In the words of the new pope, "f###'em and feed 'em beans"!

I have no idea if this is an actual pope quote, but, like Billy Graham, he mighta said it.

The whole God problem stems from one little phrase our framers wrote: "Look at the ass on that little redhead."

Oh sorry, that's actually a phrase I heard from a window framer down at Hooters.

The framers of our constitution wrote about the "separation of church and state!" BINGO! That's the phrase that's allowing libs and atheists and the ACLU to remove the Ten Commandments from the courthouse quicker than a redneck juror telling a Dirty Johnny joke. This little phrase is causing more problems than rap music in suburbia.

But when you really read the phrase and understand what the framers intended, "separation of church and state" doesn't mean "take God outta government." It means the government is supposed to let people have the freedom to worship as they wish without fear of persecution. If the framers believed that the government shouldn't discuss God or his existence, they wouldn't have mentioned him in almost every sentence they ever wrote.

You can cry about it till Wang Chung reforms, but this country was founded on Judeo Christian principles and you can't change that.

It pisses me off that atheists and other libs want the Ten Commandments removed from everything. Like there's not more important things for these bored, pathetic whiners to attack? The Ten Commandments don't hurt anyone. It's not like you walk by 'em and a hand pops out to rack your nuts or grab your wife's tits or somethin' like that. As a matter of fact every time someone wants a display removed, I didn't even know it was there until they started bitchin' about it.

And what's wrong with the Ten Commandments? At least it teaches good things. God forbid we display something in public that's uplifting. The main point of these ACLU penis lickers is that it's offensive to other religions.

Here we go again with that PC sensitivity crap. If a Ten Commandments monument in front of a government building is so offensive, how come in 125 years of it sittin' out there, y'all's the first people that have complained about it? Nobody gave a rat's ass about this issue until the birth of political correctness. Now all of a sudden Christian monuments are as dangerous as Chinese drivers.

I got an idea; maybe it's just offensive to uptight, trouble-makin' liberal assholes that live pathetic empty lives and have nothin' better to do but bitch about something that's been sitting on a lawn for 125 years! But then again maybe a man and woman walked by it and a hand reached out to rack his nuts and grab her tits!

I understand the point the government makes about religious symbols. I know they wanna respect all faiths in order to keep public property from being overrun with every religious symbol known to man. Being of the Christian faith, I would hate to go to court for a drunk-and-disorderly and have to walk through a passion play, pictures of Allah, a copper Buddha, a sacred cow, a menorah, and some dude stabbing a goat before I saw the judge. I can sort of understand why in today's sensitive political climate, they're banning all religious symbols from public property. I don't agree with it but I understand the dilemma.

However, with that said, it seems to be open season on the Christian religion, while it's hands off for other practices. Case in point: the other day I was scanning the personal ads in the newspaper, looking for bisexual twin sisters. I came across a story about a woman who lost her job for attending a Baptist church youth function. She had asked her boss for permission to leave early so she could get to the function on time. He refused, she left early anyway and he fired her.

Now let's switch to another article where a business not only had to build an extra room for Muslim employees, but also had to let them take six breaks every day so they could go bow before

Allah in that room. How come these sonsa-bitches get special treatment while the Christian chick gets canned? Good thing she didn't ask for a prayer closet or they probably would have arrested her. I didn't see the ACLU helpin' out this girl, but they sure as hell were first in line to assist the Muslims. And it's certain members of that religion that's tryin' to kill everybody!

It's that kinda crap that pisses me off. I mean if we're gonna do this "treat all religions the same" crap, then let's poop or get off the pot. I could give you tons of examples like this.

Let's look at holidays. People that believe in Jesus got like what, two holidays. Easter and Christmas. Okay, three if ya count the Daytona 500. That's it! And the PC crowd is even tryin' to screw them up. It's ridiculous! Ya can't even say the name "Christ" in connection with Christmas anymore because apparently mentionin' "Christ" offends some people.

You believe that? That's like celebrating Abraham Lincoln's birthday without being able to say Abraham OR Lincoln!

The politically correct crowd argues that saying "Christ" during Christmas excludes kids that don't believe in Jesus. Well, no shit Sherlock, Christmas is a Christian holiday! That's who it's for, people that celebrate the birth of Christ! What's so hard about this equation? Did everybody get whacked in the head with a retard stick?

If other people wanna celebrate their God's birthday I couldn't care less. God bless ya! Live it up! It ain't gonna bother me. If anything, it'll give me another long weekend! But quit bitchin' and let me celebrate the birth of my Lord! Fair is fair.

ED NOTE: I have a friend that's never been very religious. However I think he's starting to come around. Last night he watched an Amy Grant video and got a boner.

Iraqi Prisoners

Here's a topic that makes me wish members of our American news media would all die of some sort of serious ass cancer. Here ya have a bunch of terrorists that have been captured tryin' to kill not only our soldiers, but also women and children with bombs, and our media is pissed because these prisoners are being mistreated.

What are we supposed to do, powder their nuts and take 'em to the carnival for funnel cakes? They're killers!

Why don't these assholes from the *New York Times* ask the relative of some guy that just had his head cut off on videotape if those terrorists are bein' mistreated? Most people in this country wouldn't mind seein' those prisoners get hammer whacked every two minutes just for entertainment purposes! Here's a bunch of extreme Muslims that got caught tryin' to kill people and the *New York Times* wants to make sure they have rooms at the Hyatt.

I remember when they showed pictures of all those Iraqis in a big naked pyramid pile lookin' like an Elton John after-party. Everyone in the PC crowd was up in arms. "How can we be so cruel?" they wanted to know. Meanwhile, most of the country was laughin' at it like it was a sketch from Comedy Central.

My favorites are all these lib senators that came on TV and said, "George Bush is spitting in the face of the Geneva Convention." I flunked history twice, but even I know that the Geneva Convention doesn't pertain to terrorists that hide behind women and little girls to detonate bombs! Ya want to see these senators get outraged. Force all them terrorists to sit through Greta Van Susteren on Fox News for an hour. Now that's inhumane!

My favorite loudmouth against the war is that human beer keg Ted Kennedy. This guy hasn't taken a piss in the last 25 years that wasn't flammable. I can't believe people still take this liberal can of lager seriously. Here's a guy that drowned a woman and he's gonna tell us right from wrong. When he dies and goes to hell, I wonder who Satan's gonna sodomize first, him or O.J.

I never understood these anti-war people. I also never understood why Ally Sheedy never became as big a star as I thought she would, but that's for another chapter. I hate war as much as anyone. I even hate it more than guacamole. I wish we lived in a world where dogs could lie with cats, and sheep with lions, and strippers with strippers (I actually know for a fact that the "stripper lyin' with stripper" thing can happen for 600 bucks).*

The problem with the peace process is that there's always someone that wants to rule the world, just as there's always someone that wants what you have. Sometimes you need to defend yourself or your property from scumbags. The scumbags in this case are extreme Muslims!

Now Ted Kennedy and all his friends may think that a terrorist who just butchered a family of five is worthy of three meals a day and a free weekend at the Bellagio in Vegas. But the majority of Americans—at least those who haven't drowned any women in rivers—couldn't care less if the terrorists' guards played "Wipe Out" on their exposed testicles while usin' road flares as drumsticks. They're terrorists, for God's sake, not Santa's Helpers!

Two years ago, I was washing my car when these two bisexual sisters came over wearing nothing but little red . . . oh, sorry, this is for a thing I'm writing in the *Penthouse Forum*.

Let's see, now, where was I . . . Oh ya, Iraqi Prisoners!

I remember seeing those pictures of that female soldier standing next to those captured terrorists who were all tied up naked and piled on top of one another. She had her thumb pointin' up like she had just shot a trophy buck.

*average Vegas price

Now that's the kinda stuff that should replace Mary Worth in the comics. It was hysterical. It was the kind of uplifting thing that we here at home needed to see. All we kept hearing was how the terrorists had the upper hand, and that our soldiers were hating every minute they had to spend in Iraq.

And the media kept complaining that these terrorists were so hard to find. Then we get pictures showin' terrorists posed in a naked round bale next to a smiling soldier who's smokin' a cigarette and havin' the time of her life! It was nice to see. Some friends and I actually went to Denny's and had a "moons over mihammy" in celebration of it.

Then along comes the liberal press and everyone else in their PC glory, jumping on the "We're mistreating the prisoners and violating the Geneva Convention" bandwagon. They were so pissed off at this girl, you would have thought she'd just cut off someone's head on TV!

Then again, if she had done that, she probably wouldn't have generated the same level of outrage. I've never seen the *New York Times* so pissed! You'da thought someone had accused them of false reporting. They were like, "How can this be happening?"

Reporters could ask questions like that because they weren't gettin' shot at 24 hours a day by scumbag Muslim terrorists and didn't have to watch friends die right next to them. So it's hard for them to understand why anyone would want to screw with prisoners just for the hell of it. Forgive this girl for not having compassion for a group of people that want her dead. What an asshole she is, huh? You'd think she'd want to discuss theology and eat strawberry shortcake with 'em instead.

Let's get real. So she stripped terrorists naked and made 'em dry hump each other. Who cares! I say give the girl a medal. At least she didn't cut their heads off like another group of people we all know and love.

ED NOTE: I really believe our military knows what they're doing. If they want to humiliate terrorists by strippin' 'em naked then, by God, get them britches off! The media should leave Iraq so the folks in the military can do their jobs. It's just so much easier for us to shoot into a crowd of people hiding Muslim snipers when there isn't some CNN asshole around tryin' to catch it on tape to show to kids in Berkeley.

Narrow-Mindedness

OK, enough of the war stuff. Here's a phrase that left wingers and the politically correct crowd love to pull out like a knife, "narrow-mindedness." Know when you've won an argument with somebody? When they run out of actual factual information and pull out "well, you're just narrow-minded." I've also noticed that whenever you disagree with a certain activity, no matter how offensive, the people doing it are never wrong. It's just that you're being a narrow-minded jackass.

Need an example? Let's eavesdrop on this bit of dialogue:

Jim: "You mean to tell me you never blew a goat behind a Tilt-A-Whirl at a county fair?"
Jerry: "Uh, no I sure haven't. I really don't think it's right."
Jim: "I knew it! You're just a narrow-minded right-wing asshole."

ED NOTE: I admit that's not your typical conversation between two normal people. However it is quite common among carnies, and I once heard a similar conversation at a Kentucky Headhunters concert.

I don't want to leave this subject without giving you one more example. One afternoon, a buddy was watching some rap video on MTV. I walked in and said, "Oh man I hate that crap!"

He said, "You're just narrow-minded."

"No I'm not. I just hate rap. I have watched rap, I have even enjoyed the videos that show chicks half naked with asses the size of Miatas. However I have come to the conclusion that I hate the music."

Now that's not narrow-mindedness. It's called forming an opinion! What? Ya can't form an opinion anymore without catching flack for it. That's the great thing about this country; you have the right to your own opinions.

Gun Control

Here's my favorite gun story: I was listening to some radio show last summer while eating a Heath bar with my pants off and fanning my balls with a *TV Guide,* after jogging for an hour with no underwear on, and they said that during some interview, Sharon Stone announced that guns are bad, so she's getting rid of hers.

The next day her house got robbed.

Brilliant! Not only did she get rid of her gun, she announced it on TV so every felon in the country knew about it. This woman's an idiot. I love how everyone says, "But she's such a wonderful actress" (well not everybody, just my sister'n law). I never even heard of her until she flashed us all a beaver shot in the movie theater. One thing's for sure, though, the next time she gets rid of her home protection, I bet she keeps it to herself.

I also find it retarded that some people think they should sue the gun manufacturer if somebody uses a gun in a crime. Like it's the manufacturer's fault that DeWayne needed crack cash and knocked off a 7-Eleven. If that's the case, then I'm gonna sue Snackwell cookies for making my stomach big—I thought they said "fat free."

All this campaignin' against guns makes no sense. A gun is a tool like anything else. If I shoot myself in the foot, it ain't the gun's fault. I'm the jackass. Just like if I misspell words, I can't blame it on the pencil!

A gun is a good tool when used by good people, and in the case of this country more people use them properly than don't. Look it up, its true. And while you're researching those facts on the Internet, check out the website that shows people pooping on each other. (Better yet, don't.)

You're gonna find that there's way more positive stories about guns but the anti-gunners don't want anyone to see those. We never hear about the thousands of cases a day where Grandma cocks a shotgun and scares away burglars. But we always hear about dumbshit Shawn shooting his drunk buddy over 10 bucks.

There were two other issues that have inspired heated debate in this country. One was the argument over trigger locks. The other was, did Britney Spears buy herself some fake tits?

Let's deal with the big one first: yes on the Britney thing.

The debate over trigger locks was far less heated, though almost as important. One night some news show had on this guy who was supposed to demonstrate how easy it was to attach and detach a trigger lock. He couldn't figure it out! Talk about backfiring. That was funnier than watching fat women do Tae Bo back in early 2000.

I love how we always make gun laws that hamper only law-abiding gun owners. Criminals are all for trigger locks, especially after watching that anti-gun retard struggle tryin' to figure out how to take off the lock on national TV. Not one of the anti-gun faction's better moments. If they really wanted to get our attention, they should have Sharon Stone demonstrate trigger locks while giving us beaver shots.

I'd watch that just for the acting.

ED NOTE: Just some food for thought. Did you know that the worst dictators in the history of the world all rose to power with the same agenda:

1. Disarm the public;
2. Re-educate the youth; and
3. Get meet-and-greet tickets to a Led Zeppelin concert.

Art

Not museum art, my neighbor Art. People hate that dude for some reason.

But enough about him, let's talk museum art. Or the stuff they call art nowadays. I'll never understand it. Last year, some New York museum had (and may still have at the time this book, or whatever ya wanna call it, comes out) a picture of the Virgin Mary sitting in a jar of urine hangin' on its walls. They called that art. I got a picture of Hillary Clinton smeared with dog crap. I oughta sell it to the same museum.

Shoot, come to think of it I could crap on pictures of all sorts of lib democrats, I'd have a whole damn catalog of portraits.

Whatever happened to real art? Like pictures of meadows, valleys, mountain scenes and four chicks bent over a wagon wearin' thongs and chaps! Nowadays you could put hog nuts on a plate, spray it with no-stink spray, glaze it, and call it art. Rich people love that garbage. What is it about getting rich that turns your brain into cheese grits? I'd love to hear a conversation at the museum between two different classes of people looking at so-called art:

Rich Uppity Dude: "You know when I look at that picture of the Virgin Mary sitting in a jar of urine I think of a man's relationship to a greater being and the struggles of a world oppressed by antagonisms of a cornucopia of dreams and thoughts."

Regular Middle-Class Dude: "I see a sick son-of-a-bitch that pissed on the Virgin Mary in an old mason jar and he needs serious help."

It's really incredible that people call this stuff art. And they call me uncultured? Here I head over to the flea market and get a velvet picture of dogs playin' poker and throwin' darts, and I'm called an uncultured idiot. Meanwhile some dude defecates on the Virgin Mother, and he's called a genius! Go figure. If pissin' on religious symbols and smearing poop on 'em is being cultured, then chalk me up in the backassed-and-proud-of-it column!

The Death Penalty

I was talkin' to some guy about the death penalty over a couple of beers one day and he asked, "Would you really like to be the guy that had the responsibility of pulling the lever and being responsible for ending a human life?"

I was like, "What's it pay?"

I'm sure if one of these anti-death penalty folks had a son or daughter picked up, killed, and then cut into little pieces, the death penalty might be on their Christmas list. I just read where this country spends almost 300 thousand dollars a year for cable television in prisons. Holy DirecTV! Why don't they just steal it like everybody else?

Jane Fonda

Did you know that some theaters still won't play any Jane Fonda movies because of her anti–Vietnam War stance during the '60s? That's awesome! Now if we could just get Ben Affleck to say something negative about the war in Iraq, it would be safe to head back to the movies.

Illegal Immigration

It really ticks me off that George W. hasn't done anything about the Mexican border. We're all gung ho in this country on keeping an eye out for illegal activity yet here we got Mexicans pourin' over the border like Stetson just announced they was givin' out free hats to anyone named Rodriquez. I don't get it. I'm glad you people come to this country because your country's a piece of shit, God bless ya, but do it legal.

For some reason, the thought police call you a bigot if you say, "Illegals should get the hell out of America." I don't get it. They're fricken ILLEGALS! WHICH MEANS WHAT THEY'RE DOIN' IS AGAINST THE LAW! Hell, even legal immigrants get pissed off at illegal ones.

W. pissed me off a while back when these concerned citizens from Arizona decided to patrol the borders themselves. Bush, who's supposed to be so concerned with our safety, labeled 'em vigilantes and told 'em to stop.

So let's see, one minute he says "be vigilant and on the lookout" and then when we are vigilant and on the lookout, he calls us vigilantes! Make up your mind, for God's sake! All I know is somebody needs to do somethin' about that border before Hadji and Abdul sneak over in a donkey suits and blow up a strip mall.

The U.N.

Is there anything in this world you can think of that's more useless than the United Nations? Other than Ted Kennedy what could be more unnecessary than these sumbitches? We fund most of the organization, let them live here and give them diplomatic immunity. Basically all that means is they're allowed to park where they want, fondle tits, grab asses in clubs, cuss out valet parkers, and get away with it.

They're kinda like Colin Farrell with fewer screen credits.

Name one thing these U.N. diplomats do that we couldn't do without. Absolutely nothing. Sure they help get food to the hungry. Big deal, so do we. But they're not much good for anything else.

OK, I take that back. Every now and then, when a country gets a little threatening, they'll dictate a nasty letter that goes kinda like this:

DEAR OUT OF LINE COUNTRY:

How are you? We at the U.N. think you are bad and though we can't stop you from being bad, we will keep sending you these letters telling you to stop. If you don't listen to us then . . . well . . . you just should stop and be nice. We're warning you. If you continue to kill and threaten people, we will not invite you to that big dinner Donald Trump is hosting next week. If you do not respond to this, we'll . . . we'll . . . we'll send you another letter. We might even take away your parking pass to the Knicks and revoke your ass and titty grab privileges for one whole week.

We mean it. Let this serve as a warning.

Government Grants

I don't mind payin' taxes, but when ya learn the money's goin' for grants so people can find out whether cow farts are hurting the ozone, then I got a problem.

I just read where the government actually gave seven million of our tax dollars to some people so they could find out whether the food at Taco Bell was good for us.

Of course the food at Taco Bell ain't good for us. It's Taco Bell! That's why we go there.

After all this money was spent, and all the surveys finished, know what the study found? The food at Taco Bell may cause cancer. Talk about seven million bucks spent for nothing. Everything causes cancer!

I did my own survey on this and you wanna know what Taco Bell food really causes? It causes people to fart for 30 minutes while they lay on the floor with their pants unsnapped and their feet up on a coffee table. That's what Taco Bell causes and that's a fact, there's no maybe to it.

Know how much that survey cost me? 4 dollars and 23 cents! Just another example of how much money the private sector can save us!

India vs. Pakistan

Remember a while back when India and Pakistan were threatening to use nuclear weapons on each other over Kashmir. It reminded me of the time my buddy Gerald got into a fight and threatened to kill his lesbian neighbor over a box of flannel.

BAM!!!

Get it? Kashmir, flannel . . . nevermind.

Anyway that kinda scared me a little bit, Pakistan and India with nuclear weapons. These folks can't even count out correct change down at the convenience store, now they're gonna screw with nuclear weapons! God help us all.

Remember the Alamo

This was the dumbest thing I've heard since C.M.T. got rid of the Grand Ole Opry. A newspaper story said the Texas school system was thinking about banning the phrase "Remember the Alamo" because they thought that it was offensive to Mexican children.

Are you kiddin' me? Didn't Mexico win that battle? You'd think they'd wanna yell "Remember the Alamo" all day long. An offensive phrase would be "Remember the ass kickin' the Mexicans got after the Alamo!" The Alamo, I think, is the only thing Mexico has won since they kicked Colombia's ass in World Cup soccer many years ago.

Changes Since 9/11

I remember about a year after 9/11, I was using this newspaper article to wipe my ass after eating some bad deer meat during a hunting trip. It asked how America had changed since 9/11. I really think we've changed for the worse. All we've done is lose more of our freedoms because of terrorist threats.

Let me offer an example. A friend who works for the post office just informed me that it's against the law to poop in a FedEx box and overnight it to my other friend Marty as a gag birthday gift.

Now before 9/11 this would have been awesome, but terrorism has really taken the imagination and cleverness out of gift giving.

I'll tell you what else has changed since 9/11. Americans are being treated like criminals in our own damn airports. Our government is always sayin', "The terrorists aren't gonna win." But the next day I'm naked at some terminal with a rubber glove up my ass crack and a dog sniffin' my nuts. Meanwhile three Middle Eastern terrorists between the ages of 18 and 32 board the plane untouched like they own the sumbitch!

That's right, people from terrorist-sponsoring countries in the Middle East can roam the United States free and easy because everybody's too scared to pull 'em outta line for fear of being sued for profilin'! This is ridiculous! It's just another example of how political correctness can kill a country like a cancer. Let's get back to the good ole days when a fella could poop in a FedEx box without fear of government reprisal!

ED NOTE: I once went through the security line wearing nothing but a pair of Speedos to save time; they still accused me of stealing a roll of dimes from the gift shop!! (Have I already said that? . . . I can't remember.)

The Passion of Christ

Boy, Mel Gibson sure took some heat over this movie. At first, even I was mad at Mel. I'd heard he was going to name his film *Lethal Weapon V* and feature Jesus and some black sidekick driving around in a chariot and wasting creeps. Then I found out the film was legit. Now I'm glad he did this movie and made good money for it. He deserved every cent he made for stickin' to his guns no matter what anybody said. He wanted to do a movie that showed what Jesus went through for all mankind. He did it with conviction and he made a great movie.

Remember how everyone said that the movie would bring riots and violence to the theaters? Of course, that turned out to be false. Well, I guess one lady did die in a Cineplex and some critics claimed she had a heart attack because the movie was so violent. Actually she had the heart attack right after seeing the price of Milk Duds and a large popcorn. The movie hadn't even started yet.

Then there was that moron, a so-called priest that was dissin' it. This was around the time all those priests got hammered for nailing little boys. Remember that scandal? Seemed like every ten minutes some news agency would interview some choir boy who said he was diddled 35 years earlier by Father so-and-so. I always thought that certain priests should wear shock collars!

Anyway, this priest dude was so upset over the violence in Mel's film, he gave it two thumbs down.

Actually, he gave it two thumbs in but I won't go any further.

Of course, the Jesus movie was violent, numbnuts. Jesus didn't die after getting tickled to death by feather dusters! It's not easy to portray a crucifixion in a nonviolent way. The fact is that Jesus died a horrible death. That's the way God planned it and Mel Gibson was trying to bring that to the screen.

Jesus didn't have to die that way but he did. The violence of his death showed his deep love for mankind. I mean if God had told Jesus he was gonna die in his sleep after eating a big t-bone steak and some peach cobbler, it wouldn't have made quite the same impact! I'm glad this movie was a success and I'm a bigger Mel Gibson fan for it. I can't wait for his next movie, *Moses Meets Abbott and Costello*.

Campaign Ads

I have just a brief comment on these crazy campaign adds we see every year at election time. I can't believe people actually fall for this crap. But then again, Alf has his own talk show. Both parties get so outrageous in lying to and misleading people, I don't know if it's funny or sad that we've reached such a political low point! I'll use the Kerry and Bush campaigns for my examples here, since they went head-to-head in the last election.

Announcer: "John Kerry saved 34 kids from a burning school while George Bush degutted a live hog at a camp for kids, called Santa Claus a fag, then slapped his own mother and set her on fire at an old folk's home when she asked for a drink of water!"

Do you want that in a commander-in-chief?
VOTE JOHN KERRY FOR PRESIDENT

Announcer: "George Bush is working for affordable health care while John Kerry was injecting old people with a euthanasia drug. Then he bitch-slapped a cancer victim for touching his new tie."

Do you want someone like that in the White House?
VOTE GEORGE BUSH FOR PRESIDENT

News Media

Earlier, I wrote a little bit about the news media and the war. I forgot to mention something, so I need to interject it here if you don't mind. I hate when these absolute idiots in the news industry take it on themselves to report on possible terrorist targets that remain unprotected. A while back, a CNN story on our nuclear facilities revealed exactly which ones were still vulnerable to attacks.

Why would I or any other American care to know this? It's not like we can do anything about it. It seems the only people that would find that information interesting would be . . . gee I dunno . . . maybe . . . TERRORISTS!

I mean if someone wanted to screw with a nuclear reactor, these jackasses gave 'em everything they needed to know except directions to get to the fricken place! Hello McFly! Why didn't CNN just go ahead and mail 'em badges, keys, and a map while they were at it.

These traitors need to keep their mouths shut. It ain't like Allah and Habib don't have cable! Here I have to go get my moles checked for irregularities and now I have to worry about Habib Abdul Walla Walla Bing Bang flyin' his dumb ass into a reactor! Why doesn't CNN just send a guy over to my house and kick me in the nuts every morning since they like ruinin' my day so much!

Bill Clinton

What would a book I'm writing be without me talking about Bill Clinton? I still got tons of material on him from the early '90s and I actually kinda miss the comedy he gave the world. I want to do something different here, though. I remember when he first left office, they actually thought of bringing the *Bill Clinton Show* to television. Man, I wish they would've done that series! Bubba could have been the next Arsenio. The idea got me so excited, I wrote a treatment for a pilot show and sent it to his producers. They never did get back to me but this woulda been a great opening episode:

Announcer: "Welcome, ladies and gentlemen, to the Bill Clinton Studios in Harlem, New York. It's time for the *Bill Clinton Show*. And now, here's heeeeeeres Bill!"

A standing ovation as Bill Clinton walks into the spotlight on centerstage.

Bill: "Hoo, boy was it hot today folks! Me and Monica set the hotel bed on fire just so we could run through the sprinklers!! Hoo! Hoo! Hoo! I thought doing a show would be easy, but I gotta tell ya it's harder than my wife's wiener after she watches the ladies finals at Wimbledon! Hoo! Hoo! I kid her because I love her! Hey, anyone in here bought any rubbers lately? I've got these new lambskin rubbers that come in two sizes, wooly booly and Lil bo peep! Hoo! Hoo! Anybody care for a cigar? I have one, but it tastes like salmon and needs a comb-over! Hoo! Hoo! Hoo!

"Say, let me ask you, what do ya call a thousand-pound woman at the bar with a rubber in her hand? A half-ton pickup with a box liner! Hoo! HOO! But enough of this foolishness, we got a big show tonight, folks. Jesse Jackson will be here tonight performing magic. For his first trick, Jesse will pull his head out of his ass! And then later on he'll try and tell us what he actually does for a living since it's always been a big mystery.

"Also my good friend Janet Reno will show slides of all the fire hydrants she's peed on in Washington. Then we'll have Ted Kennedy playing 'We'll Miss That Bridge When We Come to It,' after which the audience will get to play 'Name That Stain!!' We'll be right back. Hoo! Hoo! Hoo! Hoo!"

Well, that'll do it for this chapter. Tell me you didn't want to march down the street singing "God Bless America" after readin' it. And even though I got pissed and cursed a few times, I think

Ronald Reagan and John Wayne would have written the same stuff. I know these are just my opinions; I honestly try to keep an open mind with politics. But you have to admit, there's some goofy stuff going on in this country.

ED NOTE: You can't tell me that seeing Jesse Jackson pull his head out of his ass on the *Bill Clinton Show* wouldn't have been must-see TV.

Chapter 14

THAT'S FUNNY, AND I DON'T CARE WHO YA ARE

THIS CHAPTER COVERS why retards and farts are guaranteed to get big laughs. As a bonus, we'll learn how farts brought freedom to the Jews.

Make no mistake. I know society says we shouldn't laugh at certain subjects; we chuckle at 'em anyway. Don't lie, you've done it too. Everyone has laughed at stories that make other people cringe. Half the time, it's their reaction that makes the story so damned funny. For example, my buddy Ron (Tater Salad) White talks about drinking my dip cup accidentally to swallow some aspirin. I was there when it happened and laughed my ass off. Was he amused? Of course not, but since it wasn't me drinkin' week-old Skoal spit it was downright comical! Now, should I have laughed after that happened? Probably not, but hey, I wasn't the one it was happenin' to so pass the Handy Wipes!

Here's another one: I once dated a girl with elephantitis. It's the disease that makes certain body parts swell up to four times their normal size.

Of course it never affects your penis. Go figure.

Now I know it's not right to make fun of someone's disease, but let's be honest here. If some dude came up to you and your friends in a bar with a head on him the size of a heavy-duty lawn bag full of grass, tell me you wouldn't chuckle over it later in the night.

Anyway I took this girl with the elephantitis to this nice French restaurant. I don't remember the name, it may have been Fudd-ruckers. To make another long story a little longer, I was going to tell her how good she looked but I didn't want to make her head any bigger!

I could do this all day.

There are things you can say on a date that will put your friends in stitches, but they'll make your girl disappear quicker than a set of rims at a Puff Daddy concert. Once I was in Victoria's Secret hanging out with some girl I had met at music camp. At this point, I hadn't been laid in my whole life. Even though she outweighed the entire Nebraska offensive line, I'd heard she'd show her tits for a couple of Baskin-Robbins coupons.

I won't even say what she would do for lemon squares, but it was worth the purchase.

This girl was a skank. A friend told me she was so sleazy he once took her panties off out behind the church Dumpster and a crab jumped on his leg and said, "Sorry dude, I gotta come over by you because it's a damn zoo in there!"

You believe that she banged Donny the Retard? I mean I'm all for retarded kids gettin' some ass, but this kid was obviously not all there. Rumor had it that she stripped him naked and layed him down like an open-faced turkey sandwich, then sat on his head.

Since Donny was retarded, he had no clue what was about to happen to him. He just lay still there, calmly trying to play his har-monica as her fat ass approached his face like a jumbo jet fixin' to land on runway number three. She came down on Donny the Retard so hard, the harmonica knocked out two of his remaining 11 teeth. And then the instrument disappeared up her ass crack like undershorts on a sumo wrestler.

It was a sexual disaster! Retarded Donny ran off yelling something about a giant starfish trying to kill him. She ended up with a harmonica so far up her ass that every time she gets gas, she farts "Home on the Range!"

In the words of Jeff Foxworthy, if you're farting "Home on the Range" because you accidentally sat on a harmonica trying to hump Donny the Retard . . . you might be a redneck . . .

So here I am at the Victoria's Secret with not only the sleaziest girl I've ever met, but also the fattest. This girl was the first chair trumpet in the school band. Come to think of it she was also the second through fifth chair as well. Oh, let's be honest. She actually looked like the whole damned band in one clump! Around Christmas, she wore a white dress and played the part of a blizzard in our school play!

Anyway, we're browsing though Victoria's Secret and I'm tryin' my best not to laugh. But, c'mon, what the hell is she lookin' for in here, crotchless overalls?

While she tried on the front window curtain, I snuck into the back with a pair of scissors and cut out the white cotton patches from the returned panties to sell as t-bags to hot, thirsty horny fat guys. After attaining my quota, I walked to the front of the store. My date came walking by me wearing a big white robe. When she asked, "How do I look?" I said, "Like William Conrad, the fat actor who played the detective Cannon with a big ass sheet on . . . minus William Conrad."

I guess she found the humor of my quip somewhat amiss 'cause she threw me on the ground faster than the fat Dixie Chick tearing into a box of Boston cream pies. Then she laid a piledriver on me that left me lookin' like Wile E. Coyote after a cliff fall! I wound up apologizing to her even though it was funnier then hell!

ED NOTE: I do believe this is the only book you'll ever read that uses the phrase "hot, horny, fat guys." Also the girl I just wrote about eventually went into acting. I never knew this but she apparently went to an audition 16 years ago and was William Conrad's stunt double for the last 3 years of *Cannon* and for the first season of *Jake and the Fat Man*. Who'da thunk it?

Several years ago, I had just finished taping another Soloflex commercial when I ran into a former classmate named Rita. She used to be an Olympic mud wrestler and I tell you she looked just like she did when we were back in school. Ugly.

I could see Rita was upset that day. She was on her way to the gynecologist after feeling several lumps in her vagina. She thought they were uterine polyps. The doctor gave her some tests and it turned out that all she had were dirt clods!

The Lord sure does work miracles.

ED NOTE: Now uterine polyps are not funny. However when they turn out to be dirt clods, this is comedy, I don't care who ya are!

Every year in this country, ya hear about someone who thinks he or she saw the Virgin Mary appear. About two years ago, I read about this super-Catholic woman in our town that bought a dilly bar on eBay because it supposedly had a melted image of the Virgin Mary on it. She paid 5,700 bucks for the thing!

Ya read these stories all the time. The Virgin Mary appears in a hay bale or some people line up in front of a picture of her everyday at 5 o'clock and the painting starts cryin' real tears.

I've never personally seen the Virgin Mary in a hay bale or crying from a picture. However, I've seen this virgin Sherri sit on a leather couch with no panties on at my friend Brad's 4th of July party. When she stood up, it sounded like somebody had ripped a plunger off a linoleum floor!

Virgin my ass!

Question: Is it wrong to have a threesome at a wedding? Before you answer, let me tell you this story. As you may have reckoned by now, my luck with women isn't very good. The last three words of any date I go on are usually, "That's him, officer!"

But I was at a friend's wedding and two of his mom's sisters were flat out hitting on me. Now the only three-way I've ever experienced was when I used both hands simultaneously after striking out at Hooters one night. So actually having two girls in bed at the same time would count as a real treat. I let those women get me drunk. Then they threw me in the back of a van and boom!

When I went back inside the church, I was so nervous my friend would find out, I couldn't stop fidgeting. He finally said, "Hey what's wrong, ya look like you got ants in your pants!" Damn that broke me up. Little did he know that I did have "aunts" in my pants!"

ED NOTE: Kiss my ass it's funny!

If ya didn't like that one, here's another story you'll hate. I was in a bar one night drunk with a buddy. It was late and we both went home with girls. We left the bar thinkin' we had *Baywatch* beauties on our arms. Next morning, they looked more like those music-playin' aliens from the bar scene in *Star Wars*. My friend asked me whether we should wake 'em before we left. I thought about that age-old phrase and said, "No, we better just let sleeping dogs lie."

Damn, that's funny, and I don't care who ya are!

When I was workin' as a sidekick on morning shows for extra money and coupons that gave ya half off on Hooters' buffalo wings, I would usually make some remark that the stations would have to apologize for. I thought it was funny at the time. Then again, I still think the "aunts in my pants" joke is hilarious.

One time in Austin, Texas, I did a commentary about a retarded kid who was awaiting execution on death row. Because of this case, there was a big debate goin' on about whether you should apply the death penalty to retards.

I called up to explain that there were good retard seeds and bad retard seeds. This was a bad retard seed. Then I pointed out that it would be the only case recorded in history where instead of working the fry machine, a retarded kid would be getting fried.

Remember when I said earlier that some things just strike ya funny though other people may not find it funny at all? TADA! This was one of those times.

The next morning there were short buses lined up in front of the radio station like it was a summer day at the Water Park. It was like the Million Retard March down there and every one of 'em was pissed and foamin' at the mouth.

Actually only one kid was foamin' at the mouth and it wasn't that he was pissed. He had just eaten a hot pepper breakfast burrito from El Choritos.

The program director called me and said, "Larry, I'm gonna kill you because I've got 300 Corkys down here pissed off over your commentary about the retarded kid on death row. I'll call ya back."

Now I'm the one sittin' at home all pissed off because no one has a sense of humor anymore and all these people actually took me serious. I mean, c'mon for God's sake, the phrase "retard seed" is a hoot.

The program director finally resolved this by givin' about 20 retards equal time on the radio show so they could speak their peace to the good citizens of Austin. Later that afternoon, he called and said, "Remember when I was pissed after I was ambushed by the cast of *Life Goes On* in front of the station this morning? Well we're giving you a raise because having those talking retards on was by far the funniest four hours we've ever put on the radio."

Ya see, all that worry over nothing. He never should have panicked. I knew all along that if you give 20 retarded kids a morning show microphone, all ya have to do is kick back and let the magic begin. When ya watch Stern, the funniest shows are always when they do stuff with retarded people. You don't have to have a degree from the school of broadcasting to figure that out. Is it right to laugh at retarded people? Probably not. But don't tell me, that if you were in a car driving down the road and heard the show that day you wouldn't have let out at least two chuckles.

ED NOTE: I love retarded kids. There's nothing I wouldn't do for them, but I gotta tell ya, sometimes they make me laugh my ass off!

I got a big scare the other day. I found a gray hair. I really need to stop picking woman up at bingo (this has nothing to do with anything).

A while back, I was reading a book about farting called *Lean Right, Blow Left.* I don't want to brag but I do read all the classics. Fart jokes are the greatest form of laughter next to watching a retarded choir sing the national anthem at a NASCAR event.

ED NOTE: That actually happened at Talladega in 2004. NASCAR invited an all-retarded choir to sing the National Anthem and everyone was like, "You gotta be shittin' me." You could tell all the drivers were holdin' in laughs. They were red faced and their jaws were clenched like they were holding back the turd of the century.

It was by far the funniest thing I've seen since my half-retarded cousin stood in line at the first *Star Wars* premiere dressed up in his Captain Kirk outfit, screaming, "Nanu Nanu."

As I was saying, fart jokes are the backbone of this great nation. *Lean Right, Blow Left,* the controversial farting book by L. Ron Hubbard, traces the early days of the fart joke and discloses how flatulence led to the freeing of the Jews from the rule of the Pharaoh. At the Last Supper (and this is rarely taught) Disciple Thomas actually did the first pull-my-finger joke after Peter served the fish sticks. It was one of those farts that sounded like he'd crapped himself and of course the other apostles just fell out about the place.

Many people think that story is a crock. However these guys ate nothing but fish, so ya gotta believe they were droppin' bombs left and right all the time. That's why Jesus always spoke upwind.

In *Lean Right, Blow Left,* Mr. Hubbard examines accounts written on lost college-ruled stone tablets. He discovered that Moses, who was suffering from stomach cramps, was actually about to say, "Let my people go . . . to the healers to buy Beano and Mylanta." However, the Pharaoh cut him off in mid-sentence. The only reason he freed the Jews was because he didn't hear Moses's entire question. Had he just waited for Moses to finish askin' for some stomach relief, the Jews mighta never left Egypt,

Thus we have farting playin' a major role in history. If ya don't believe me, ya can look it up for yerself. It's all right there in *Lean Right, Blow Left.*

ED NOTE: Remember all those stupid commercials for that book called *Dianetics*? The way they put it, you'da thought this fricken L. Ron Hubbard had the answer to everything in its pages:

Actress 1: "How do I achieve true inner peace?"

Faceless Announcer: "It's in the book!"

Actress 1: "How can I get caught up on my bills?"

Faceless Announcer: "It's in the book."

Actress 1: "Is there an afterlife?"

Faceless Announcer: "It's in the book."

Actress 1: "Where's my car keys?"

Faceless Announcer: "It's in the book."

Actress 1 (in different clothes this time): "What's the recipe for Kentucky Fried Chicken?"

Faceless Announcer: "It's in the book!"

Actress 1 (only now wearin' a hat and sittin' next to a made-up family): "Should we go visit Grandma or just stay home and go to the park?"

Faceless Announcer: "It's in the book!"

ED NOTE PART 2: I'd like to thank my special guest Edward James Olmos for his role as the faceless announcer. I was shocked and excited to have the star of *One Day At a Time* playing my actress. Ladies and gentlemen, please help me welcome Miss Bonnie Franklin!!

Me (Larry): "So, Bonnie, how ya been?"

Bonnie: "Awesome, I just finished a Broadway show called *Whatever Happened to Bonnie Franklin?*"

Me (Larry): "And how is that going?"

Bonnie: "Actually not too good. I was replaced by Bonnie Hunt. They felt she played me better than I could, so it's now her role. You would think a play about Bonnie Franklin would star Bonnie Franklin and not Bonnie Hunt, but that's the crappy part of this business, I guess."

Me (Larry): "Do you have any plans to return to television?"

Bonnie: "I actually am working on a reality show for Fox called *Bonnie*."

Me (Larry): "And how is that shaping up?"

Bonnie: "Very well, I think. They have the roll of Bonnie widdled down to where it's between me or Shirley Jones. I think I have a better shot at the part, though, as her name is Shirley and mine is, of course, Bonnie. I figure since the show is called *Bonnie* and that it was my idea from the start, I'm very optimistic that the chances of my getting the role are about 60–40."

Me (Larry): "Did you see *Fat Actress*? Tell me that wasn't bad."

Bonnie: "I know, it was horrible."

Me (Larry): "Hey thanks for being in my book. Now before ya go, do ya mind poppin' out those old titties just for my single male readers".

Bonnie: "For you, Larry, sure. Check out these bombs!"

Me (Larry): "Nice! Those nipples are like cup saucers, wow! OK, thanks for being cool with us. Bonnie Franklin, folks! Now let's head on to the next chapter!"

Chapter 15

RELATIONSHIPS, LOVE, AND FOUR-WHEELERS

IT SURE WAS GREAT to hear from Bonnie Franklin in the last chapter, wasn't it? I'm still giddy!

OK, we're about to trudge through a section that will no doubt win several literary awards and become a feature discussion on Dr. Phil's show. If anyone knows about the art of dating it's . . . my buddy Art! But since Art's not funny, the hell with him. I've had my share of relationships and, by God, this chapter is gonna be about all two of 'em. We're gonna cover everything you need to know about dating and relationships.

I'm gonna be honest with ya at the start. This chapter has absolutely nothing to do with four-wheelers. I added them to the title so this wouldn't look too much like a chick chapter. Don't be too disappointed. Every now and then I'll throw in somethin' about muddin' and deguttin' wild hogs just to keep it on the up-and-up!

I remember the time I met this girl and thought she was the one. I mean I was in love! She was the only girl I ever made love to with my pants completely off, so you know there was an awesome connection from the start. We broke up after she told me that we should just be friends. FRIENDS! I hate when women say that.

They say it because they don't want to hurt our feelings. Trust me, it's the worst thing to say to a guy.

When a woman says to me, "Let's just be friends," it basically means we can still go out and I'll still pay for everything but I'm never getting lucky!

Where do I sign up for that gig?

Havin' a girl say, "Let's just be friends" is like your mom telling you the dog died but you can still keep it if ya want to!

Boy, with these kinda observations this chapter will have readers scratching their heads wondering how many other people with GED's receive book deals.

When I was a kid, my first love, other than using frogs as baseballs, was Kate Jackson. She was the least popular one on *Charlie's Angels*. Everyone had pictures of Farrah and Jaclyn Smith but I loved Kate. Don't get me wrong, Farrah was for sure a hottie and never a day went by when I didn't picture her bent over a cattle feeder. And Jaclyn Smith had the Target clothes collection, so she was easily a favorite.

Kate Jackson, though, was that plain Jane, all-American girl. I've always gone for plain Janes. Either them or whores. I can easily go from one extreme to another. I don't condone picking up prostitutes but if ya have to do it, always remember these words of wisdom my grandpa told me just before he died of syphilis, "Never kiss a gift whore on the mouth!"

When I was a kid, I knew women were going to be a problem in my life. I was the only kid expelled from 3rd grade because he had a *Penthouse* lunchbox! They even took the batteries out of my thermos! Back then my hormones were raging like somethin' that . . . oh, I don't know . . . uh, uh, something that really rages a lot. I never received much advice on dating or handlin' rejection.

I could have gone to my older brother for advice on women. On second thought, he probably wouldn't have been the best person to ask. I never saw him with a girl. He was always either bowling or in trouble for doing something stupid. The only dates he ever had when we were growing up were court dates. So basically I just learned as I went along.

My brother is still single and bowls every weekend. Now I don't mind bowling, but c'mon every weekend!? One time he asked me to help him name his bowling team and I was like, "How 'bout the I Can't Get Laid on Weekends Either's."

I guess most boys grew up like me. They got their sex education out of *National Geographic* or the panty section of the Sears catalog. When I was a kid it was perfectly normal for boys to lock themselves in the bathroom, turn to page 32 of *National Geographic,* and fantasize about nailing some African chick bent over a dead wildebeest. She'd be degutting' it while her boobs dangled down in front of her about 2 inches above a fire ant mound. Sure ya look at that picture now and it's pathetic. But back when you were 12, this was better than Cinemax after midnight! There was no Internet when I was growing up, so naked African natives and women wearing bras and panties in Sears qualified as a godsend. Why, in the 5th grade, a horny crippled kid once gave me 10 bucks for a *National Geographic* that had a Zulu woman on the cover breast feeding.

As I got older, the big thing was dirty books. Boy, if you could just get your hands on one of those. And a *Hustler* was a hormone-filled 15-year-old's golden ticket to Willy Wonka's! Imagine, a magazine featurin' pictures of naked women that didn't kill for their food. Wow! Somebody grab a towel!

But here was this problem with dirty books: you had to buy them at a convenience store and in most cases there was usually a grandma runnin' the register. Nothing in the world was scarier to a kid then making that long 30-second walk into a store to buy a dirty book, only to have a grandma give ya "The Look."

I'm talking 'bout that "You're a Pervert Look."

Since you don't want some old lady thinkin' you're a freak, you have to buy something ya don't need to justify enterin' the store. Then ya have to drive from store to store looking behind each register for an old man or some foreigner who doesn't speak English in order to buy what you really want.

Believe it or not, that happens even now even though I'm an adult. Just the other day me and my buddies went to buy a copy of *Barely Legal* and every register in the place had somebody's grandma running it. So instead, we ended up buyin' 34 Coors Lites, 21 bags of Beef Jerky, and 65 cans of Skoal long-cut berry blend! It was so pathetic! I can't imagine what it was like when I was a kid. But, hey, it's all part of growing up and we've all been through it, right?

OK, maybe not everybody, but I have and so has . . . well, I have.

ED NOTE: Cyberspace is so full of porn it's downright wrong. I believe they need to monitor the Net to get rid of all the scumbags. You can't even do an honest work on it anymore without some a-hole sending ya naked crap. I mean kids lookin' at dirty books is part of growin' up but the Internet is Satan in a keyboard!

Last Christmas, I wanted to send fudge to my friends, mostly because it was something unusual and I'm a cheap bastard. I went on the Internet, looking for a company to order it from. Well, here's a tip: if you ever do a search on "Internet fudge" when you're at your computer, make sure there's no kids around because you may get something totally different from what you had in mind!

Now that I'm older I look back on some of the goofy things I did to satisfy my hormonal desires and I laugh my ass off. If I had a dollar for every time I was behind the barn with a copy of *Penthouse,* spittin' Bloodhound chewin' tobacco with my friends, I'd be retired by now.

Come to think of it, I did that last week!

But, hey, when I was a kid, the breeze made me excited. Every week, I had to lock myself in the bathroom after watching Daisy Duke, for Pete's sake! Nothin' to be ashamed of. It's called hormones and it's a normal fact of life.

ED NOTE: I also locked myself in the bathroom after the Atlanta Braves won the National League Eastern Division in '91, and that, my friends, is NOT normal!

I was single for 40 years, so I've had some real dating experiences. But due to time constraints, the fact that I can't remember half the girls I've dated since I've been alive and the fact that the *O'Reilly Factor* comes on in 20 minutes, I'll just list a few of my stranger girlfriends and explain why they didn't work out. Following this chapter, I will test you on these girls. Whoever gets the most right answers will receive two tickets to that hit Broadway play, *Whatever Happened to Bonnie Franklin?* starring Bonnie Hunt. So pay close attention.

I once dated a girl with a club foot. She was nice and all, but I hated it that we could never go dancing at the country bar. However you should have seen her on the driving range. Unbelievable!

I also dated a Mormon girl but I broke up with her because I never made any progress in the sex department. Have you ever tried to get to third base with a Mormon girl? It's easier to get into Area 51!

I once had a buddy set me up with a 24-year-old virgin. Now I think chastity is a fine virtue, but, to be honest, at the time I wanted someone with experience. I kinda liked my women to be like Wal-Mart bookcases, pre-drilled! Is that wrong?

OK, enough of this, you get the drift. I did date some nice girls. I actually went out with Jimmy Cramps's sister Early. I loved Early Cramps but she was so damn moody!

ED NOTE: Let me apologize right now for the last few ridiculous paragraphs. I never dated any girls like I described here except for all but the last one.

I always hated the "Ask Me a Question" game women like to play on dates. That's the game where you can ask each other anything and you both have to answer truthfully. It's a game women play so they can get to know you better.

A few years ago, I was on a date with a girl I really liked. Puttin' my best foot forward, I wore a nice sleeveless shirt (the same one I wore to my brother's wedding) and bought the girl one of those flowers that squirted water.

I picked her up on my four-wheeler and took her to Checkers because I had a crap load of coupons good for free cheese fries that were fixin' to expire by the end of the week.

Anyway, we were getting kinda huggy and kissy when she said, "Lets play Ask Me a Question." Here we go. Even though I'd been happy with the burpin' game we'd been playing for the previous 20 minutes, I agreed to her request. This is a game that shows how men and women really think differently. For example, her questions were:

1. "If you could vacation anywhere in the world, where would it be?"
2. "What's your favorite color?"

Now in contrast, here were my questions:

1. "Do you shave yourself totally bald or do you leave a landing strip?"
2. "Do you wear panties when you're bowling?"

If you ask me, my questions—though they may sound superficial and out of line—were legitimate. That's the difference between men and women. We guys ask questions that are important in starting a relationship. Finding out in the first couple of dates whether the girl you're with likes cheese fries, bowls without panties, and has a landing strip is pertinent dating information! Finding out someone's favorite color is not.

Now I love women to death. If it wasn't for women this country'd be . . . full of queers! But here's another big difference between the two sexes: the female wins all the arguments. Always. And you know why the ladies always win the arguments? Because they have more friends that they can share stuff with than we do. So whenever ya get into an argument with your girl, you can never win.

For example, if a guy is pissed at his girlfriend, he'll get together with some buddies over a beer and some Merle Haggard tunes and eloquently explain the situation (or as eloquently as you can after 8 beers and 4 shots of Wild Turkey). He'll open the discussion with somethin' clever like, "She's a bitch!"

They'll say, "What did she do?"

"She's a bitch, that's what she did!"

BOOM! That's all they need to hear. Now I know that's hard for women to comprehend, but in Guyspeak every dude in the room understands what the angry boyfriend just said. "Bitch" by itself is worth a thousand words and it saves you from all the long details. Maybe you can't really pinpoint what made you call her that word, but it's all you need with a few beers and Merle Haggard on the jukebox.

Of course, it's not the right way to deal with the situation but sometimes a guy just gets pissed off and has to vent.

That's where women are different from us. They have lots of girlfriends, and they'll go to each and every one of 'em and explain exactly what an a-hole thing you just did. Women know what you do, don't kid yourself. They remember everything you've ever done over your whole life and they even know when you've just thought about doing somethin'.

And how do they know all this? Because women have diaries, charts, graphs, and computer printouts! They'll even hire stenographers and get mimes to act out what you did. Women can prove you're an a-hole! They all oughta be state prosecutors, they're that good. It's really not fair.

And the worst part is that somewhere, someday, when you least expect it, you're going to run into one of their girlfriends. Oh man that sucks! You may not even know this girl but, by God, she knows you. She's seen the slides and read the synopsis at the last "girl's night out" gatherin'. You'll recognize her when she gives you the famous "I heard about you, a-hole" look. Back in the day I got that look 12 to 15 times a week.

Here's another thing that bugs me. Women love those decorating shows. I really don't watch 'em. However I did remodel my brother-in-law's trailer after watching one of those home improvement shows. It was pretty nice. I put about 1,500 bucks into it and I was happy to find out last week that it just got appraised for 1,650 bucks.

But when it comes to decorating shows on TV, I gotta tell ya I'm not a fan. I did however once watch one with my girlfriend (now my wife) and I did a real dumb thing. She said, "Let's watch this show and get some decorating ideas for the bedroom." And I said "Well, I'm no decorator, but I think your feet would look good over the headboard!"

Not really the right thing to say at that particular time. Hey, I was tryin' to get laid. It was funny, but my timing was bad.

ED NOTE: Women also love that show *Queer Eye for the Straight Guy*. I've never watched an episode, but it's so popular, I just read that they have a spinoff comin' on. It's a new dating show called *Brown Eye for the Queer Guy!*

I don't care who ya are, that's gut-splittin' hilarious.

I hate home chores. Women love doing things around the house. When they start a project, they finish it. Men have projects but they all have snooze alarms on them. Your wife or girlfriend will say, "Ya gotta cut the grass!" You hit the snooze and say, "I'll get to it in a little while, right after this game."

Yeah, right after this game and the game after that and the game after that and the game after that and then after *SportsCenter* is over, you'll get it wrapped up. Maybe. By the time you actually cut the grass, she's remodeled the bedroom and painted the barn.

But women love doin' that stuff. That's why we just stick to the couch and watch TV; we don't want to get in the way of the contentment they get from household chores. My girlfriend (now my wife) kept nagging me last week to take out the garbage and I was like, "Hey, Rome wasn't built in a day." She said, "I ain't askin' ya to build Rome, I'm asking ya to take out the trash."

OK, she had a good point. But boy when they want you to do something, they don't let up. I bet she said something about the garbage 10 times in an hour. Sometimes I think that women really need to listen to those three calming words: LET IT GO!

By the way, I just bought a Grizzly 660 camo four-wheeler and put the winch on the front and then I bought my girl a Big Bear camo with the upgraded tire package. Sumbitches kick ass! We then went out muddin' and ended up shootin' and deguttin' a wild hog.

ED NOTE: That should cover the four-wheeler section of this chapter, the one I promised to throw in up front.

I've touched on just a few of the differences between the sexes in this chapter and shared a bit about growing up with women on the brain. I'm for sure no Dr. Phil in the relationship and love field. However, if I could give only one piece of advice on the subject, it would be this: don't look for "The One," just let it come to ya.

I think a lot of people have this problem. They want to be with someone so bad, they rush things and get stuck with the wrong person. That's never a good thing. I can't tell you how many people have asked me, "Pew, did you shit your pants?"

But on days when I didn't have a breakfast burrito, people would say, "Don't worry. There's someone out there for everyone. Just be patient, and when you meet 'em, you'll just know."

I never thought that was true. I always thought I'd die single, fat, and penniless from buying too much lotion. After all, I'd been alive for 39 years and never felt anything like that! Well, guess what? As soon as I hit 40, I experienced that "You'll just know" moment for myself. It's incredible! What they say is true. Right when I saw her I said, "This is the one."

I also said, "That's the best lap dance I've ever had in my life!" But that's beside the point.

The point is I had that feeling. The best part was I never looked for her. She just showed up outta nowhere. I'm telling ya it's true, when it happens you just know. And, no, she wasn't a stripper. I was kiddin' about that part, so lighten up a little bit! I actually did find the love of my life and it happened just like everyone told me it would. So hang in there if you're looking for your soul mate. Believe me, the "one" is gonna happen when you least expect it.

ED NOTE: For the record, my girl could strip if she wanted to, she's that hot! It's true she's got a deformed leg and is semi-retarded, but what an ass! And isn't that the main thing?

Now we head to my final chapter. I call it "The Last Chapter." That's the working title. As of right now, I don't know what I'm going to write about, but by the time you turn the page, I'd have thought of it.

Oh, yeah. Earlier I said that we'd have a quiz on this chapter and the winner would get tickets to *Whatever Happened to Bonnie Franklin?* on Broadway. Unfortunately, I have just been informed that it has closed. Bonnie Hunt, who was playing Bonnie Franklin, left the show to pursue other ventures. However, cross your fingers because I'm trying to get tickets to a new Broadway play called *Whatever Happened to Ben Vereen?*

It stars Bonnie Franklin.

Chapter 16

HODGEPODGE

O K, THIS BOOK IS FILLED with tremendous exaggerations, truths, half-truths, more smaller exaggerations, a few more half-truths, one three-quarter truth, twelve full-on lies, a half-dozen small fibs, four tiny exaggerations with some truth in the middle, all followed up by an embellishment of a truth and concluding with an absolute truth.

But the one thing I'm happy about in this book is that I didn't *confuse* the truth.

I originally was going to end the book after the last chapter, which is where books normally end. However I decided to add another chapter after the last chapter called "The Last Chapter After the Last Traditional Last Chapter."

ED NOTE: I've been drinking heavily.

In this untraditional last chapter. I will cover whatever topics I missed earlier. This will basically be a hodgepodge of long and short random thoughts that fit all categories. To be honest, I really didn't have to write this untraditional chapter but I always said that if I ever wrote a book, I wanted to use the words *hodge* and *podge* somewhere in it. So now, having used those two words, I must search through my notes for some hodge and some podge or else this chapter will be ridiculous. And now . . .

Have you ever eaten grits out of a fat woman's butt crack?

OK, maybe this is the wrong direction for this chapter to go in. Let me start again.

A while back I saw a story about the news agency Al Jazeera runnin' another Al Qaeda video that was being used to recruit more terrorists.

Ain't that somethin'? Even Al Jazeera plays more videos than MTV! MTV really sucks now. It's turned into a huge left wing, lib brainwashing machine for kids.

Speaking of MTV, did Jessica Simpson get her boobs at Sharper Image? If Martha Quinn was alive today she'd . . . wait, I think she is . . . nevermind.

Next question: How long have we had microwaves in this country—20, 30 years? How come every time I microwave a burrito I get third-degree burns on my lips from the first bite? Then I chip a tooth on a frozen bean with the next bite. You mean to tell me we can put a man on the moon, get laser hemorrhoid removal, and watch celebrity sex tapes on the Internet, yet we can't manufacture better microwaves! You gotta be shittin' me!

TV shows just keep getting worse. I saw where they now have a TV show about a blind detective. Now how dumb is that show? Can you just hear the hero: "Don't worry, ma'am, I'll find your son. Now where's the door?"

I don't know about you, but I'd rather watch Kirstie Alley hula-hoop for an hour.

Local newscasters really bug me when they try to act so smart. If it wasn't for the cue-cards, they'd be like Cindy Brady when she froze speechless onstage in that quiz show episode on *The Brady Bunch*. I was watching some local news show the other day while laying on my back naked and drunk over at my neighbor's house.

This smart-assed anchor man suddenly popped up on the screen and said, "Learn how to protect yourself, tonight at 11 o'clock."

What a moron! What if something happens to me at 8:30?

There's a contraceptive out now with a warning sign that says, "Not recommended for women over 200 pounds." That's crazy! Women that heavy already have contraception. It's called 200 POUNDS!!!!

I grew up in the church and I still go every Sunday. I even try to hit Wednesday prayer meetings if I can get outta Hooters on time. But the altar call has always bugged me. Now for y'all that never seen one, that's when everybody stands up towards the end of the church service and sings, "Just as I Am, Without One Plea." Meanwhile, people go up to the altar so everyone can pray with them to get saved.

I'm all for these altar calls but I'm wonderin' can we maybe speed them up a little bit? I stood there one Sunday squeezin' together my butt cheeks, tryin' to hold back a turd, and we were well into the twelfth stanza of "Just as I Am, Without One Plea."

Not one person moved. But we just kept on singin'.

Look, if after seven stanzas nobody has found Jesus, I think ya need to move on! I mean, good Lord, I was fixin' to run up there myself just to ask the preacher where the toilet was! I understand, ya need to sing a few lines of "Just as I Am" in case a backslid cripple, or a wheelchair sinner needs time to wiggle his way through the pews.

But after twelve stanzas, it's time to wrap things up and head for home. Some people have lives; they don't have time to sing thirty verses of "Just as I Am" while waiting on the town whore to decide whether she should head down the aisle to get saved.

Let's poop or get off the pot! The Lord ain't going nowhere. I'm pretty sure he'll be there again next Sunday! I'm all for saving souls but let's try and get it in before the football game starts!

I was watching the news one day last summer when the government actually issued a warning saying Americans shouldn't travel to Yemen on their vacations. I was like, "Damn, now what do we do? I was so looking forward to my yearly visit!"

As if anybody had family reunion plans over there. That's like the government issuing a warning to please not eat the green meat in the Dumpster behind Wendy's. It's retarded!

I have a cat. Or at least I did have one until he ran off after I tried to baptize him. Here's my only problem with cats—all of 'em are whores. When they use the phrase "humpin' like cats" they mean it.

I've also heard the phrase "humpin' like Paris Hilton" but I don't use it as much.

Every time I turn around, there's somethin' humpin' my cat. The neighbor's cat, a squirrel, raccoons, my little brother . . . you name it. Cats are whores. My dad once told me to get my cat fixed. I refused to waste hard-earned money on a pet. Instead, I bought some plumber's caulk at Wal-Mart and caulked her butt shut!

I actually tried to teach safe sex to one of my tomcats but he kept licking off the rubbers!

Th-th-th-that's all folks!

ED NOTE: I was going to leave this cat thing out of my book altogether. But my publishers said that if I left it in, I'd be the only author in the country that has ever written the phrase "caulk her butt shut" in a book. This is a proud moment.

*   *   *

I now would like to say something that I may regret later.

I saw the movie *Coyote Ugly*.

PLEASE DON'T SHUT THE BOOK! YA GOTTA HEAR ME OUT! I had to see it because I'm a guy and anytime you have babes in chaps dancing on bars half-naked, your attendance is mandatory. I don't make the rules, I just follow them.

The producers oughta just rename the movie *Women I'll Never Have.* Of all the great story lines ya could have for a film, this is the crap they come up with. Damn, if this picture could get made, I'm going to pitch these sumbitches an idea I've been working on. It's an animated movie that'll make millions called *The Adventures of Dickweed and Pussywillow and Their Little Boy Cumquat!*

Liberal talk radio cracks me up. They bitch because conservative radio has taken over. You don't have to be head sandwich maker at the Subway to figure out that conservative talk radio has taken over because most people in this country are conservative and they like listening to it.

Ever look at that blue states–red states map crap? If ya took out five major cities, that map would be redder than Ted Kennedy's eyes after 8 p.m. on . . . pick a day. Maybe if libs had someone worth listening to, someone entertaining that didn't bitch and whine every two seconds about losing elections and who actually offered solutions to problems instead of just rehashing the same old liberal bullshit over and over again, year after year, they might attract some listeners.

I mean if I gotta hear one more time from some lib that we don't spend enough on education, I'm gonna stab myself in the fricken neck! Every year we dump more and more cash into schools, and they get worse and worse. Ya ain't gotta be head floor mopper at the quarter slot porno booth to figure out money ain't the problem.

But every year since I've been alive, there's been some lib crying on TV about putting more money into the school system. That's like puttin' oil in a car with no tires! The lack of oil ain't the problem!

Is that a good example? I can't tell.

Look, I love talk radio and listen to a whole variety of hosts. I even listen to Al Franken's liberal show but, I gotta tell ya, demon possession is funnier than that program.

ED NOTE: Now I'm sure that's going to piss off someone but it's my opinion. Let me lighten things up a bit. Did you hear the one about the guy that dated Siamese twins? They broke up because everything he said to her went in one ear and out her sister's!

Thank you, two shows on Friday. Now are we all friends again?

Here's another news item from the freak section: some guy was arrested in a mall for shooting women with a squirt gun full of semen. No joke, it really happened.

My question is how the hell do you fill up a whole squirt gun with semen? I have a hard enough time working up enough DNA to put on a microscope slide down there at the doctor's office and this goof ball's fillin' up super soakers!

I must be outta the loop.

You know who can kiss my ass other than the head of the WB Network? The French. These folks would be eating pastries with sauerkraut filling if it wasn't for the United States of America kickin' Germany's ass for 'em. And now they do nothing but bitch and moan about everything we do militarily. How soon people forget. But every time their pansy ass needs somethin', who's the first country they come cryin' to? Bingo! The U. ESH. of A. (Donna Fargo).

It's the same with a lot of these other third world nations. America's always the bad guy, and we suck as a country, blah, blah, blah! But they sure as hell risk life and limb to find every way imaginable to get over here to live, don't they? It almost reminds me of how the rest of the country treats us rednecks. Everybody makes fun of us until their car breaks down!

I think t-backs on women are awesome! However I do think they should be a privilege and not a right. I was at a beach one time and two girls came walkin' by me, both of them easily tipping the scales at 230 apiece. They were wearing thongs!! I haven't seen that much hail damage since '78, when some July thunderstorms tore through corn crops in Lincoln, Nebraska! Don't people have mirrors anymore? Why would you wear a thong when you're 130 pounds overweight?

I mean I love all folks, but I'm a big guy and I know better than to wear nut huggers and nipple clips when kids are around! Every time I see a big gal in a t-back, it looks like she's about to go somewhere and pull a jeep out of a ditch with her ass crack, like some kind of a weird Victoria's Secret tractor pull.

ED NOTE: One time I did wear nipple clips for some girl. I had never worn them before and when I came out of the bathroom with this seductive look, all happy about gettin' 'em on right, she just kinda stared at me and said, "What are you doing? Those clips are supposed to keep the chips fresh!" Another beautiful moment, wasted!

*   *   *

Just a real quick note about Home Depot: the plumbing department needs to make it clear that the toilets are for display only. I
mean, for God's sake, those hot dogs they sell up front go right
through ya.

There was a news story a while back about some guy on death row
that claimed he was Jesus. So they delayed his execution to find
out if he's crazy.

Who's working that case, Barney and Goober?

A guy killed somebody and now he thinks he's Jesus. Hello
McFly! Which part of this equation is stumpin' ya, Officer Fife?
Maybe he doesn't think he's Jesus of Nazareth that saved sinners.
Maybe he thinks he's just a guy named Jesus from Albuquerque
that stocks shelves at a Walgreen's. Ya know, there are Mexicans
named Jesus so it could be a case of mistaken identity.

I got an idea, to find out which Jesus he is, electrocute the guy
anyway. If he takes the helmet off his head after a few volts and
walks off unscathed, we'll know he was the real deal. If he takes a
few volts and dies, then all we did was kill the Walgreen's Mexican
Jesus that killed somebody else.

There ya go, another problem solved!

I have a buddy that's a gynecologist and his office is right by a college campus. On top of that, he's good-lookin' and single. Talk
about willpower. It's like putting an Ethiopian in a bakery and
telling him not to eat anything!

My cousin was a gynecologist and had to quit because he got
tunnel vision. You must have self-control in that job. Hell, I can't
even get five minutes into seein' a good-lookin' girl on the Weather
Channel before I'm naked on a folding chair.

*   *   *

I see where this might be the last year for the Jerry Lewis telethon.
Too bad, I'm sure he helped cure a lot of people. Let's face it, if 36
hours of watchin' Jerry Lewis doesn't make ya wanna walk, nothing will!

My grandpa used to drink a lot. One Christmas Eve, he really got
really hammered and told us kids *The Christmas Story*. Only his
version was a little different from anything you've ever heard. So
now, readers, I'd like to present *The Christmas Story* as told by my
drunk grandpappy:

Many years ago a child was born to Fred and Doris Hollister. He
was a very special child for he was conceived at a Fog Hat concert
in the third row during the song "Slow Ride." Fred wasn't earnin'
much money when he learned Doris was expectin'. He worked as
a hush puppy fry cook down at Long John Silver's at the time and
the pregnancy scared the bejesus out of him.

So the couple decided to name the child "Bejesus."

Fred and Doris (who was pregnant with Bejesus at the time)
were driving home from a Foreigner concert at the State Fair when
Doris's water broke. So they stopped at a Best Western for the
night. The bad news was that the Best Western was booked solid
with a convention of Kiwanis so Fred and Doris had to sleep in
their van in the parking lot.

That night Bejesus was born.

They swaddled him in Richard Petty bed sheets and laid him in a
milk crate. Just then three kinda smart men with two-year degrees
from Devry Institute of Technology arrived bearing gifts of cola,
frankfurters, and buns. They grilled out and spoke of love and
hope and whether restrictor plates should be used at Talladega.

Little Bejesus grew and studied. He spoke philosophical phrases such as "Whoever smelt it, dealt it" and "It's better to burp and taste it, than to fart and waste it." He once brought back to life a 69 Formula Firebird by replacing the engine with that of a Delta 88 he got at a junkyard.

Bejesus was loved by all and the whole town was at his funeral after he was killed while humpin' Beverly Pritchie in his truck. They were goin' at it pretty heavy when her ass hit the shifter and knocked the truck outta gear and they rolled into the river. The End.

ED NOTE: This is a lot funnier when ya hear me read it with my accent.

I must admit to being disappointed when the media threw a roast for Bill Clinton. These folks could have really nailed him but it was all PCed up. As usual, anything with politically correct restrictions sucks. You can't have a roast with political correctness. For pete's sake a roast is supposed to be a whole night of political incorrectness.

I remember the blast we had roasting Jeff Foxworthy on Comedy Central. The cool thing is you can blast your buddy and in the end, everybody remains good friends. I wish they'd have put me in charge of the Clinton roast:

Host: "Ladies and Gentlemen, welcome to the Bill Clinton roast. Here's your emcee, a man with a vision and a notebook full of penis jokes, Larry the Cable Guy!"

Me: (Larry): "Thank you and please stay standing. Sorry I was a little late tonight but Congressman Barney Frank stopped me in the elevator, took out his privates, and asked me if they looked infected!

"Only jokin'! I kid the queers!

"I see where Janet Reno couldn't be with us tonight. She's still in production for her feature film *It's Pat, Part 2*. I kid

Janet. I actually gave her a pad and pencil the other day and bet her 50 bucks she couldn't draw a straight line!

"I see Hillary at the end of the table. Nice outfit. I've never seen suede overalls! By the way, congrats on your prostate check coming out negative!

"Folks, I kid her because I love her!

"Hey, there's Al Gore. Do you dye your hair brown or is that color from your head being up your ass for eight years?

"Thank you, it's a gift!

"Speaking of asses, is it me or does Donna Shalala's look big enough to smuggle Elian Gonzalez in and out of a Chuck E. Cheese?!

"I kill myself.

"There's Monica in the second row. Ya know when I see her two words come to mind: SALAD BAR!!

"Enjoy the meatloaf.

"And Ted Kennedy, God bless ya. Sittin' right by my wife. Do me a favor and give her a ride home.

"I kid Ted only because he's drunk!

"And Mr. President. Did you just get some earlier in the day or is that tapioca on your pants!

"Well I need to go now because the ATF is going to show me how to get rid of scandal witnesses!"

ED NOTE: I'm pretty sure that show never would have aired. Even if it did, folks would have been pissed but, hey, it's a roast. By the way, notice all the familiar names? Damn they gave us great comedy.

Back before we went to war with Iraq and we told everyone they had weapons of mass destruction, Saddam Hussein wouldn't allow us to check on them for about two years. When he finally

backed off and let the inspectors inside, he said we could go anywhere we wanted except for Saddam's Palaces. Every one in the
U.N. was like, "That seems fair."

Ya, that's really fair. That's like a pot head saying to the cops, "I
don't have any bags of marijuana in here, I swear. Go ahead and
check anywhere ya want, just don't look underneath the bed or in
the third drawer on the right." That makes a lot of sense!

A while back, the government folks who track and watch asteroids
and other intergalactic matter said that an asteroid the size of a
football field had just missed hitting the U.S. Now get this, they
didn't see it until it passed us!

How the hell do you miss a football field–sized rock headed
your way? Here our government has these sophisticated spy satel-
lites that can tell what color our pee is from 300 miles up in space,
yet they can't see a football field–sized boulder zingin' by. I bet if
that big-assed rock was talking about Jesus and was heading to the
gun show with a copy of the Ten Commandments attached to it,
they'da monitored it pretty easy!

Boy, getting slammed by an asteroid. That would be a shitty way
to die:

Ed: "Hey boss I need off on Tuesday for my uncle's funeral."
Jim: "How'd your uncle die?"
Ed: "He was headed to Wal-Mart and a football field landed on
him!"
Jim: "Yeah right, and my grandma was crushed by a falling hockey
rink. Now shut the hell up and get back to work!"

Here's something that makes about as much sense as A&E doing a
True Hollywood story on Corbin Bernsen. McDonald's banned

smoking in their franchises to protect our health. The next day they brought back the McRib.

I actually think smoking is better for you!

This next story demonstrates why political correctness is a big joke. Bill Maher was fired from his show *Politically Incorrect* for being . . . envelope please . . . POLITICALLY INCORRECT! That's the name of the show, for God's sake. That's like getting mad at a show called *Kick a Midget in the Nuts* because all the guests appearing on it were midgets getting nut kicked! In fact, this is the biggest television outrage since they canceled *Kick a Midget in the Nuts!*

ED NOTE: I used to TiVo that show. Like I said earlier, there is nothing funnier!

I read an article a while back that said kids are overweight, watch too much TV, don't exercise enough, and eat too much junk food.

No wonder I feel like a kid again!

Well that's the last of my hodgepodge. I hope you enjoyed this untraditional last chapter. I also I hope you enjoyed reading this book as much as I enjoyed writing it. I appreciate the fact that my fans love to laugh as much as I do. That's one thing that most people in our great nation have lost, the ability to laugh at ourselves.

Everyone that has ever seen one of my live shows knows how much I appreciate you, the fan, for enjoying my work. I will always be grateful to you and I'll continue tryin' to make you laugh as long as ya support me. Thanks for buying this book. If you can ever make it to a live show, I'd love to have ya!

And now with all that said, I am about to write the last words of my first book while sitting in my camo underbritches and watching *The Match Game '73* on the Game Show Network on my tour bus as it rolls through Atlanta at 3 in the morning.

God bless America, God bless my fans, and God bless Ronald Reagan! YIPPER DIPPER RIPPER STRIPPER!

END CREDITS

Announcer 1: ....Jim Hauser
Announcer 2:..Rikki Fredrick
Boss...Myself (Larry the Cable Guy)
Brother...Danny Whitney
Guy on TV from Verizon..Ed Lambert
Guy walking by him...Phil McCrackin
Man..Bill Alderman
Wife..Sheri Alderman
Jerry Seinfeld..Henry Skokel
Jim the dietitian...Dick Gozinya
Merel the dietitian ....Marty Hill
Andy the supervisor ....Brad Ward
Brad Ward..Andy the Supervisor
DeWayne...Jimmy Folk
Bill ....Randall Meyers
Operator ....Cara West
Panicked man..PJ Walsh
Reporter ....Reno Collier
Judge ....Jerome McComb
Lawyer...Ron White
Jim ....Bill Egvid*
Jerry..Jeff Foxworthy
Faceless Announcer...Edward James Olmos
And Special Guest star ....Miss Bonnie Franklin

* I know it's Engvall. I'm just screwin' with him 'cause nobody can pro-
nounce his last name!

Special thanks to:

The Mexican government
The UNICEF Foundation
Boobla Boobla and family
Jim Beam
Apple Power BookG4
The cast of *Whatever Happened to Ben Vereen?* starring Bonnie
    Franklin
Kraft Singles: "Anytime's a good time for cheese!"

Color by Technicolor
    Written in Panavision inside a Vantari Featherlite Prevo H3
in various cities across the United States.
    No animals were harmed in the writing of this book.
    The words written and expressed in this book are solely for
the entertainment purposes of only those reading it. They can-
not be reproduced or used as part of any kind of "see what
happens when you don't get a college education" speech in
family meetings or school functions without written consent
from Larry the Cable Guy or Major League Baseball.
    If someone has been offended by this book, then I give you
my expressed written consent to pucker up your uptight commie lips and kiss the author's ass!
    Lord, I apologize!

RUM BALLS RECIPE

Place in a mixing bowl:
   2 cups finely sifted, toasted sponge cake or graham cracker crumbs

Add:
   2 tablespoons cocoa
   1 cup sifted powdered sugar
   ⅛ teaspoon salt
   1 cup finely chopped nut meats

Combine in a cup:
   1½ tablespoon honey or syrup
   ¼ cup rum or brandy

   Powdered or granulated sugar, for rolling

Add the liquid ingredients gradually to the crumb mixture. Use your hands in order to tell by the "feel" when the consistency is right. When the ingredients hold together nicely, stop adding the liquid. If the mixture is too dry, add a few more drops of the liquid. Roll the mixture into 1-inch balls. Roll the balls in powdered or granulated sugar.

Set the balls aside for 12 hours to ripen.

AUTOGRAPHS

AUTOGRAPHS

AUTOGRAPHS

AUTOGRAPHS

AUTOGRAPHS

AUTOGRAPHS

AUTOGRAPHS